After Imperialism

Studies in Chinese Christianity

G. Wright Doyle and Carol Lee Hamrin,
Series Editors

A project of the Global China Center

www.globalchinacenter.org

After Imperialism
*Christian Identity in China
and the Global Evangelical Movement*

Edited by
RICHARD R. COOK
and
DAVID W. PAO

◆PICKWICK *Publications* • Eugene, Oregon

AFTER IMPERIALISM
Christian Identity in China and the Global Evangelical Movement

Studies in Chinese Christianity 3

Copyright © 2011 Richard R. Cook and David W. Pao. All rights reserved. Except for brief quotations in critical publications or reviews, no part of this book may be reproduced in any manner without prior written permission from the publisher. Write: Permissions, Wipf and Stock Publishers, 199 W. 8th Ave., Suite 3, Eugene, OR 97401.

Pickwick Publications
An Imprint of Wipf and Stock Publishers
199 W. 8th Ave., Suite 3
Eugene, OR 97401

www.wipfandstock.com

ISBN 13: 978-1-60899-336-9

Cataloguing-in-Publication data:

After imperialism : christian identity in China and the global evangelical movement / edited by Richard R. Cook and David W. Pao.

Studies in Chinese Christianity 3

xviii + 238 pp. ; 23 cm. Includes bibliographical references and index.

ISBN 13: 978-1-60899-336-9

1. Christianity—China—20th Century. 2. Christianity—Social Aspects—China. I. Cook, Richard R. II. Pao, David W. III. Title. IV. Series.

BR1288.C24 2011

Manufactured in the U.S.A.

Contents

Contributors / vii
Acknowledgments / ix
Introduction—Richard R. Cook and David W. Pao / *xi*
Abbreviations / xvi

1. Modern Evangelicalism and Global Christian Identity: Promise and Peril as Seen through the Eyes of a North American Church Historian—*Douglas A. Sweeney* / 1
2. Missions, Cultural Imperialism, and the Development of the Chinese Church—*Ka Lun Leung* / 23
3. Overcoming Missions Guilt: Robert Morrison, Liang Fa, and the Opium Wars—*Richard R. Cook* / 35
4. Chinese Evangelicals and Social Concerns: A Historical and Comparative Review—*Kevin Xiyi Yao* / 46
5. The Old Testament in Its Cultural Context: Implications of "Contextual Criticism" for Chinese and North American Christian Identity—*K. Lawson Younger Jr.* / 73
6. "Holy War" and the Universal God: Reading the Old Testament Holy War Texts in a Biblical-Theological and Postcolonial Setting—*Tremper Longman III* / 96
7. "Holy War" and the Universal God: Reading the New Testament Conquest Accounts in a Postcolonial Setting —*David W. Pao* / 112

8   The Group and the Individual in Salvation: The Witness of Paul—*Frank Thielman* / 136

9   Boundaries in "In-Christ Identity": Paul's View on Table Fellowship and Its Implications for Ethnic Identities —*Maureen W. Yeung* / 154

10 "Who Am I?" Theology and Identity for Children of the Dragon—*Robert J. Priest* / 175

11 Chinese Contextual Theology: A Possible Reconstruction? —*David Y. T. Lee* / 193

12 Forging Evangelical Identity: Integration of Models of Theological Education in the Global Context —*Carver T. Yu* / 220

Contributors

RICHARD R. COOK, Associate Professor of Mission History and Global Christianity at Trinity Evangelical Divinity School, Deerfield, Illinois.

DAVID Y. T. LEE, Associate Professor of Theology at Evangel Seminary, Hong Kong.

KA LUN LEUNG, President and Professor of Systematic Theology at Alliance Bible Seminary, Hong Kong.

TREMPER LONGMAN III, Robert H. Gundry Professor of Biblical Studies at Westmont College, Montecito, California

DAVID W. PAO, Professor of New Testament and Chair of the New Testament Department at Trinity Evangelical Divinity School, Deerfield, Illinois

ROBERT J. PRIEST, Professor of Mission and Intercultural Studies and Director of the Doctor of Philosophy in Intercultural Studies Program at Trinity Evangelical Divinity School, Deerfield, Illinois.

DOUGLAS A. SWEENEY, Professor of Church History and the History of Christian Thought, and Director of the Carl F. H. Henry Center for Theological Understanding at Trinity Evangelical Divinity School, Deerfield, Illinois.

FRANK THIELMAN, Professor of New Testament at the Beeson Divinity School, Birmingham, Alabama.

KEVIN XIYI YAO, Associate Professor in Theological Studies at China Graduate School of Theology, Hong Kong.

MAUREEN W. YEUNG, President and Associate Professor of Biblical Studies at Evangel Seminary, Hong Kong.

K. LAWSON YOUNGER JR., Professor of Old Testament, Semitic Languages, and Ancient Near Eastern History at Trinity Evangelical Divinity School, Deerfield, Illinois.

CARVER T. YU, President and Professor in Dogmatic Theology at the China Graduate School of Theology, Hong Kong.

Acknowledgments

WE WOULD LIKE TO acknowledge some of the many people who made the Hong Kong Conference and this book possible, most importantly President Maureen Yeung and Dean Robin Fung of Evangel Seminary who served with us in the Steering Committee. The Carl F. H. Henry Center of Theological Understanding at Trinity Evangelical Divinity School, under the leadership of Director Douglas Sweeney and Managing Director Owen Strachan, also played an indispensable role. The conference was jointly organized by Evangel Seminary and Trinity Evangelical Divinity School, and the cosponsors were China Evangelical Seminary and the Evangelical Free Church of China. We received enthusiastic support from President Craig Williford at Trinity International University and Dean Tite Tiénou at Trinity Evangelical Divinity School. President Paul Lai led a delegation of faculty from China Evangelical Seminary in Taiwan. Danny Cheng, Director of Administration at Evangel Seminary, provided vital support in Hong Kong. Because of the limited scope of this published work, we could not include all of the papers or the formal responses to the papers. Others who provided a valuable contribution to the Conference include: Elaine Cheung, Dorothy Chiu, Andrew Lam, Thomas Loong, Alfred Suen, and Gregory Wong from Evangel Seminary; Miriam Parent from Trinity Evangelical Divinity School; Samuel Chiow, Joshua Mak, and Timothy Wu from China Evangelical Seminary; Suk-Ming Tam from China Graduate School of Theology; Paul Cheung from Alliance Bible Seminary; Fook Kong Wong from Hong Kong Baptist Theological Seminary; and Colleen Yim from CHRISTAR.

April 2010

Introduction

RICHARD R. COOK *and* DAVID W. PAO

THIS COLLECTION OF ESSAYS arises from a commitment to the belief that evangelicalism continues to provide the historical assets and intellectual (hermeneutical and theological) tools for the global church. Evangelicalism possesses assets with explanatory power able to address significant theological and cultural issues arising out of the churches in the global south. We believe evangelical approaches to contextualization and biblical studies can produce valuable fruit. One such issue is that of identity. In May 2008 over a dozen evangelical scholars, Chinese and Western, from the United States, Hong Kong, and Taiwan, came together to address issues of Christian and evangelical identity. The "Inter-Cultural Theological Conversation" was titled, "Beyond Our Past: Bible, Cultural Identity, and the Global Evangelical Movement." This collection of papers from the conference demonstrates the value of the careful balancing of judicious appropriation of the social sciences and thorough biblical inquiry. Questions of evangelical identity in China and around the world are addressed through the disciplines of history, biblical studies, and systematic theology/contextualization.

The first section on history contains four papers. Douglas Sweeney leads off the collection with incisive insights into the history of evangelicalism, its continuing value in the contemporary world, and its future utility in an increasingly global church. Ka Lun Leung provides a Chinese perspective on the historical background to the introduction of Protestant Christianity into China. He shows the close ties between the Christian missions movement and the growth of imperialism in China, and spells out the long-term consequences in the life of Chinese Christians and churches as a result of linking missions and imperialism. Richard Cook acknowledges the historic ties Protestant missions has with Western imperialism, but goes on to ask how those ties were formed. Looking at the lives of Robert Morrison and Liang Fa, he presents a sympathetic interpretation for missionary involvement in the political activities surrounding the Opium War and the Nanjing Treaty in the late 1830s and early 1840s. Kevin Yao concludes the historical section with an article demonstrating how house churches in China may now be moving beyond traditional limitations. Yao suggests that the evangelical house churches in China may now, starting in the 1990s, be moving beyond their aversion that emerged in the 1920s to social and political involvement. Yao examines Chinese evangelicalism profitably through the lens of social action. He starts by noting the complex history of evangelical involvement in social action, and then turns to the story in the Chinese churches.

The second section is foundational: five articles focused on the Bible. Lawson Younger opens the biblical section of this collection with a clarion call for attention to the context. Younger notes that many in missions and intercultural studies have argued persuasively for attention to the modern context, yet he believes the biblical context deserves equal attention. In order to comprehend Scripture in the multiple contexts of the emerging global churches, Younger argues we must learn to attend to the Ancient Near Eastern cultures of the biblical texts.

The biblical section next includes two papers on the provocative biblical themes of Holy War. Tremper Longman puts the issues of Holy War into a coherent framework. He identifies five phases of "Holy War" and argues that today we live in the fourth phase, "Jesus fights spiritual enemies." Some thought-provoking questions Longman addresses include: What is the moral ground to take the land and kill all the people (*herem*)? How are these Old Testament texts relevant today? Longman concludes that Holy War is not applicable in the redemptive age. David Pao picks up the discussion of Holy War in the New Testament (focusing on the divine warfare motif in Acts, Ephesians, and Revelation). Pao specifically locates his discussion of Holy War in the context of the colonial and post-colonial eras, and provocatively provides a prophetic critique of "both the dominant power and those who see themselves as victims." Thus, the "conquest narratives can fulfill their prophetic function in calling all nations to repent and acknowledge the one and universal Lord of all."

Introduction

In the fourth paper in the biblical section, Frank Thielman addresses issues of biblical scholarship in the West that have correlated ramifications on the churches in the global south. Some recent observers believe North American scholarship has been unduly influenced by American individualism at the expense of a more biblical collectivism. The thinking goes, then, that this imbalanced view of individualism has been passed on to more collectivist cultures through the western missions movement. Through attentive exegesis, Thielman counters that "there is an indelibly individual element in the gospel as Paul explains it, and that this individual element is as important as the social element in Paul's soteriology." Thielman calls on Christians from both the West and the majority world to strive to find the balance between individualism and collectivism found in the biblical texts.

Maureen Yeung, in the fifth paper, anchors her study of the question of Chinese Christian identity in the New Testament as she tackles one of the perennial problems faced by Chinese Christians: ancestor rites. Based on careful exegesis, she urges a nuanced approach stressing both that ancestor practices "should never be seen as good works meriting salvation," yet "cultural elements which are not idolatrous should be respected."

The third and final section includes three case studies of contextual theology. First, from the perspective of anthropology and intercultural studies, Robert Priest looks at several relevant questions of contextualization for the Chinese context. Priest's central case study is a perceptive examination of the "dragon." Priest questions whether the Chinese word for "dragon (*long*)" appropriately translates the biblical term "dragon" in the New Testament. While there are some similarities in the description of the biblical dragon and the Chinese dragon, Priest, after meticulous (and often witty) investigation, concludes that the association of the dragon in Revelation with the Chinese *long* is problematic, creating potentially unnecessary dislocations between Chinese and Christian identities. Priest encourages fidelity to the Bible and the appropriate use of the social sciences to address thorny questions of identity and contextualization.

David Lee moves the discussion to the positive development of a contextual Chinese theology, and calls for the comprehensive utilization of multiple sources. Lee looks at the comparative history of the contextualization of Christianity, Judaism, and Islam in China, the contemporary insights of theologian Kevin Vanhoozer, and Chinese wisdom literature. He aims to "triangulate" the various sources to provide a robust Chinese Christology. Lee affirms, at the same time, that the Bible is still at the center. As Lee writes, "Without undermining the *sola Scriptura* principle, this paper asserts that it is possible to construct a Chinese theology that regards Chinese culture as an interpretative tool or communication vehicle that may be "allied" with the Bible." Lee finds help from Chinese wisdom in avoiding a narrow understanding of Christ that has emerged in the West. He writes, "Rather than indiscriminately importing nineteenth- and twentieth-century Western religious thought, Chinese Christian interpreters and cultural agents may explore the God-man—the human and divine Christ—as the pivotal stand on which they can triangulate Scripture, culture, and the world of wisdom."

Carver Yu, writing on theological education, provides a fitting concluding chapter to this collection of papers. Yu begins with a broad overview of the current context of theological education. He highlights the growing secularization of Europe and the West ("global north"), and contrasts that with the rapid expansion of Christianity in Asia, Africa, and Latin America ("global south"). After discussing definitions of church, theology, and theological education, he dives into the question of evangelical identity and the task of theological education in a global context. He writes, "Fluid identity and the loss of inwardness is the hallmark of our age.... Theological students coming into seminaries today can be expected to have been deeply affected by such fragmented identity." Yu then creatively draws on the Asian context to advance three proposals for theological education: 1) Restoring piety in the loss of inwardness. Drawing on Chinese theologians and the Chinese classics, Yu writes, for instance, "Theology needs to recover the long forgotten practice of 'emptiness, unity of knowing and being, quietude' in the Chinese tradition." 2) Theological education with a missional orientation. Yu notes that while the western missions movement was on "drastic retreat following World War II, with a deep sense of guilt and remorse," the post-1949 churches in China imbibed the "missional orientation of faith left behind by the missionaries" which has "proved to be highly explosive." 3) Prophetic critique of culture. Yu asks some provocative questions, such as: Can we as evangelicals send students not just to seminary, but also to study the "theology of economics, aiming prophetically at the Chicago School of Economics?" After mentioning an array of current philosophical, economic, political and cultural issues, Yu concludes, "Theological education must empower future ministers to be able to think through these issues."

This "intercultural dialog" in Hong Kong among scholars from China and the West brought rich insights into the Bible, theology, and the future of evangelicalism. We came away encouraged that evangelicals could continue to contribute to the global churches and help pave the way for an evermore fruitful global theological discourse. In their papers, several of the contributors provide optimistic assessments of the future role of global evangelicalism. Douglas Sweeney concludes his paper, "Perhaps Chinese evangelicals will lead the way in showing their brothers and sisters in God's family how to contextualize the faith without domesticating it—how to render the faith their own without repeating the sins of the past and universalizing their social and cultural preferences." David Lee adds, "Indeed, there is an urgent need to construct or reinherit an evangelical Chinese theology.... The role of the church is vital in the process of contextualizing the Christian message. In the end, the mission of the Christian church in China is to demonstrate that the world of wisdom is found only in the person and work of Jesus Christ who is both the Divine Wisdom and holy sage."

Robert Priest concludes with an urgent call to the global churches, "I believe that Chinese and Africans and Indians and Koreans need theologians who are addressing the distinctive identity challenges and opportunities provided within their own contexts out of a deep understanding of Scripture, but also out of profound skills in understanding the cultures both of their own societies and of the societies that first mediated the gospel to them.... [W]hen Chinese evangelical theologians, while retaining a deep knowledge of Scripture and submission to its authority, also direct their efforts towards contextual challenges of identity—honing their own skills in studying and exegeting culture, and doing so through a positive engagement with the human sciences—they will carry out theologizing that serves the Chinese Christian community and that also provides correctives for the global Christian community."

Abbreviations

AB	Anchor Bible
ABD	*Anchor Bible Dictionary*
AOAT	Alter Orient und Altes Testament
BASOR	*Bulletin of the American Schools of Oriental Research*
BECNT	Baker Exegetical Commentary on the New Testament
Bib	*Biblica*
BibInt	*Biblical Interpretation*
BJS	Brown Judaic Studies
BN	*Biblische Notizen*
BNTC	Black's New Testament Commentaries
BR	Biblical Research
BZAW	Beiheft zur Zeitschrift für die alttestamentliche Wissenschaft
CAD	*The Assyrian Dictionary: Of the Oriental Institute of the University of Chicago*, ed. Ignace J. Gelb et al. 21 vols. Chicago: The Oriental Institute, 1956–
CANE	*Civilizations of the Ancient Near East*, ed. Jack M. Sasson. 4 vols. New York: Scribner, 1995
CBQ	*Catholic Biblical Quarterly*
EvQ	*Evangelical Quarterly*
HBT	Horizons in Biblical Theology
HDB	Harvard Divinity Bulletin
HUCA	Hebrew Union College Annual
IEJ	*Israel Exploration Journal*
Int	Interpretation
JANES	*Journal of the Ancient Near Eastern Society*
JAOS	*Journal of the American Oriental Society*
JBL	*Journal of Biblical Literature*
JES	Journal of Ecumenical Studies
JETS	*Journal of the Evangelical Theological Society*
JNES	*Journal of Near Eastern Studies*
JSNT	*Journal for the Study of the New Testament*
JSNTSup	Journal for the Study of the New Testament Supplement

JSOTSup	Journal for the Study of the Old Testament Supplement
JTS	*Journal of Theological Studies*
KTU	*Die keilalphabetischen Texte aus Ugarit*, edited by M. Dietrich et al. AOAT 24/1. Neukirchen-Vluyn, 1976
NAC	New American Commentary
NIBC	New International Biblical Commentary
NICNT	New International Commentary on the New Testament
NICOT	New International Commenatry on the Old Testament
NIGTC	New International Greek Testament Commentary
NIVAC	NIV Application Commentary
NovTSup	Supplements to Novum Testamentum
NTS	*New Testament Studies*
Opif.	*De opificio mundi* (Philo)
OTL	Old Testament Library
PittTMS	Pittsburgh Theological Monograph Series
PTMS	Princeton Theological Monograph Series
RB	*Révue Biblique*
RlA	*Reallexikon der Assyriologie*
SAAB	*State Archives of Assyria Bulletin*
Sacr.	*De Sacrificiis Abelis et Caini* (Philo)
SBL	Society of Biblical Literature
SNTSMS	Society of New Testament Studies Monograph Series
TDNT	*Theological Dictionary of the New Testament*, edited by Gerhard Kittel and Gerhard Friedrich, translated by Geoffrey W. Bromiley. 10 vols. Grand Rapids: Eerdmans, 1964–1976
TynBul	*Tyndale Bulletin*
VT	*Vetus Testamentum*
VTSup	Supplements to Vetus Testamentum
WTJ	*Westminster Theological Journal*
WUNT	Wissenschaftliche Untersuchungen zum Neuen Testament
ZAW	*Zeitschrift für die Alttestamentliche Wissenschaft*
ZNW	*Zeitschrift für die neutestamentliche Wissenschaft und die Kunde der ältern Kirche*

1

Modern Evangelicalism and Global Christian Identity

Promise and Peril as Seen through the Eyes of a North American Church Historian[1]

Douglas A. Sweeney

According to the demographers who study global religion, more than one out of every eight people in the world is an evangelical. By the dawn of 2008, the world population had exceeded 6.6 billion people. Nearly a third of these identified with Christianity. Roughly 900 million were evangelicals. A century ago, Christians of any kind were much fewer in number, and the vast majority lived in Europe and North America. But the twentieth century witnessed a major explosion of evangelicalism, a blast that rocked the two-thirds world more powerfully than the West. By the early 1970s, most Christians lived outside the West, a result of evangelical growth that shifted their churches' center of gravity and reminded thoughtful members of their churches' ancient bases in North Africa and Asia. Global evangelicalism is now an enormous movement of which Americans and Westerners comprise a small minority.[2]

---

1. Some parts of this chapter have been adapted from Douglas A. Sweeney, *The American Evangelical Story: A History of the Movement* (Grand Rapids: Baker Academic, 2005).

2. Estimating the size of Christian groups is complicated. The best estimates of the number of evangelicals in the United States suggest there are roughly one hundred million of them today (2008). See the Web site of the Institute for the Study of American Evangelicals, Wheaton College: www.wheaton.edu/isae. For statistics on the size and spread of global evangelicalism, consult the tables updated by David B. Barrett, Todd M. Johnson, and now Peter F. Crossing as well in every January issue of the *International*

But since I have been assigned to write about Western evangelicalism, I plan to approach our subject from the movement's early history. After addressing the recent debates about the label "evangelical," I will sketch the rise of the modern evangelical tradition, noting its spread around the world through Christian witness and local efforts to contextualize the faith, before concluding with reflections on the state of evangelicalism across the globe today. I hope these considerations will pave the way for discussing the question: "Is 'evangelicalism' still a useful category for understanding our faith traditions within our own cultural contexts?"

WHAT IS AN EVANGELICAL?

Defining evangelicalism is difficult to do—no matter where in the world one lives. In fact, the most contested issue facing scholars of evangelicalism pertains to its definition. Evangelicals are diverse—exceptionally diverse, even for a modern movement. Men and women on every continent count themselves as evangelicals. Some of them are rich, but even more of them are poor. Some are highly educated, others largely self-taught. Evangelicals belong to hundreds of different denominations—several of which were founded in opposition to some of the others. Most of them are Protestant, but even among Protestants there are Lutheran, Reformed, and Anabaptist evangelicals. Anglicans, Methodists, Holiness people, and Pentecostals are also evangelicals. In addition, there are untold millions of "independent" evangelicals, some of whom attend extremely large worship centers. There has never been a *comprehensive* evangelical church. Evangelicals do not possess a formal constitution. Although they rally around plenty of famous leaders and institutions, none has final authority to govern the whole movement.

The best-known theologian to attempt a definition of evangelicalism is Oxford's Alister McGrath. In his book on *Evangelicalism and the Future of Christianity*, McGrath suggests that, "evangelicalism is grounded on a cluster of six controlling convictions, each of which is regarded

---

Bulletin of Missionary Research—for the most recent statistics, see "Missiometrics 2008: Reality Checks for Christian World Communions," *International Bulletin of Missionary Research* 32 (January 2008) 27–30. (I include Pentecostals, charismatics, and neocharismatics in my estimates of the size of evangelicalism.) Global population estimates are offered in many places. I have used the World POPClock Projection of the United States Census Bureau: http://www.census.gov/ipc/www/popclockworld.html.

as being true, of vital importance and grounded in Scripture... These six fundamental convictions can be set out as follows:

1. The supreme authority of Scripture as a source of knowledge of God and a guide to Christian living.
2. The majesty of Jesus Christ, both as incarnate God and Lord and as the Savior of sinful humanity.
3. The lordship of the Holy Spirit.
4. The need for personal conversion.
5. The priority of evangelism for both individual Christians and the church as a whole.
6. The importance of the Christian community for spiritual nourishment, fellowship and growth."[3]

Among historians, David Bebbington's definition is best known. In his widely-used book entitled *Evangelicalism in Modern Britain*, Bebbington writes that, "there are ... four qualities that have been the special marks of Evangelical religion: *conversionism*, the belief that lives need to be changed; *activism*, the expression of the gospel in effort; *biblicism*, a particular regard for the Bible; and what may be called *crucicentrism*, a stress on the sacrifice of Christ on the cross. Together they form a quadrilateral of priorities that is the basis of Evangelicalism."[4]

Both McGrath and Bebbington grant that there is more to evangelicals than can be stated in such definitions, but neither is keen on defining the movement further. Consequently, some complain that they have neglected to distinguish evangelicalism from Protestantism, or even from Christianity broadly. Such critics contend that *most* Christians define their faith in these terms, whether or not they think of themselves as evangelicals. A few contend more strongly that self-professing "evangelicals" have commandeered this label, ignoring its use by groups that predate their movement by centuries.[5] Still others have decided to *cease*

3. Alister McGrath, *Evangelicalism & the Future of Christianity* (Downers Grove, IL: InterVarsity, 1995), 55–56.

4. David W. Bebbington, *Evangelicalism in Modern Britain: A History from the 1730s to the 1980s* (London: Unwin Hyman, 1989), 2–3.

5. This argument is usually made by confessional Lutherans, though it could be—and has been—made just as strongly by other Gospel-centered groups, some of which were using the label before the evangelical *movement* existed.

defining evangelicals. They claim that the movement defies all neat and tidy definitions.

Donald Dayton, an American, has led this latter group. He has gone so far as to call for a "moratorium" on the label, which he rejects as "theologically incoherent, sociologically confusing, and ecumenically harmful."[6] It is theologically incoherent, in Dayton's estimation, because evangelical theologians are always at war with one another and have never united around a common doctrinal platform. Dayton believes the label is sociologically confusing because it obscures more than it reveals about most of the groups who are so labeled. And he regards it as ecumenically harmful because its most prolific definers represent what Dayton refers to as a myopic, rather elitist, even bourgeois "Presbyterian" model of evangelical history.

This last point is the one to which Dayton has given the most attention. It is also the one that requires the most unpacking. In Dayton's view, the very scholars who spill the most ink discussing evangelicalism are responsible for misleading us as to its nature and significance. Their writings focus primarily on the movement's intellectuals, or intellectual power brokers—privileged white men with Calvinistic worldviews and cultural pretensions that put them at odds with most of their followers. According to Dayton, most *real* or *everyday* evangelical Christians hardly ever fit this description. White men are in the minority. Few are intellectuals. Their beliefs seldom conform to standard Calvinistic worldviews. In fact, a simple head count will confirm that most evangelical Christians hail from humble "Pentecostal" backgrounds—a blanket term that Dayton uses in opposition to "Presbyterian" that covers a wide array of Arminian, Wesleyan, Holiness, Pentecostal, and Charismatic Christians. These groups rarely resonate with the views of leading Calvinists.

This is not the place to flesh out the rest of Dayton's argument.[7] Suffice it to say that he is so taken by the scope of evangelicalism's diver-

---

6. Donald W. Dayton, "Some Doubts about the Usefulness of the Category 'Evangelical,'" in Donald Dayton and Robert Johnston, eds., *The Variety of American Evangelicalism* (Knoxville: University of Tennessee Press, 1991), 251. See also Donald W. Dayton, "The Holy Spirit and Christian Expansion in the Twentieth Century," *Missiology: An International Review* 16 (1988) 403; and Dayton, "'Evangelical': More Puzzling Than You Think," *Ecumenical People Programs Papers*, Occasional Paper no. 29 (May 1988) 5–6.

7. For more on Dayton's perspective, see the *Festschrift* published recently in his honor: Christian T. Collins Winn, ed., *From the Margins: A Celebration of the Theological Work of Donald W. Dayton*, PTMS 75 (Eugene, OR: Pickwick Publications, 2007).

sity, and so concerned to avoid the hegemonic rule of Christian elites, that he has called us to boycott the evangelical label as well as efforts to define it.

Debates over the nature of the evangelical movement can be terribly confusing, as they complicate efforts to understand the millions of people who associate themselves with it. Are their differences so great that they share nothing at all in common? Does their label really distinguish them from other kinds of Christians who do not regard themselves as evangelicals? Does it refer to anything more than gospel-centered Christianity? Has the evangelical movement grown so large in recent years that its promoters no longer see it as being at odds with the rest of the church? Or, to phrase this more tendentiously, has evangelicalism lost its saltiness?

I believe that evangelicals do comprise a common movement, one that is possible to define in more than vague generalities. Evangelicals are certainly diverse. Most resist attempts to pigeonhole them with precision. And Dayton is right to warn against the totalizing tendencies of many evangelicals who seek to fashion the movement after their own personal, cultural, and theological preferences. For the purpose of analysis, though, it is possible to define evangelicals in terms of their common ancestry: *modern evangelicals comprise a religious movement rooted in ancient Christianity, shaped by a largely Protestant understanding of that faith, and distinguished from other such movements by an eighteenth-century twist.* Or, put more simply (though less precisely), *evangelicals are a movement of orthodox Protestants with an eighteenth-century twist.* They are certainly not the only authentic Christians in the world. Nor are they the only ones with a right to use their label.[8] But they are unique in their commitment to spreading the Christian gospel message. And their uniqueness is best defined by adherence to: 1) beliefs most clearly stated during the Protestant Reformation, and 2) practices shaped by the revivals of the so-called "Great Awakening." Something close to this definition is used by other scholars as well, most significantly in the recent *Cambridge Companion to Evangelical Theology.*[9]

---

8. The English word *evangelical* comes from the Greek word *euangelion*, meaning "gospel" or, more literally, "good news" or "glad tidings." In the Bible it refers to the good news about Jesus Christ. Thus the word is important to all the world's Christians.

9. In his introductory chapter, "Defining and locating Evangelicalism," coeditor Timothy Larsen develops a definition of evangelicalism similar to mine, unpacking the meaning of "orthodox Protestant" very helpfully: "An evangelical is: 1. an orthodox

It may well help us later on if I here unpack a few key terms in this definition of evangelicalism: *movement, orthodox Protestants*, and *eighteenth-century twist*. First, evangelicals comprise a *movement*, not a church or denomination. They are a coalition of Christians from all sorts of different backgrounds working together in pursuit of a vibrant, ecumenical witness. Second, evangelicals are descendants of the *Protestant Reformation* with a commitment to the *orthodoxy* (i.e., right doctrine and right worship) expressed in the ancient Christian creeds, which were hammered out in Asia and repackaged by Reformers in the early modern West. Some disparage "orthodoxy" as incorrigibly repressive, but not most evangelicals. They are not socially, politically, and culturally conservative—at least not necessarily—but most of them are conservative theologically. Finally, modern evangelicals differ from other Christian groups in that their movement emerged from a definite, *eighteenth-century* spiritual context, which yielded a *twist* on older forms of Protestant orthodoxy. Modern evangelicals, as distinguished from others who use the word or share their view of the gospel, stand as heirs of the Great Awakening—a Christian renewal movement that reconfigured the Protestant world over the course of the eighteenth century.

THE RISE OF THE MODERN EVANGELICAL MOVEMENT

Modern evangelicalism emerged three centuries ago out of a spiritual movement, the likes of which the world had never seen. Known then and since as a "Great Awakening"[10] of Protestant Europe's state churches, this

---

Protestant; 2. who stands in the tradition of the global Christian networks arising from the eighteenth-century revival movements associated with John Wesley and George Whitefield; 3. who has a preeminent place for the Bible in her or his Christian life as the divinely inspired, final authority in matters of faith and practice; 4. who stresses reconciliation with God through the atoning work of Jesus Christ on the cross; 5. and who stresses the work of the Holy Spirit in the life of an individual to bring about conversion and an ongoing life of fellowship with God and service to God and others, including the duty of all believers to participate in the task of proclaiming the gospel to all people." See Timothy Larsen, "Defining and locating Evangelicalism," in Timothy Larsen and Daniel J. Treier, eds., *The Cambridge Companion to Evangelical Theology*, Cambridge Companions to Religion (Cambridge: Cambridge University Press, 2007), 1.

10. Scholars have long debated the accuracy, analytical utility, and theological significance of the term "Great Awakening." For information on this debate, see Allen C. Guelzo, "God's Designs: The Literature of the Colonial Revivals of Religion, 1735–1760," in Harry S. Stout and D. G. Hart, eds., *New Directions in American Religious History* (New York: Oxford University Press, 1997), 141–72; and Christopher Grasso, "Appendix

movement began in the middle of Europe, quickly spread to the British Isles and Britain's North American colonies, and impressed the entire West with the spiritual power of the new birth.

Before the Great Awakening, the Protestant world had been divided in both its worship and its witness by various ethnic and cultural boundaries. The heirs of the Reformation had long been fighting among themselves over matters of doctrine and control of their churches' resources. The Protestant movement also yielded an enormous spiritual harvest, blessing its members with biblical knowledge, a brand-new sense of gospel freedom, and the tools with which to practice their faith in lives of personal service. As a result of their infighting, though, the movement broke apart—and its state churches were not the only signs of division. Its theologians developed competing doctrinal statements, or confessions, which buttressed their rulers' tendencies toward intramural partisanship. They granted religious support to the rise of European nation states, fracturing the superficial unity of Christendom.[11]

During and after the Great Awakening, much of this would change for good—not overnight, and never completely, but considerably and noticeably. Hundreds of Protestant leaders began to join hands across the boundaries that had long divided their churches and collaborate in the work of gospel ministry. They did not establish a new church. Rather, they labored ecumenically—*inter*-denominationally and *pan*-geographically—co-sponsoring revivals, "concerts of prayer," and other spiritual exercises. They traded pulpits with one another, promoting itinerant gospel preaching and thereby undermining the zoning system that had long divided their churches.

These Protestant leaders accomplished such things with the help of a new communications network, which linked all kinds of evangelicals living in Europe and North America. Historians refer to the eighteenth

---

3: A Note on the Historiography of the Great Awakening," in Grasso, *A Speaking Aristocracy: Transforming Public Discourse in Eighteenth-Century Connecticut* (Chapel Hill: University of North Carolina Press, 1999), 495–98.

11. The term "Christendom" refers to the territory, and the ideal, of state-sponsored Christian nationalism, both of which date back to the conversion of the Roman Emperor Constantine (in AD 312), the establishment of Christianity by Emperor Theodosius I as the *only* legal religion of the ancient Roman Empire (in AD 380), and the geopolitical agenda of the "Holy Roman Empire" (which emerged in AD 800, lasted in one form or another through the period treated here, and gave to Christendom its definitive, medieval shape).

century as the great age of letter writing. Evangelicals, for their part, exchanged tens of thousands of letters. This was also the time of the rise of British magazines and newspapers, media used by Christians to promote the cause of revival. Spiritual books outsold all others in this age of American history, uniting evangelicals and helping those who struggled to make sense of the revivals. Such media offered Christians a new sense of religious identity that transcended their readers' national and denominational ties. Many now felt that they were part of a new *international* movement of God. Their horizons expanded dramatically. They often grew more excited about reaching out together for Jesus than about propping up much older and more parochial Protestant projects.

In short, the Great Awakening engendered a new sense of gospel urgency and spirit of partnership. Of course, its evangelical leaders would never experience perfect peace. And the new movement that they founded would know its fair share of sibling rivalry. During and after these revivals, however, a host of evangelicals pushed their differences aside and worked together for the cause of the gospel. Led by the Anglican George Whitefield (said by many to be the greatest preacher in all of Christian history), Congregationalist Jonathan Edwards (known as "America's theologian"), and the Methodist John Wesley (the revivals' organizational genius), they transgressed their state-church boundaries, said that the *world* was now their parish, and labored diligently to promote what they considered "true religion." Many made new friends with Protestant leaders in other places. They learned to trust each other's judgments. They came to see that their numerous differences need not keep them from working together.[12]

It is no coincidence that the rise of the modern evangelical movement took place at roughly the same time as the last gasp of Christendom.[13] Throughout much of Christian history, the faith was extended most dramatically by the territorial expansion of Christian nations—nations with legally "established" churches, the will to colo-

---

12. Of course, it has always been the case that some evangelicals are more interested in collaboration than others. Further, some evangelical partnerships themselves have proved divisive, leading to reconfigurations of their members' Christian allegiances (more on this below).

13. On this theme, see especially Andrew F. Walls, *The Missionary Movement in Christian History: Studies in the Transmission of Faith* (Maryknoll, NY: Orbis, 1996); and Walls, *The Cross-Cultural Process in Christian History: Studies in the Transmission and Appropriation of Faith* (Maryknoll, NY: Orbis, 2002).

nize foreign lands, and the audacity to Christianize their populations by force. But in the eighteenth and nineteenth centuries, most state churches in the West began to weaken—as did their goal of imposing religious unity. Modern thinkers began to defend the right to freedom of religion, official leaders of state churches lost much of their secular authority, and the kind of toleration many Christians now expect began to find its champions in the halls of power.

Early on, most evangelicals were nervous about these trends. They feared a loss of influence on their nations' cultural developments and opposed the "infidelity" of the more open, liberal champions of religious toleration. Eventually, however, evangelicals would embrace the transformation these trends produced—and exploit it to promote their *transdenominational* movement. In America, especially, they learned that "disestablishment" could unleash a spirit of voluntarism that boosted the work of evangelism and spiritual renewal. On the one hand, it would yield an exponential increase in religious institutions, none of which was able to claim a legally sanctioned authority. On the other hand, however, it deregulated the marketplace, enabling new religious groups to flourish like never before. Evangelicals have always excelled at "marketing" their faith. Disestablishment created a "free market" for religion in which their entrepreneurs enjoyed tremendous success.[14]

A couple of examples from the U.S. confirm this claim: On the eve of its Revolution (that is, in 1776), more than half of the nation's churchgoers attended Congregational, Presbyterian, or Anglican worship services and supported the legal establishment of their churches. By 1850, though, these denominations boasted fewer than 20% of churchgoers, while evangelical Protestants predominated the landscape. Baptists and Methodists alone comprised over half of the nation's attenders. Scores of other denominations seemed to be sprouting up overnight. A democratization of religion accompanied American independence. All kinds of previously marginal groups—evangelicals, Roman Catholics, people of color, many women—began to enjoy the new opportunities for ministry.

---

14. On these changes, see especially Nathan O. Hatch, *The Democratization of American Christianity* (New Haven: Yale University Press, 1989); and Roger Finke and Rodney Stark, *The Churching of America, 1776–1990: Winners and Losers in Our Religious Economy* (New Brunswick, NJ: Rutgers University Press, 1992).

Most prodigious by far was the growth of Baptists and Methodists. Historians estimate that at the outbreak of the American Revolution there were 494 Baptist congregations in the colonies. By 1795, however, this number had more than doubled (to 1,152), and Baptists were poised to exert an enormous effect on the church of the next century. They proved most powerful in the South and on the expanding western frontier, largely due to their flexibility in forming rural congregations. The Southern Baptist Convention, which has now become the largest Protestant body in the U.S., coalesced in 1845 to facilitate this growth. German and Swedish Baptist groups emerged at roughly the same time (in 1843 and 1852, respectively). By 1850, Baptists trailed only Roman Catholics and Methodists in size among America's Christian churches.[15]

America's Methodist Church did not exist until 1784, when it was founded at the historic Christmas Conference in Baltimore under the leadership of Thomas Coke and Francis Asbury. In 1770, fewer than 1,000 Americans had identified with Methodism. By 1844, however, the first year that Methodists topped the denominational charts, they claimed 1,068,525 members, 3,988 itinerant preachers, and 7,730 local ministers. Needless to say, their impact was great. Much like the Baptists, they enjoyed their greatest numerical successes in the mid-Atlantic states, the Southeast, and on the frontier, serving people often neglected by the older denominations. In an era when the U.S. grew faster than ever before or since—and when most of the growth took place to the west of the Appalachian Mountains—their rough and ready approach to ministry proved essential. Thousands of "circuit riders" took up the cause of preaching out in the country. Their work was grueling. They were poorly paid. They often lived out of saddlebags, slept outside, and died young (from exhaustion and frequent exposure to the elements). But they evangelized the country like no other Christian group. Consequently, the nineteenth century is often called "the age of Methodism."[16]

---

15. Gregory A. Wills, *Democratic Religion: Freedom, Authority, and Church Discipline in the Baptist South, 1785–1900*; Religion in America Series (New York: Oxford University Press, 1997); Isaac Rhys, *The Transformation of Virginia, 1740–1790* (Chapel Hill: University of North Carolina Press, 1982).

16. On the rise of American Methodism, see especially Dee E. Andrews, *The Methodists and Revolutionary America, 1760–1800: The Shaping of an Evangelical Culture* (Princeton: Princeton University Press, 2000); John H. Wigger, *Taking Heaven by Storm: Methodism and the Rise of Popular Christianity in America*; Religion in America Series (New York: Oxford University Press, 1998); and David Hempton, *Methodism: Empire of*

As a result of the revivals, and in the wake of disestablishment, evangelical institutions moved to the center of American culture, rendering the nation what some have called a "righteous empire" (a term that appalls most post-colonial evangelicals).[17] During the early nineteenth century, evangelical groups provided most of the country's social services, prefiguring the nationalization of America's civic life. They founded special needs asylums for the disabled and mentally ill. Some of them worked for temperance reform, abolition, and Indian outreach. They raised millions in support of education for the needy. They printed tens of millions of books, tracts, and Christian periodicals. They organized on a grand scale at a time when the Bank of the United States comprised their country's only truly national corporation, and the United States Postal Service comprised its only national government agency.

As they sidled to the center of the Protestant "mainline," however, critics complained that they had sold out to secular, "worldly" values. They needed revival once again—a common refrain throughout the history of the evangelical movement. Ever since the Great Awakening, in fact, evangelical leaders imagined their movement on a cycle of revival and decline, making its greatest spiritual strides in major seasons of renewal. Attempting to regularize revival, bottle their leaders' moral charisma, and coordinate the projects needed to shore up the life of the spirit, they built new structures that would preserve, channel, and multiply their energies. Over and over again, however, the structures themselves became corrupt, disenchanting the movement's purists and leading to further reformation. The Second Great Awakening and many subsequent revivals—not to mention the Holiness, Pentecostal, and Charismatic movements—have been launched in efforts to purify and revitalize evangelical Christianity.

Ironically, this cycle of revival and decline has proliferated countless evangelical institutions, each one needed to resurrect the life of its predecessors. These institutions, even while laboring ecumenically, have often proved schismatic—severing families, congregations, and even entire denominations and restructuring the landscape of the evangelical

---

the Spirit (New Haven: Yale University Press, 2005), which interprets that rise within an international context.

17. The classic work on this theme is Martin E. Marty, *Righteous Empire: The Protestant Experience in America*, Harper Torchbooks (New York: Harper & Row, 1977; orig. ed., 1970).

movement nearly everywhere in the world. They have also sponsored the rise of a massive evangelical subculture—a counterculture of sorts, but one that is now nearly self-sufficient in its institutional life and frequently isolated from those institutions it originally sought to renew. Evangelicals have long been eager to work with kindred spirits, but their partnerships have often placed a strain on old relationships. When blessed with new wine, they rarely store it in old wineskins (Luke 5:37–39).

WESTERN MISSIONS, OTHER CULTURES, AND THE CHALLENGE OF CONTEXTUALIZING EVANGELICALISM

This very evangelical movement played the most significant role in fueling the rise of the modern, international, Christian missions movement. It should come as no surprise, then, that the work of modern missions has been shaped by some of the same dynamics as evangelicalism.

Devoted disciples of Christ have eagerly borne witness to the gospel ever since His resurrection. But a special development occurred after the birth of evangelicalism. Unprecedented numbers of people engaged in missions abroad, with the backing of an unprecedented evangelistic network. The nineteenth century soon became the "age of Christian expansion."[18] Many hoped that the twentieth century would become "the Christian century" and witness the eschatological climax of world history.

The early Protestant reformers understood the Reformation to be a wonderful work of God that spread true faith amidst their world in preparation for the second coming of Christ. They thought the end of the world was near and that their job as Protestant pastors was to purify the church, restore its apostolic faith, proclaim the gospel fearlessly, and thus resist the final ravages of sin, death, and the devil. They favored missions, to be sure, in their pursuit of these urgent goals. But in their age of Christendom, Protestant missions often looked different from what we have come to expect from missions on this side of the Great Awakening.[19]

---

18. The classic source of this notion is Kenneth Scott Latourette. See especially *Christianity in a Revolutionary Age*, 5 vols. (New York: Harper, 1958–1962).

19. For recent essays on the history of evangelical world missions, see Martin I. Klauber and Scott M. Manetsch, eds., *The Great Commission: Evangelicals and the History of World Missions* (Nashville: Broadman & Holman, 2008).

Magisterial reformers,[20] like their Catholic counterparts, thought of missions largely in terms of what we call "confessionalization." With the help of the civil authorities, they inculcated their doctrinal views within their jurisdictions, using preaching, catechesis, visitation, and church discipline; they evangelized the newly Protestant regions of Christian Europe, training their neighbors, first and foremost, in the faith. To the detriment of the cause of *intercultural* missions, though, their lands were usually ruled by people with little concern, and less capacity, for work beyond their borders. They were embroiled in a series of battles over the boundaries of their churches that curtailed the spread of the gospel for over a century. Some of their leading Protestant thinkers taught that the Great Commission only applied to the first Apostles anyway—that God had *decreed* to spread the gospel through the rest of history by the organic growth of covenant communities.[21]

All in all, then, early Protestant efforts at cross-cultural missions work did not amount to much, at least not by the standards of the evangelical movement. The Puritans and Pietists would mount significant efforts to evangelize the "heathen" in their rulers' distant colonies. Moravian Pietist missionaries would pioneer in methods of evangelism untethered from the power of the state—crossing national, racial, ethnic, and denominational boundaries with remarkable success. However, none of these early forays would come close to the size and scale of the missions boom that shook the world in the wake of the transatlantic revivals. Although Protestants had always sought to witness to the gospel, and had capitalized on missions opportunities where they could, their opportunities expanded exponentially soon after the modern, evangelical movement coalesced.

Indeed, impelled by the momentum established by early Protestant missions and quickened by the supernatural force of their revivals,

---

20. The *magisterial* reformers were leaders like Luther (1483–1546), Zwingli (1484–1531), and Calvin (1509–1564) who promoted the Reformation with the help of their civil *magistrates*—frequently by the power of the sword, as it was said. They are distinguished in the textbooks from the *radical* reformers—commonly called the Anabaptists, many of whom were avowed pacifists and all of whom were sectarians—who favored what we would call the separation of church and state (though at times they took up arms and tried in vain to establish independent municipalities).

21. I have explored these themes in greater detail in Sweeney, *The American Evangelical Story*, 79–106, where I also detail the missions work of the early Protestant leaders.

evangelical leaders organized the modern missions movement during the final years of the eighteenth century. Like the Moravians, they surmounted older denominational boundaries. But, positioned as they were so close to the end of Christendom, they had more freedom than their predecessors to found a broad coalition of "true" Christians who would evangelize the nations. They also completed a telling transition in evangelistic method begun in fits and starts by early Protestant leaders: a change from practicing evangelism by means of confessionalization to evangelizing by calling people to genuine conversion that transcends all prior confessional allegiances.

Stories abound regarding evangelical missionary heroes who ignited the globalization of the church. From William Carey to Samuel Mills, Lottie Moon to John R. Mott, a wide array of Christian leaders from a multitude of churches changed the world by means of their international labors. By the end of the nineteenth century, there were nearly 5,000 from the United States alone. But, like the English who preceded them, American missionaries often packed more than the Bible in the bags with which they sailed. (The Christendom model died hard—even among those who opposed it!) Western culture often suffused their presentations of the faith. And Western military and economic force too often guaranteed that those they went to serve would bear the weight of *all* their baggage. As a host of history writers has made clear in recent years, modern evangelical missionaries have often been seen as agents of imperial expansion on the part of Western powers. And, as Brian Stanley has shown, this view has nowhere been more prevalent than in the land of China, where the Opium Wars were only the most egregious sign of aggression on the part of Western "Christians."[22]

---

22. Brian Stanley, *The Bible and the Flag: Protestant Missions and British Imperialism in the Nineteenth and Twentieth Centuries* (Leicester, UK: Apollos, 1990): "The earliest significant example in modern times of an indigenous society developing an articulated case against Christian missions in terms of their relationship to Western expansion is provided by China in the 1860s. The rapid influx of both Catholic and Protestant missionaries into inland China after its opening to Western penetration in 1858 [during the Second Opium War] called forth a spate of tracts written by Chinese intellectuals attacking Christianity as a foreign religion and missionaries as agents of the Western powers which had foisted opium and then gunboats upon China." Not surprisingly, later Chinese Communists would make "common currency of the theory that Christian missions were in essence the ideological arm of Western imperial aggression. Events in China had irrevocably placed the issue of missions and imperialism on the agenda of both historical scholarship and missionary thinking" (14–15). On this theme, see

This is not the whole story, though, as Andrew Porter explains. Many missionaries repudiated imperialistic methods, as did many local Christians who contextualized their faith more fully than foreigners ever could. In China, a country that has a long history of Christianity and high-level Christian efforts to indigenize the faith, Hudson Taylor and his nineteenth-century China Inland Mission favored "faith mission" strategies for raising their support, clearly distancing their ministries from Western money and might so they could embrace indigenous cultural forms authentically. As Porter describes the varied practices of other English missionaries, he argues that scholars should recognize their *spiritual* motivations and resist the common temptation to dismiss them all as imperialists:

> The growing scale of Britain's worldwide presence of course made it impossible for missionaries to escape all involvement either with empire or with other facets of Britain's expansion abroad. However, that involvement was both patchy and discontinuous ... Attitudes ranged from total indifference or harsh criticism of empire, through discomfort and toleration, to enthusiastic support. The great majority of missionaries displayed a fitful interest in empire, giving it their temporary and often grudging attention chiefly when it hindered evangelization.[23]

Further, as Andrew Walls insists, Christianity has always been an incarnational faith, spread through limited, cultural forms: "no one ever meets universal Christianity in itself; we only ever meet Christianity in a local form, and that means a historically, culturally conditioned form." Walls continues, "We need not fear this; when God became man,

---

also Stephen Neill, *Colonialism and Christian Missions* (New York: McGraw-Hill, 1966); and Andrew Porter, *Religion versus Empire? British Protestant Missionaries and Overseas Expansion, 1700–1914* (Manchester: Manchester University Press, 2004).

23. Porter, *Religion versus Empire?*, 323–24. Porter deals in detail with missions to China on pp. 191–224. For more on the gradual rise of non-imperial, indigenous forms of Chinese Christianity, see especially the following chapters in *Christianity in China: From the Eighteenth Century to the Present*, ed. Daniel H. Bays (Stanford: Stanford University Press, 1996): Daniel H. Bays, "The Rise of an Indigenous Chinese Christianity" (265–68); Jessie G. Lutz and R. Ray Lutz, "Karl Gützlaff's Approach to Indigenization: The Chinese Union" (269–91); and Daniel H. Bays, "The Growth of Independent Christianity in China, 1900–1937" (307–16); and see R. G. Tiedemann, "Indigenous Agency, Religious Protectorates, and Chinese Interests: The Expansion of Christianity in Nineteenth-Century China," in *Converting Colonialism: Visions and Realities in Mission History, 1706–1914*, ed. Dana L. Robert, Studies in the History of Christian Missions (Grand Rapids: Eerdmans, 2008), 206–41.

he became historically, culturally conditioned man, in a particular time and place. What he became, we need not fear to be. There is nothing wrong with having local forms of Christianity—provided that we remember that they *are* local." We need not fear intercultural contact, or assume that culture is best approached as a timeless, changeless form, always corrupted by interference from outsiders. Interference can enrich us. Cultural change is not all bad. Our concern as gospel witnesses, rather, should be to oppose all instances of cultural chauvinism and imperial aggression, unilateral cultural force exerted with ethnocentric prejudice. Or, as Walls concludes the matter, "[t]he principal dangers of [cultural contact] come when one party insists that its own local features have universal validity."[24]

Gambian church historian Lamin Sanneh has applied this incarnational theme insightfully in a spate of recent writings. As a convert from Islam, Sanneh is well positioned to see the beautiful cultural diversity intrinsic to Christianity and the cultural malleability of an incarnated faith. "Christianity," he writes, "is the religion of over two thousand different language groups . . . More people pray and worship in more languages in Christianity than in any other religion in the world. Furthermore, Christianity has been the impulse behind the creation of more dictionaries and grammars of the world's languages than any other force in history." Christianity, then, "is not . . . a religion of cultural uniformity." And its pluralism "is not just a matter of regrettable doctrinal splits and ecclesiastical fragmentation." Rather, the Christian faith is meant to spread and grow through multicultural exchange, witness, dialogue, and partnership in ministry. The Christian church is built by God as faithful, humble witnesses put flesh on His grace, mercy, and love—without exhibiting favoritism (Jas 2:1-13).[25]

The challenge for cross-cultural Christian witnesses, says Walls, is mainly to balance what he calls our faith's "indigenizing principle" with its twin, the "pilgrim principle." The indigenizing principle, for Walls, reminds us that Christian faith is always and only expressed in terms of *concrete* cultural forms. "The fact . . . that 'if any man is in Christ he is a

---

24. Andrew F. Walls, "The American Dimension in the History of the Missionary Movement," in Joel A. Carpenter and Wilbert R. Shenk, eds., *Earthen Vessels: American Evangelicals and Foreign Missions, 1880-1980* (Grand Rapids: Eerdmans, 1990), 19, 24.

25. Lamin Sanneh, *Whose Religion Is Christianity? The Gospel beyond the West* (Grand Rapids: Eerdmans, 2003), 69, 130.

new creation' (2 Cor 5:17) does not mean that he starts or continues his life in a vacuum, or that his mind is a blank table. It has been formed by his own culture and history, and since God has accepted him as he is, his Christian mind will continue to be influenced by what was in it before. And this is as true for groups as for persons. All churches are culture churches—including our own."

The pilgrim principle, by contrast, states that all Christianity is also *universal*. Christians are pilgrims and strangers here. They have no abiding, earthly city. They and their cultures need to be transformed by the heavenly King of Kings. Walls unpacks this pilgrim principle with profound historical wisdom:

> The Christian is given an adoptive past. He is linked to the people of God in all generations (like him, members of the faith family), and most strangely of all, to the whole history of Israel, the curious continuity of the race of the faithful from Abraham. By this means, the history of Israel is part of Church history, and all Christians of whatever nationality, are landed by adoption with several millennia of someone else's history, with a whole set of ideas, concepts, and assumptions which do not necessarily square with the rest of their cultural inheritance; and the Church in every and, of whatever race and type of society, has this same adoptive past by which it needs to interpret the fundamentals of the faith. The adoption into Israel becomes a "universalizing" factor, bringing Christians of all cultures and ages together through a common inheritance, lest any of us make the Christian faith such a place to feel at home that no one else can live there; and bringing into everyone's society some sort of outside reference.

Walls's principles speak volumes about the focus of this chapter. The question of our identity, our place, within the church—as evangelicals, or Christians, whether in China or the U.S.—must be answered in reference to both our cultural *differences* and our *unity* as pilgrims, brothers and sisters, fellow heirs of God with Christ (Rom 8:14–17).[26]

THE CHINESE SITUATION

I admit, however, that this assignment is easier for me to announce than it is for us to complete. In Chinese history alone, there is a host of good

---

26. Andrew F. Walls, "The Gospel as Prisoner and Liberator of Culture," in Walls, *The Missionary Movement in Christian History*, 3–15 (quotations from 8–9).

reasons to resist the call to recognize the pilgrim principle—to suspect it as a ruse, a Trojan horse put forward to conquer Chinese differences and co-opt the Chinese churches into a Eurocentric faith. Such suspicion, furthermore, sorely complicates the task set before us in this chapter. It is difficult, even daunting, to define one's Christian identity in a context of concern regarding the history of the church, in a time and place where many remain uneasy about appearing too dependent on, or rooted in, those parts of the pilgrim throng which they associate with the West.

Christianity is growing as fast in parts of mainland China as it has ever grown, anywhere, before. Over the course of recent decades, further, this growth has been indigenous—*far* less dependent on the churches of the West than Western churches are dependent on their ancient, Asian forebears.[27] Chinese missionaries today are risking their lives in untold numbers, spreading their own faith abroad and playing a major role in the history of the evangelical movement.[28] And as Daniel Bays has quipped, "on any given Sunday there are almost certainly more Protestants in church in China than in all of Europe."[29] Nevertheless, many Chinese complain that Christian faith is "foreign," or that Chinese Christianity is not Chinese enough. "One more Christian, one less Chinese," as the well-worn slogan goes. People continue to think of Christian faith as a form of Western culture.[30]

---

27. On this theme, see especially Bays, "The Rise of an Indigenous Chinese Christianity," 265; Tiedemann, "Indigenous Agency, Religious Protectorates, and Chinese Interests"; Tony Lambert, *The Resurrection of the Chinese Church* (London: Hodder & Stoughton, 1991); and Kevin Xiyi Yao, *The Fundamentalist Movement among Protestant Missionaries in China, 1920–1937* (Lanham, MD: University Press of America, 2003), which shows indigenous forces shaping Chinese Protestant developments as long ago as the early twentieth century.

28. For an introduction to missions from China (and other eastern Asian lands), see Richard R. Cook, "The Great Commission in Asia," in Klauber and Manetsch, eds., *The Great Commission*, 149–63, who writes: "The global center of the church has shifted several times during Christian history. And that center may now be shifting to Asia, most of all to East Asia" (150).

29. Daniel H. Bays, "Chinese Protestant Christianity Today," *The China Quarterly* 174 (June 2003) 488.

30. On the notion that Chinese Christianity is not Chinese enough, see Ralph R. Covell, *Confucius, the Buddha, and Christ: A History of the Gospel in Chinese*, American Society of Missiology Series 11 (Maryknoll, NY: Orbis, 1986); and Alex Buchan, "Is the Chinese Church Chinese Enough? The Search for a More Chinese Theology," *ChinaSource* 3 (Spring 2001) 1–3, 8–10.

In their efforts to contextualize the Christian faith, moreover, many Chinese have sought to sever the cords that bind them to the West, to the history of its churches and their doctrinal distinctives. Kevin Yao has shown that this began at least a century ago, when local Chinese leaders assumed control of their own congregations and then distanced them from Western denominations:

> As Chinese Christian communities grew stronger and more independent in the early twentieth century, Chinese Christians started to take leadership roles in the life of churches. For them Western denominationalism was irrelevant and even absurd in the Chinese setting and harmful to the progress of Christianity in China ... Liberal church leaders and intellectuals viewed denominationalism as the obstacle to indigenizing Christianity in China ... On the other hand, many conservative and evangelical church leaders viewed denominations as an unbiblical invention.[31]

Philip Leung, among others, adds that many Chinese Christians also ignored their *own* history, as it was formerly taught from what he calls a "Western-centric" perspective. Though a "China-centered" history has emerged in recent years,[32] the habit of leaving history behind has helped

---

31. Kevin Yao, *The Fundamentalist Movement among Protestant Missionaries in China, 1920–1937*, 185.

32. Philip Yuen-Sang Leung, "Mission History versus Church History: The Case of China Historiography," in *Enlarging the Story: Perspectives on Writing World Christian History*, ed. Wilbert R. Shenk (Maryknoll, NY: Orbis, 2002), 54–74. Cf. Ryan Dunch, "Protestant Christianity in China Today: Fragile, Fragmented, Flourishing," in Stephen Uhalley Jr. and Xiaoxin Wu, eds., *China and Christianity: Burdened Past, Hopeful Future* (Armonk, NY: Sharpe, 2001), 195–216; and Philip Yuen-Sang Leung, "Conversion, Commitment, and Culture: Christian Experience in China, 1949–99," in *Christianity Reborn: The Global Expansion of Evangelicalism in the Twentieth Century*, ed. Donald M. Lewis, Studies in the History of Christian Missions (Grand Rapids: Eerdmans, 2004), 87–107, which sheds much light on both the conservative and liberal Chinese tendency to sever most ties with the past. Regarding conservative and liberal Chinese Protestantism in general, I have found two books on the most important twentieth-century spokesmen on each side very helpful: Thomas Alan Harvey, *Acquainted with Grief: Wang Mingdao's Stand for the Persecuted Church in China* (Grand Rapids: Brazos, 2002), on the conservative house-church leader; and Philip L Wickeri, *Reconstructing Christianity in China: K. H. Ting and the Chinese Church*, American Society of Missiology Series 41 (Maryknoll, NY: Orbis, 2007), on liberal Three-Self leader Bishop Ting. See also David Aikman, *Jesus in Beijing: How Christianity Is Transforming China and Changing the Global Balance of Power* (Washington, DC: Regnery, 2003); and Miikka Ruokanen, "K. H. Ting's Contribution to the Contextualization of Christianity in China," *Modern Theology* 25 (January 2009) 107–22.

all kinds of Chinese Christians to discard the heavy baggage often brought to their country by missionaries. It has helped these Christians to develop their own, uniquely Chinese faith—and to base that faith more squarely on the Bible.

As Mark Noll has written, this rather ahistorical manner of contextualizing the faith is certainly not unique to China. At a symposium in Oxford held in 1999, he noted that "Worldwide evangelical movements today are much less self-conscious about the Reformation origins of Protestantism than were evangelicals in the eighteenth century." They exhibit what one might call a typically evangelical "willingness to set aside the authority of tradition, evangelical tradition, in appropriating the faith." Such a willingness is rooted in the ecumenical impulse of the eighteenth-century revivals, which led to varied efforts to find a least common denominator for evangelicalism, but was strengthened by the desire to spread the faith beyond the West. "Even more than a willingness to sit lightly to tradition, it [is] an assumption that authoritative Christianity *must* set aside the baggage of its history if it [is] to thrive in the new environments lying beyond historic Christian regions."[33]

Ironically, then, this ahistorical style of self-fashioning perpetuates a typically Western evangelical problem. It exacerbates the long-standing evangelical habit of holding doctrines rather loosely, standing only on the Bible, reinventing the faith for themselves, and thus ignoring the rest of the church—indeed, isolating themselves from others whose faith they seek to renew—allegedly for the sake of moving beyond the confessional boundaries and the socio-cultural practices that divided them in the past. Not only does this approach impoverish their Christian faith and practice, it also renders identity questions difficult to resolve in any but presentist and ethnocentric terms.[34]

WHERE DO WE GO FROM HERE?

So where do we go from here? What are we to do about these questions of identity posed in church historical terms? Is "evangelicalism" still a

---

33. Mark A. Noll, "Evangelical Identity, Power, and Culture in the 'Great' Nineteenth Century," in Lewis, *Christianity Reborn*, 34, 40.

34. For more on the typically evangelical flavor of much of Chinese Protestantism, see Daniel H. Bays, "Christian Revival in China, 1900–1937," in Edith L. Blumhofer and Randall Balmer, eds., *Modern Christian Revivals* (Urbana: University of Illinois Press, 1993), 161–79.

useful category for understanding our faith traditions within our own cultural contexts? I would like to answer *yes* as I conclude this chapter, while suggesting that this category is useful only insofar as we understand its history, as we recognize the promise and the peril of identifying with evangelicalism.

God has used this modern movement to facilitate the spread of the gospel all around the world. He has done so, however, in a variety of ways, all of them culturally conditioned and historically particular—and many plagued with what I am calling ahistorical tendencies. Some evangelicals have proved more ethnocentric than others. But all of them have shared their faith in idiomatic terms, in contemporaneous forms. Only recently, moreover, have we come to see with clarity—and embrace with sensitivity—what Philip Leung has called "a multi-centered view of the church," a view in which genuine Christianity has no single, earthly center, but is "polycentric" in nature, to borrow a term from Tite Tiénou. As Zhang Kaiyuan reminds us, "Christianity does not belong to any particular nation or nationality. The process of Christianity's spread worldwide is also the process of its transplantation into one new culture after another. Meanwhile, for many centuries the dream of converting non-Christian areas actually involved the indigenization of Christianity in these areas. Of course, normal cultural communication is a two-way interactive process. From the perspective of us historians, the universality of Christianity lies in its theological core, and is formed through multilingual and multicultural interpretation, development, and gradual integration."[35]

So the challenge that faces those who want to make good on the rich legacy of the evangelical movement is to deepen their sense of identity with reference to the past without becoming more parochial in the process. We need to join hands with the *whole* church—past and present,

35. See Philip Yuen-Sang Leung, "Mission History versus Church History," 74; Tite Tiénou, "Forming Indigenous Theologies," in James M. Phillips and Robert C. Coote, eds., *Toward the Twenty-First Century in Christian Mission* (Grand Rapids: Eerdmans, 1993), 248–9; and Zhang Kaiyuan, "Chinese Perspective—A Brief Review of the Historical Research on Christianity in China," in Stephen Uhalley Jr. and Xiaoxin Wu, eds., *China and Christianity: Burdened Past, Hopeful Future* (Armonk, NY: Sharpe, 2001), 29. Cf. Tite Tiénou, "Christian Theology in an Era of World Christianity," in Craig Ott, and Harold A. Netland, eds., *Globalizing Theology: Belief and Practice in an Era of World Christianity* (Grand Rapids: Baker Academic, 2006), 37–51; and Lamin Sanneh, *Disciples of All Nations: Pillars of World Christianity*, Oxford Studies in World Christianity (New York: Oxford University Press, 2008), esp. 13–56.

at home and abroad—a church that first arose in Asia but now nearly spans the globe.[36] We need to reject the common assumption that our faith is a Western product. And we need to be more honest about the sins of the Christian past that keep us from living and working together as the body of Christ in the world.

Perhaps Chinese evangelicals will lead the way in showing their brothers and sisters in God's family how to contextualize the faith without domesticating it—how to render the faith their own without repeating the sins of the past and universalizing their social and cultural preferences. As Lamin Sanneh has suggested, "It is clear that in the [Christian] religion's eastward shift what happens to the church in China will have incalculable consequences for the rest of the world generally, and for the post-Christian West in particular. China could correct the one-sidedness of Western Christianity."[37] Let us pray that, by God's grace, this may be so.

---

36. Significantly, Martin Marty begins his recent history of Christianity on the continent of Asia, "the birthplace of the church," and does not move west to Europe until much later in his narrative (i.e., until chapter 4, nearly a third of the way through the book). See Martin Marty, *The Christian World: A Global History*, Modern Library Chronicles (New York: The Modern Library, 2007). Relatedly, see Philip Jenkins, *The Lost History of Christianity: The Thousand-Year Golden Age of the Church in the Middle East, Africa, and Asia—and How It Died* (New York: HarperOne, 2008).

37. Sanneh, *Disciples of All Nations*, 282.

2

Missions, Cultural Imperialism, and the Development of the Chinese Church[1]

KA LUN LEUNG

DEVELOPMENTS IN THE TWENTY-FIRST century are altering perceptions of Christianity and the relationship of Christianity to culture around the world. Churches in Asia, Africa, and Latin America now have an opportunity to challenge the Western-American monopolization of Christianity. While local expressions of Christianity might in some ways hinder global fellowship, I believe now is an ideal time for churches around the world to share resources and experiences and to develop strong local cultural identities as well as strong global bonds. The churches in China have begun this process of local indigenization and have also initiated global networking. This chapter will chart the development of the Chinese Protestant churches and show how they have broken away from the Western missionary movement to which they were once closely tied. Following loosely the major divisions of modern Chinese history, the chapter will examine missions and imperialism, missions and culture, the Gospel and social change, and, finally, contextual theologies.

If the nineteenth century was a period of imperialism (or New Imperialism, to distinguish it from colonial movements begun in the seventeenth century), then the twentieth century was an era of nationalism and anti-imperialism. World War II dealt a heavy blow to the great powers in Europe and left the colonial domains created during

---

1. Chinese materials referred to in this chapter are mostly omitted.

the previous century no longer sustainable. Colonies in Asia, Africa, and Latin America declared their independence one by one after the war. National independence movements roared, all making anti-imperialism their goal.

However, World War II was soon succeeded by an era of the Cold War, when most countries were compelled to ally with either the United States or the Soviet Union. Nationalism was suppressed, replaced by ideological dichotomies such as capitalism versus communism and liberalism versus totalitarianism. It was not until after the Soviet Union dissolved during the 1980s and the Cold War ended that nationalism began to flourish again. It is in the current period that local expressions of Christianity, in China and around the world, have also begun to prosper.

MISSIONS AND IMPERIALISM, 1807–1911

The growth of Western imperialism in the nineteenth century was coupled with Christian missionary expansion all over the world. The two movements, therefore, were interlocked in many ways. The coalition was especially notable in the way Western powers employed their military force to back missionary work. China is an example of this. The privileges to evangelize and to build churches were actually "benefits" listed in the unequal treaties that China was forced to sign after being defeated on the battlefields. In other words, the right to evangelism was both a form of compensation and penalty that the West placed on China. From 1844, when the first treaty containing terms about missionary work was signed, until 1943, when all unequal treaties were abolished, the Christian missionary enterprise had an official documentary relationship with Western imperialism. This is a fact that Chinese Christians could neither deny nor explain away.[2]

Motives for missions and of various missionaries were diverse. However, they were generally all committed to protecting or even supporting foreign missions out of the belief that the spread of Christianity was a crucial element for the expansion of Western culture in other countries. Westernization—assimilating the entire world into the Western epistemological system and social order—was regarded as instrumental

---

2. Brian Stanley, *The Bible and the Flag: Protestant Missions and British Imperialism in the Nineteenth and Twentieth Centuries* (Leicester, UK: Apollos, 1990).

in building a world dominated by Western values and Christianity. Not only was Christianity a Western religion, but it was also an essential constituent of Western culture. As Yale University historian Jonathan Spence puts it: "Diplomats, merchants and missionaries all came to China for one single reason, i.e., to change China."[3]

This was also the general understanding of the Chinese people. Since the 1920s, many Chinese had criticized Christianity for being a tool of invasion into China, with missionaries acting as pioneers of Western imperialism. Cultural imperialism had become a constant accusation against Christianity.[4] Ironically, the so-called "cultural imperialism" of the missions movement did not really refer to the import of Western cultures and religions that threatened traditional Chinese cultures and faiths. In fact, many of the Chinese who made such accusations had already lost their attachments to traditional Chinese culture and were longing for Western democracy and Western science. This was especially true for the Marxists, who could not in any way claim that they opposed Western thought.

According to the critics of missions, all Westerners who came to China, including diplomats, merchants, and missionaries, were from the same camp and had consciously or unconsciously participated in the same cultural invasion scheme against China. It is just that they had played different roles in such invasion. The role played by missionaries was to increase the cultural impact of the West on China, to construct a positive image of Westerners, to reduce the hostility of the Chinese against Westerners, and to diminish Chinese awareness of the invasion of Western imperialism.

The laudatory work of missions in China, then, was instead seen as sinister by these critics. The establishment of mission schools and hospitals and involvement in charity work were viewed merely as attempts to curry favor with the local people by convincing them that the good deeds performed by Westerners stemmed from good intentions. Although their intentions were generally good, the missionaries were also, either consciously or unconsciously, helping invade China with Western

---

3. Jonathan Spence, *To Change China: Western Advisers in China, 1620—1960* (Boston: Little, Brown, 1969).

4. See for example Paul W. Harris, "Cultural Imperialism & American Protestant Missionaries: Collaboration & Dependency in Mid-Nineteenth-Century China," *Pacific Historical Review* 60 (1991) 309–38.

cultural and epistemological ideas. For the missionaries, this created a paradoxical phenomenon: The more good they did, the more they were intricately tied with the cultural invasion of China. They thereby were working at cross-purposes with the Chinese anti-imperialist efforts.

Nevertheless, it is difficult to verify or falsify this kind of accusation from the critics of missions. People on both sides could easily offer supporting evidence for their own arguments. Yet the fact remains that Christianity has had to face such a charge from Chinese critics fueled by nationalism and anti-imperialism during the last century.

MISSIONS AND CULTURE, 1911–1949

After the missions movement took root in China, the problematic relationship between missions and culture became more prominent. In addition to the challenges that cultural imperialism posed for the Chinese churches, the churches also had to negotiate the complex relationship between missions and culture.

Gospel and culture are inseparable. Christianity is not just a set of abstract concepts. It is, rather, a living religion that has grown during the past two thousand years, and it always manifests itself in a particular cultural form. Thus, Christianity has always appeared as a form of culture. Furthermore, as a "positive religion," Christianity is informed by a whole set of ideologies and values that its adherents apply directly in cultural or social occasions. For instance, Christians define marriage as being between one man and one woman, and this itself is a cultural orientation.

When Christian missionaries enter a new community, with their Christianity dressed in their own foreign culture, conflict with the local culture is natural. This results in the perception that there is a conflict between Christianity itself and culture. However, it is important to point out that major conflicts between Christian teaching and the local culture are not common. Conflicts often arise, rather, as missionaries bring their own cultural agenda into a new place and attempt to create changes in the local society and culture. Missionaries can be classified as cultural reformers, and many of the cultural conflicts are caused by their intention to renew culture.[5]

---

5. Paul A. Varg, *Missionaries, Chinese, and Diplomats: The American Protestant Missionary Movement in China, 1890–1952* (Princeton: Princeton University Press, 1958).

Ever since the nineteenth century, missionaries to China, both conservative and liberal, sought to change China. Not only were they purveyors of Western culture, but they were also catalysts for the Westernization of China.[6] On one hand, some conservative missionaries viewed traditional Chinese culture as a heathen culture that was completely based on false beliefs and false knowledge. These missionaries thus believed that traditional Chinese culture had to be changed, and this created tensions for new Chinese Christians. In addition to abandoning their previous religions, these Christians also had to abandon their traditional ways of thinking and living. Thus, conflicts often arose when, for example, Chinese Christians were instructed by their Western mentors not to participate in ancestral worship. Missionaries in the liberal camp, on the other hand, did not put as much emphasis on eradicating traditional Chinese culture and religion. Instead, they tended to focus on espousing certain social or cultural ideals, believing that the values contained within Christianity and Western culture were universally superior.[7] They regarded these values as setting the one and only proper direction in which all human societies should proceed. Their strategy was to help China embark on this path through education and social reforms.[8]

I do not believe it was wrong for foreign missionaries to promote their own cultural agenda, nor was it wrong for them to have aimed to change China, for all peoples have ideals for culture and society. Missionaries should thus not be blamed for either of these objectives, which often resulted in conflicts between the missionaries and those whom they sought to reach. As noted previously, these conflicts were cultural and not religious in nature. In the nineteenth century, the Chinese gentry acted to protect the traditional Chinese culture and social order. Their opposition to Christianity was not necessarily due to their belief

---

6. My intent is not to understate the contributions of missionaries in China to the modernization of the country. See for example Dan Cui, *The Cultural Contribution of British Protestant Missionaries and British-American Cooperation to China's National Development During the 1920s* (Lanham, MD: University Press of America, 1998).

7. Xi Lian, *The Conversion of Missionaries: Liberalism in American Protestant Missions in China, 1907–1932* (University Park: The Pennsylvania State University Press, 1997).

8. William R. Hutchison, "Modernism & Missions: The Liberal Search for an Exportable Christianity, 1875–1935" in *The Missionary Enterprise in China and America*, ed. John K. Fairbank; Harvard studies in American–East Asian relations 6 (Cambridge: Harvard University Press, 1974); William R. Hutchison, *The Modernist Impulse in American Protestantism* (Durham: Duke University Press, 1992).

that Christianity is a false religion, but sprang, rather, from their strong conviction that Christianity was harming the social order of Chinese society. Moving into the twentieth century, many Chinese had participated in the massive reformation movements to transform traditional China, but they held different cultural and social agendas. They thus held different points of view toward Christianity—most of them negative. For example, those who promoted communism and communist reformation saw Christian eschatology as conflicting with their own utopianism, and the leftists who worked among the young people regarded the YMCA as their biggest competitor.

Most of the time, then, Christianity was not regarded merely as a new religion and a new religious option, but as a representation of Western power, culture, and social ideals. In this sense, Christian mission was more of a political and cultural concern than a religious initiative.

GOSPEL AND SOCIAL CHANGE, 1950S–PRESENT

China, like most Asian or African countries, has gained its political independence and is gradually moving toward prosperity. The age of the invasion of imperialism has come to an end, and anti-imperialism is no longer a major concern for government officials or the people. However, this does not mean that Christianity has disassociated itself from imperialism. As a means to achieve more effective social control, the Chinese Communist government regards officially unauthorized Christian communities, especially those with overseas connections, as imperialistic in nature. Like many non-governmental organizations, Christian organizations regularly show concern for the social and cultural circumstances in developing countries, targeting particularly inhumane or tyrannical political systems. Western capitalistic powers have sometimes generously funded NGOs, occasionally using them as tools to overthrow "unqualified" governments. Since the 1980s, the government in the Peoples Republic of China has repeatedly trumpeted warnings lest Christian missionaries should become a tool to force changes upon China's political system, making the nation another Soviet Union or Eastern Europe. This threat by NGOs and missionaries is regarded by the Chinese Communist Party as yet another form of cultural imperialism.

The threat posed by this kind of cultural imperialism, however, is only directed at political regimes, rather than at the people in general. On one hand, the Chinese government accuses Western powers of using religion as a tool to bring about regime evolution; on the other hand, political dissidents today are actively appealing to Christianity as the basis for making social-political critiques. In the 1980s, "Christianity fever" aroused the interest of Chinese intellectuals in the religion, who viewed it as a source of intellectual and spiritual power to change China. Thus, in a sense, the PRC government has not been wrong in its warnings. Religion does have the power to effect social change, and it has used both violent and peaceful activism as means to achieve that goal.

The critical question centers, however, on who the active player is: foreign NGOs or the native people? If local Chinese citizens are promoting Christian values as part of their own social agenda and cultural movements, imperialism would not be indicated. But if overseas Christian organizations are involved in political or social movements in China—especially those related to nationalism, such as independence movements of ethnic minorities or events to address territorial sovereignty issues, anti-imperialist reactions would be triggered at once. For instance, Western societies' general support for the independence movements in Tibet and Taiwan are surely not acceptable to many of the Chinese people. Active participation by foreign Christian organizations in, for example, Tibet's independence movement, would likely be opposed by Chinese Christians. Thus, Chinese churches have always emphasized their independence from Western Christian movements. This, unfortunately, inhibits the global fellowship of Christian communities to a certain degree.

Western postmodern societies are gradually excluding religion from the public square, limiting it to the private sphere. However, in many African and Asian countries, religion still has broad influence on politics and society. Religion in these nations is a major source of all kinds of political disputes, both internal and international.

Are missions and evangelism then necessarily imperialistic in nature? In modern societies where relativism and nihilism are popular, any proselytizing activities with the objective of changing another person's faith would be regarded as cultural imperialism. Little consideration is given to whether the missionary's intention is benign, nor to whether he or she respects religious freedom and individual choice. In the eyes of the nearly nihilistic postmodernists, anyone who claims to possess universal truth would be seen as a threat to the pluralistic society. Similarly, anyone actively sharing his or her faith would be regarded as invading the private domain of others. This is the reason why some liberal Christians appeal for the abandonment of global evangelism, or at least urge a transition from evangelistic activities to religious dialogue that seeks better mutual representation of personal worldviews.[9]

Evangelicals have never accepted this "religious dialogue" point of view. They maintain, rather, that Christianity aims to change both the society and the individual. Such change includes internal religious beliefs as well as external cultural behavior. As Christian believers, we should not hide our desire that Christianity transform the Chinese people and China. Furthermore, evangelicals, at their best, have always insisted that political power is not the proper means to achieve this end. "Not by might nor by power, but by my spirit," says the Lord Almighty (Zech 4:6).

ON CONTEXTUAL THEOLOGIES, 1980S–PRESENT

As churches began in the 1980s to experience revivals and relaxed religious restrictions, they could engage in more earnest deliberations concerning the contextualization of Christianity in China.

To quell accusations of critics who viewed evangelism as culturally imperialistic, the usual solution of both missions and the Chinese churches was to build national and contextual churches. This gave rise to the popularity of "three-self" principles: self-governance, self-propagation, and self-support. It was thought that adherence to three-self principles would lead to an integration of traditional ideas and Christian theology, thus fostering the development of a contextual theology for a specific location.

Fruitful discussions on contextualization of the Chinese churches began a hundred years ago, and ever since then the "three-self" principles have played a critical role. However, the question of how a contextual theology should be constructed remains. Whether Christianity ought to be contextualized through dialogue with traditional culture or modern thinking, or whether contextualization should occur in the cultural or political arena, are still unanswered questions. In the past century, drastic changes have taken place in Chinese societies and culture, and a huge gap now exists between tradition and modernity, with neither of the two monopolizing the mainstream culture. Thus, even if Christian thinkers

---

9. See William E. Hocking, ed., *Re-thinking Mission: A Laymen's Inquiry after One Hundred Years* (New York: Harper, 1932).

desired to seek a contextualization through dialogue, it would be difficult to find a generally accepted representative of the various Chinese cultures with which to converse. Even if Chinese theologians could contextualize Christianity with Confucianism, Buddhism, or communism, they still could not say that the result would be regarded as the general Chinese theology. In the current pluralistic era, theologians must construct various types of contextual theologies that accommodate different cultural backgrounds and subcultures.

Therefore, theoretical discussions about what constitutes contextualization may well be meaningless, as the word "Chinese" does not point to a single type of people, but to a vast group of peoples whose differences are as numerous as their similarities. What Christian theologians should thus do is recognize a people group within a particular time and space and make every effort to demonstrate the relevance of Christianity to that group.

Chinese Christians have often only participated in reactive discussions about contextualization. That is, they first ask what the needs and problems of Asian and specifically Chinese societies are, and then ask what Christianity can do in response. This has been the basic mode of thought behind twentieth-century contextual theologies, based on an assumption that the reason the church exists is to respond to the needs of society. Theologians seemed to concur that the theological agenda should be set by the secular world, and that the churches would only then provide an antithetical response, regardless of whether it was a negation or a supplement to the needs of society.

During the nineteenth and twentieth centuries, major Asian countries faced two predominant issues. The first was political reformation. Nationalism arose quickly when Asian peoples encountered imperialism from the West. Internally, feudalism and traditional monarchies were overthrown, whereas externally the Western invasion was resisted and thus movements for national liberation were promoted. The second issue was cultural reformation. Traditional societies strived to depart from their old mode of thinking and to fit into the Westernized world, yet paradoxically sought at the same time to keep Western cultural and social impacts to a minimum. Many Christians participating in discussions concerning contextualization worked hard to address these two issues. They often believed that the universal claims inherent in Christianity could provide a solution for peoples and countries suffering from regional problems.

In the nineteenth century, missionaries were not only spreading the Gospel in non-Christian nations, but were also disseminating Western culture. By educating people, building hospitals, printing newspapers, translating books, and contributing to the work of social charities, these missionaries injected Western culture into their mission-field countries. Moreover, with the goal of winning more young intellectuals to the faith, missionaries overtly claimed that Christianity was the core value of Western culture, asserting further that belief in God was the key factor that led to democracy and science. According to these missionaries, Westernization, modernization, and Christianization were inseparable, if not identical.

In the twentieth century, non-Christian modes of thought (especially naturalism and positivism arising with the Enlightenment) began to gain popularity in Asia, Africa, and Latin America. Christianity was no longer regarded as the equivalent of Western culture. Moreover, atheism and Marxism were attracting significant numbers of people to embrace Western ideas and culture. Still, many of these adherents of Western culture were nationalists who despised the invasion of cultural imperialism, and they had found Christianity and the missions movement to be convenient targets to attack. According to these critics, Christianity represented the parts of Western culture that should be rejected. For instance, many Chinese intellectuals in the early twentieth century believed that two kinds of Western civilization existed, characterized by two revolutions: the French Revolution and the Russian Revolution. Chinese intellectuals believed the people had to choose one or the other. During the period of the Cold War, many intellectuals contrasted the Christian West with the Socialist East. They sometimes even argued that Christianity was a tool used to stop communism from spreading around the world.[10] They believed Christianity supported political democracy, social freedom, and capitalism.

Globalization emerged as a central issue as the period of the Cold War came to an end. I believe there is a predominant culture today in the progress of globalization. Francis Fukuyama's claim that "Globalization is Americanization" is largely true. For him, globalization is the general-

---

10. See George Hood, *Neither Bang Nor Whimper: The End of a Missionary Era in China* (Singapore: The Presbyterian Church, 1991).

ization of American culture all around the world, manifest by everything from McDonald's to Hollywood. This Americanization prompts non-Americans to rethink the position of their own national culture in the face of globalization. They may realize they cannot wholly resist cultural forms and values emitting from around the globe, but at the same time believe they should not assimilate them so readily.

Apparently, China, and all of Asia, could not resist globalization (in other words, Americanization) in the arenas of economics and politics. As a result of economic globalization, consumer and production modes of all the countries in Asia are now more or less similar to that of the Western world. Even in education, medicine, society, and politics, Asians have come to accept the operational modes and values set by the West. No matter how much the PRC government insists on its situational differences from Western societies, it cannot completely deny democracy, freedom, human rights, and the rule of law as vital cultural values. Thus, the government argues that different countries are in different stages of progress, and that the timetables for adopting these values therefore also vary.

There is also no urgency in non-Western countries to accept religious globalization. It is even thought that religious localization is a way for non-Americans to resist globalization. Globalization is creating identity crises both nationally and culturally. Many people are thus looking to traditional religions for a sense of continuity between the past and the present in their attempts to keep Western culture at bay. Religions are most resistant to globalization. In the global world today, economic and political non-conformity are practically impossible, but many people believe they have strong reasons for holding onto traditional religions. This is probably partly why many traditional religions have regained their status today, and it also led Samuel P. Huntington to predict that major conflicts throughout the world after the Cold War would be among different religious civilizations.

While the idea of non-religious globalization has become popular, I remain a holdout. Generally speaking, I believe that it is not practically possible in most of the regions in the world; it can do no more than create superficial similarities. For instance, college education programs and traffic systems are similar all around the world. However, I do believe that the globalization of religions is not only practically possible, but is a concept that we must ponder seriously. Churches must strive to complete their global mission in evangelism, at the same time actively asking local questions such as: What is the specific individual or social need in this area? What unique message can Christianity deliver in this context? What functions can Christian churches play in this particular society? To put it simply, at a time when globalization and Americanization have become synonymous, Christianity must stand firm in its effort to de-Americanize and remain intentionally localized. However, de-Americanization must involve more than merely constructing a church that is distinct from American churches. To focus exclusively on the latter would result in a kind of "antithetical" contextual theology that would be only another kind of vassal to Western cultures. I believe it is only when Christians can develop different readings of Christianity in, for instance, Asia, Africa, and Latin America that the churches will be able to halt the Western-American influence that now tends to monopolize Christianity. By developing local theologies in the global context, churches could finally alter the perception of the relationship between missionaries and imperialism. Disassociating Christianity from imperialism should also foster effective evangelism in China and around the world.

It is my belief that localization of Christianity will not hinder global fellowship, and that more and more opportunities will present themselves for churches around the world to share resources and experiences at this level.

3

Overcoming Missions Guilt

Robert Morrison, Liang Fa, and the Opium Wars

RICHARD R. COOK

INTRODUCTION

THE PROTESTANT MISSIONARY MOVEMENT had a profound impact on China, but also left an unintended legacy in the West. Western missions guilt is an unanticipated backlash from the missionary movement, which still reverberates today. Did the missionary movement draw the missionaries inexorably into the imperial project and, thus, the sins of the West? Popular culture in America has castigated the missions movement for decades, and missions in America has seemed to be in a defensive mode. Although missions, particularly North American evangelical missions, continued to expand—with an estimated more than 110,000 American and Canadian long-term Protestant missionaries serving today—the missionary movement is nonetheless, in the minds of many Westerners, forever tied with the often discredited imperialistic project. Thus while Chinese Christians and many others in the majority world surely struggle with questions of Christian identity given this association, evangelical Christians in the West find themselves facing their own quandary.

The nineteenth-century missionaries were in many ways a product of the age in which they lived. Clearly, they said and did many things that reflected the broader imperialist, and often racist, era. These "sins" of imperialism, and, by extension, the missions movement, have created the tremendous backlash of missions guilt. This guilt does not seem to have curtailed missions participation, at least among evangelicals, but it may have other ramifications. I sometimes worry that missions guilt impedes the ability of those of us in the West to understand our past, and thus our evangelical identity. My objective in this chapter is to ask: How can we as Evangelicals in the West today relate to our missions past? How can we identify with this past? How can we get beyond Western guilt stemming from imperialism?

If missions is indelibly tied to imperialism, then it may be impossible to forge a Christian identity apart from the sins of imperialism. And now, as greater numbers of Chinese Christians join the missions movement, how might Chinese evangelicals identify with this period of imperialism and missions history? How will they relate to the past? How might the imperialist past shape Chinese evangelical identity?

In my studies of missions history and missions in China, I have found that in a number of the most egregious interfaces of missions involvement with politics and imperialism, a complex context comprised of multiple factors influenced missionary behavior. Certainly someone unsympathetic to missions and the missions mandate could categorically wave off missionaries as mere tools or stooges of their home governments, but the missionaries involved may be deserving of a better understanding of the sometimes excruciating circumstances surrounding the decisions they made. Such an understanding seems important for Western evangelicals and also for Chinese Christians.

This chapter will focus on one of the thorniest issues in China and the West's shared past: the Opium Wars. Although several critical issues could be evaluated, the Opium Wars and the subsequent Nanjing Treaty ("unequal treaties") should show how a fresh perspective might help offer a new understanding of the legacy of missions in China. The missionaries in the 1830s and 1840s, as will be seen, faced an impossible predicament. In the face of the sometimes brutal persecution of the Chinese converts, the missionaries had to choose to remain silent or to enter into the political discussions on behalf of their Chinese colleagues.

For the missionaries, who often served as official translators for international political negotiations, to fail to speak up in defense of the persecuted Chinese Christians might have been perceived (at the time) as unacceptable, perhaps even unethical. Thus, when presented with the opportunity at the negotiating table, the missionaries made the fateful decision to advocate for legal protections for Chinese Christians at the conclusion of the Opium Wars. And the die was cast: Christianity and imperialism have forever been tragically linked together. Christianity in China has paid a high price for this decision, which was enshrined in the Nanjing Treaty. However, what other path might the missionaries have followed? They either could have attempted to provide some legal protection for the vulnerable and fragile Chinese Christians, or remained apolitical and continued to witness the brutal suppression of the churches and of the missionary movement in China.

While this chapter takes a more sympathetic approach in examining the early missionaries in China, I am not advocating a naïve return to missions hagiography. Nor do I advocate a celebratory history, which simplistically narrates the "triumph" of God and the Church. I do not intend to provide an apologetic for missions in the past. But, rather, my aim is to ask: How can we as evangelicals today relate to our past? How can we get beyond Western guilt over imperialism? How can we positively define our identity based on our past? I suggest that careful attention to the context of the Opium Wars, avoiding both undue guilt over imperialism and Christian triumphalism, can provide a more satisfying narrative of nineteenth-century missions history in China.

This chapter will first consider the volatile climate in China when Robert Morrison arrived in 1807. Next, a brief sketch of Morrison and his early ministry in the extreme edges of China will be presented. His early convert, Liang Fa, will then be introduced, with a particular look at how their lives intersected. The multifaceted dynamics of their relationship serve as a prototype for the types of complex concerns missionaries would face in 1840 regarding the negotiations of the Treaty of Nanjing. Finally, the Opium War and the Nanjing Treaty will be summarized.

CONTEXT IN CHINA:
THE ARRIVAL OF PROTESTANT MISSIONS

To understand the role that missionaries played in altering Chinese society and culture, it is valuable to recognize how China was already changing even before the arrival of missions and Western imperialism. China had been a more or less unified empire for at least two millennia, but there was a regular rise and fall of imperial families and even outside intervention in internal Chinese leadership. Most prominently, the Mongols ruled the Yuan Dynasty in China from 1271 to 1368. When Robert Morrison arrived in 1807, the Manchurian Qing Dynasty had been ruling since 1644. The lengthy and successful rule of the emperor Qianlong ended just before 1800. During the closing years of his reign and throughout the first decades of the nineteenth century, China was undergoing a relentless chain of crises that served as a harbinger of coming radical convulsions. Even without the series of challenges from the West through the nineteenth century, China, it seems, was bound for change.

Eminent Chinese historian John K. Fairbank offers a lengthy list of changes occurring around 1800 in China. This chapter will mention only three. The reign of Qianlong marked one of the many peaks of Chinese civilization, but China was in the midst of tremendous population growth when the missionaries began to arrive in 1807. While in 1741 the population was 142 million, by 1851 it had exploded to around 432 million. Among the many problems accompanying the rapid population growth was the tremendous pressure placed on the government bureaucracy and the traditional civil service exam system. With the government moving slowly to respond to population growth, more and more people were competing for the same number of civil service positions.

With the sharp rise in population growth, more work was needed for ever-diminishing returns. The term "immiseration" has been used to describe the worsening living standards in China. For instance, land of inferior quality took more effort to cultivate and produced less. Also, with the large population, labor was inexpensive and suppressed industrialization. While the West was developing labor-saving ideas, inexpensive labor in China reduced producers' motivation to innovate similar solutions for production. This led to increased stagnation in China. Indeed, Fairbank argues that the very superiority achieved by Song China would become by 1800 a source of her backwardness, as though "all great achievements carry the seeds of their ossification." Thus, for instance, the early development of the abacus in China might have later led to stagnation in the area of mathematics.

When Robert Morrison arrived in 1807, China still seemed to be one of the leading civilizations in the world. However, the reality may have been different. In hindsight, it would appear that China was already in decline and may have been moving toward inevitable crises. Western imperialism may have amplified those problems, but China was probably already on the brink of change and a new era.

ROBERT MORRISON: THE FIRST PROTESTANT MISSIONARY

The powerful Protestant missions movement in Britain could not have emerged in a political or social vacuum. The British missions movement grew up alongside Britain's surging imperial power around the globe. Robert Morrison (1782–1834) of the London Missionary Society (LMS), the pioneer missionary to China, developed his missions calling and passion in this context. He arrived in Canton in 1807 and served in China most of the rest of his life, from 1807 to 1834. With only limited access to the southern coast of China, in 1809 Morrison took on the official role of interpreter working for the East India Company. He also served the British government on two British missions to China. His work as a translator allowed him to retain his residence in China.

In 1818, Morrison started the Anglo-Chinese College outside of China in Malacca,[1] and William Milne[2] was appointed as the first headmaster. The dual goals of the school were to train future missionaries in Chinese and to educate local Chinese boys. In 1823, Morrison and Milne finished a complete Chinese translation of the Bible. Morrison was a recognized expert on China and the Chinese language and authored around forty works in Chinese and English, the most significant being his six-volume publication *A Dictionary of the Chinese Language* (1815–1822). Although Morrison numbered only about a dozen converts during his twenty-seven-year career in China, he laid the foundation for future missions and rightfully earned the informal title, "Father of Protestant Missions in China."

LIANG FA: THE FIRST ORDAINED CHINESE MINISTER

Robert Morrison, spurred on by his homeland's zeal for Protestant missions, discovered a new world when he arrived in mid-Qing China, a land with an ancient civilization stretching back thousands of years. Although already possibly in decline by 1807, the early missionaries might not have perceived the dramatic changes that would convulse China in the coming decades. Given the extreme limitations placed on foreigners in China by the central Chinese government, only a small

---

1. Malacca was on the Malay Peninsula. It was conquered by the Portuguese in 1511 and became a strategic base for Portuguese expansion in the East Indies. In 1641, it was taken by the Dutch and in 1824 ceded to the British.

2. Milne, from Scotland, was the second Protestant missionary in China, arriving in 1813.

handful of Chinese had access to the missionaries and an opportunity to evaluate their message. Not surprisingly, Liang Fa's background matched the profile of a potential early convert to Protestant Christianity.

Liang Fa was born near Canton in 1787, twenty years before Morrison established the tentative Protestant outpost on China's southern coast of Canton. As with many of the Chinese who had an early interest in Christianity, Liang had little education, and missions would offer him an unprecedented opportunity for education and to improve his lot in life. Although not well educated, he brought to the mission the valuable skill of woodblock cutting.

Liang was a prime candidate for work in Malacca, and he accompanied William Milne there in 1815. In Malacca, Liang's skills as a printer were put to good use. With China still almost entirely closed to missions efforts, Christian and evangelistic literature was a high priority of the early missionaries. Liang Fa's publishing skills were thus highly coveted.

While in Malacca, Liang became an early Chinese convert to Protestant Christianity and was baptized by William Milne on November 3, 1816. Liang, who had memorized the Confucian classics and dabbled in Buddhism, had a sense of the importance of moral integrity, but found he lacked the power to achieve his moral ideals. Confucianism had not freed him from his "licentious thoughts," and Buddhist chanting could not relieve his moral guilt. In Christianity, he found the moral and spiritual power he desired.[3] Together in Malacca, Milne and Liang produced the *Monthly Chinese Magazine* for seven years. They also produced a number of Christian tracts. Best known was Liang's evangelistic tract "Good Words to Admonish the World."[4] Liang would also later be involved in the printing of the Chinese Bible in 1823.

In 1819, with China still essentially closed to the missionaries, Liang Fa returned to Canton. As a Chinese person, he was able to penetrate the inland and distribute Gospel literature. While Milne, who died in 1822, and Morrison were still only on the fringes of the Chinese mainland, Liang Fa became an invaluable co-laborer as the first Chinese evangelist. Morrison ordained Liang as an evangelist in 1824. Liang traveled extensively in Guangdong (Canton) Province and regularly distributed

---

3. Samuel Hugh Moffett, *A History of Christianity in Asia*, Vol. 2, *1500–1900* (Maryknoll, NY: Orbis, 2005), 291.

4. That tract would have profound influence on Hong Xiuquan, leader of the violent, quasi-Christian, midcentury Taiping Rebellion.

Christian tracts. One priority for Liang was to pass out tracts at the civil service literary exams offered every three years. It was through this literature ministry that a number of the exam candidates converted to Christianity and even become co-workers in the ministry.

During the 1820s Liang Fa was arrested in China, an incident that surely dismayed his Western colleagues. He was severely punished, suffering thirty blows with a bamboo cane. Liang wrote, "I call to mind that all who preach the Gospel of our Lord Jesus must suffer persecution; and though I cannot equal the patience of Paul or Job, I desire to imitate the ancient saints, and keep my heart in peace."[5]

Persecution would become a hallmark of the early Protestant converts in China.

How might the missionaries have responded to such persecution of their beloved Chinese colleagues? Should Morrison, who had now been in China for more than ten years and had developed many contacts among the British and Chinese leaders in Canton, have helped Liang Fa if he had the ability to do so? As one of the key British translators, should Morrison have spent his political capital to help his friend? Morrison did intervene on behalf of Liang, and Liang was released. Thus began a long tradition of Protestant missionary intervention on behalf of Chinese Christians. With persecution still a problem, Liang then returned to Malacca.

Along with Morrison, Liang Fa would continue to pay a high cost for his faithful service. While Morrison was still limited to the periphery of China, Liang again returned to the interior of China where he continued to defy imperial edicts against Christianity. Chinese people were not allowed to convert to Christianity, nor were they allowed to distribute Christian literature. In 1834, about the time of Morrison's death, a number of Liang's Chinese co-workers were arrested. One was severely beaten, and another was put to death. During the brutal investigation, one of the Christians revealed that Liang Fa was the chief leader of their activities. Liang Fa was again forced to go on the run, escaping eventually to Singapore.

Several years after fleeing persecution in China to Singapore, Liang, China's "first Protestant evangelist" and close colleague of Morrison and Milne, was able to return to China in 1839. The persecution had

---

5. Scott W. Sunquist et al., eds., *A Dictionary of Asian Christianity* (Grand Rapids: Eerdmans, 2001), 482.

mercifully subsided. Again, the political context was destined to play a key role in missions and Chinese church history. What had changed in 1839 that allowed Liang Fa to return to China?

THE 1840 OPIUM WAR

Throughout the early nineteenth century, Britain had been expanding trade around the world. China, however, resisted Britain's trade overtures. With China's scant interest in trade and British goods, British merchants searched for a product that would foster trade with the Chinese empire. They found that product in opium. Missionaries did not necessarily support trade in opium, and in some cases opposed it, but they owed their precarious positions in China to the merchants and the British crown. The missionaries found themselves in an almost impossible position, needing to serve the interests of both China and Britain.

As Britain, strengthened by the Industrial Revolution, expanded trade in Asia, Confucian Chinese perceived the commercial activities as bad for society and thus severely restricted trade. The Chinese limited trade to only a small handful of government-approved agencies (called "*hongs*"). Britain found the limitation intolerable and demanded, for instance, printed tariff rules in order to avoid corruption. Different perceptions of national sovereignty and global relations also led to inevitable diplomatic tensions. For example, in 1793 Lord Macartney was sent to China where the Imperial Court, largely unaware of Europe and Britain's growing economic and military might, treated him as a representative of a vassal state. But the diplomatic mission failed, when, as a "representative of her majesty the queen," Macartney refused to kowtow to the emperor.

Even minor diplomatic crises could also leave missionaries, especially those serving as official interpreters, with potential delicate conflicts of interest. For instance, when a British gunner accidentally killed a Chinese bystander during a cannon salute, China demanded that all parties responsible for the tragedy be turned over. This incident raised complex questions regarding national sovereignty and the adequacy (in the eyes of the British) of Chinese law. The British did reluctantly agree to turn over the guilty party, and an Englishman was executed by the Chinese authorities. These types of events prompted consideration of issues of extraterritoriality and the extent of British interest in protecting British citizens (including missionaries) abroad.

In the 1830s, the Chinese finally made the decision to outlaw opium. Lin Zexu (Commander Lin) was sent from Beijing to the South to halt the existing trade, and he demanded that the British merchants hand over their stock of opium. The British refused, but Lin would not allow the British ships to depart from the Chinese port. After several weeks the British relinquished the opium, and, dramatically, Lin had it washed into the sea. Furious, the traders demanded that the British government pursue war with China in order to force trade concessions. The merchants financed the war, and a small fleet of British ironclads easily defeated China's outdated navy, capturing several coastal cities.

The Chinese were thus forced to the negotiating table. While the missionaries were not necessarily involved in the events surrounding the war, they served as official translators when the two sides sat down to forge an agreement after the war. Robert Morrison had died in 1834, but his son, John Robert Morrison (1814–1843), served as the chief interpreter. He served as the "Chinese Secretary" and prepared the final text of the Nanjing Treaty. Also on the translation team was the well-known German missionary Karl Gützlaff (1803–1851). Both John Robert Morrison and Karl Gützlaff were involved in the translation of the Bible that was completed in 1847.[6] Morrison died prematurely of fever in 1843, but Gützlaff traveled extensively—passing out literature and evangelizing along the Chinese coast. He also founded the China Evangelization Society.[7]

Given the opportunity to sit at the negotiating table for the Nanjing Treaty, how might the missionaries have responded? Conversion to Christianity was still illegal, the missionaries worked with stringent limitations, and the Chinese converts, such as Liang Fa who had fled to Singapore, were brutally persecuted. While the missionaries may have been willing to forgo military protection themselves, an even more problematic question was in view. Should they, for the sake of Christ and the Gospel, push for more access in China? And, more importantly, should they try to provide protection for persecuted Chinese Christians? Would it be right, or even ethical, not to provide protection when they could?

---

6. The translation team of this exceptional version in classical Chinese also included Walter Henry Medhurst and Elijah Coleman Bridgman.

7. See his colorful story in his *Journals* (Karl F. A. Gützlaff, *Journal of Three Voyages along the Coast of China in 1831, 1832, & 1833* (Boston: Elibron Classics, 2005), and in Jessie G. Lutz, *Opening China: Karl F. A. Gützlaff and Sino-Western Relations, 1827–1852*, Studies in the History of Christian Missions (Grand Rapids: Eerdmans, 2008).

The Chinese believers were not only the missionaries' most effective colleagues in ministry, but surely, in many cases, were, along with their spouses and children, their dearest friends in the world.

The Nanjing Treaty, signed in 1842, opened five new ports to British trade: Canton, Shanghai, Fuzhou, Ningbo, and Amoy (Xiamen). The Treaty also ceded Hong Kong to Britain. Missionaries were allowed residence in the Treaty ports, Chinese Christians were to receive protection, and the die was cast. Christianity was forever tied to imperialism.

The "treaty century" would last from 1842 to 1943, when Britain and the United States formally gave up their unequal rights of extraterritoriality. During those decades, the Western powers put increasing pressure on China, forcing an opening to trade. The concessions from China also provided Western missionaries with greater access to China, and greater power—first on the Chinese coast, and, after 1860 and the Second Opium War, in the inland.[8] Chinese Christians also received greater rights and freedoms, while also, at least in some cases, losing credibility among the broader Chinese population.

CONCLUSION

Liang Fa returned to China in 1839 and continued his invaluable ministry as an indigenous evangelist and ordained pastor. The end of the First Opium War began a new era in the evangelization of China, and both missionaries and Chinese Christians quickly took advantage of the new opportunities. Foreigners were allowed to learn Chinese and to build houses, schools, and churches in the Treaty ports. Liang served as pastor of a small church of about thirty Chinese believers, and in 1848 he assisted the LMS in starting a hospital in Canton. By the time he died in 1855, Christian missions and the Chinese churches had developed a strong and lasting foundation.

Hindsight reveals the intractable problems that the missionaries created during the first half-century of missions in China. To this day, the church's perceived tie to imperialism hampers Christians and evangelism in China. Yet, to condemn the missionaries outright, based on twenty-first century sensibilities and the unforeseen consequences,

---

8. J. Hudson Taylor took immediate advantage of the concessions that opened the Chinese interior to Western missions after the Second Opium War when he founded the China Inland Mission in 1865.

seems blatantly unfair. It seems, rather, that these missionaries deserve an impartial evaluation that attends to their excruciating context.

A balanced and nuanced understanding of missions in the imperialist past may help missionary efforts in the twenty-first century. As China emerges as an economic superpower, Chinese perceptions of nineteenth- and twentieth-century imperialism may shift. China, seeking markets and resources around the globe, may eventually attribute slightly more benign motives to previous forms of Western imperialism. Moreover, Chinese Christians may see more clearly the potential hazards of pursuing missions in the context of national global expansion. If China emerges as a Christian force in global missions, questions of Chinese evangelical identity will also continue to evolve.

In the United States, popular views in American academies may also be challenged. The sometimes selfish motives behind imperialism might begin to be seen as not peculiar to Western civilization, but as a universal proclivity. Further, the more pure and enlightened motives of the earlier missionaries might also be appreciated. And understanding the nineteenth-century context may help Americans today be more sympathetic to the difficult plight of the missionaries in China, who were trying to serve the interests of the Chinese people they loved while furthering opportunities to share the Gospel.

Missions continues to go forward, and it seems that the most effective missions will forge global partnerships. For healthy partnerships, it seems critical to face the past of Western imperialism tied with Christianity. But the evaluation of that past should not only result in criticism, but also be fair to the men and women involved. Though I am not suggesting a return to Christian triumphalism, I do hope to avoid a paralyzing missions guilt.

4

Chinese Evangelicals and Social Concerns
A Historical and Comparative Review

Kevin Xiyi Yao

SOCIAL CONCERN AND INVOLVEMENT is undoubtedly one of the major indicators of the changing ethos of the evangelical movement in the twentieth century. Take the example of North America, where the evangelical movement has been influential not only in the Protestant church but society as a whole. From evangelicals' balanced approach to soul-saving and social services, to the "Great Reversal" completed during the fundamentalist-modernist controversy of the 1920s and 1930s, to the re-emergence of the sense of social responsibility among evangelicals since the 1970s, the rise of American evangelicals' social consciousness and commitment is quite dramatic. Nevertheless, American evangelicals' experience is not unique, and similar phenomena can be found among evangelical Protestants of different nations. To this end, D. W. Bebbington acknowledges that evangelicals' "activism often spilled over beyond simple gospel work," in his identification of "activism" as one of four universal evangelical characteristics in his well-known essay on the definition of evangelicalism.[1]

The evangelical Protestants in China are no exception. Changing attitudes toward social engagement have also been a crucial part of their story. What were Chinese evangelicals' thoughts and struggles regarding social issues and involvement? What can they tell us about the character-

---

1. D. W. Bebbington, *Evangelicalism in Modern Britain: A History from the 1730s to the 1980s* (London: Routledge, 1995), 12.

istics of the evangelical church in China? Are there any significant differences between Chinese evangelicals and their American counterparts in this regard? In what way are Chinese evangelicals' attitudes toward society currently changing? These are the questions I intend to answer in this chapter.

I

Robert Morrison's arrival in China in 1807 is regarded as the starting point of the Protestant missionary movement in that country. Generally speaking, the nineteenth century was an era of great missionary expansion and church planting in the midst of continuous tensions between traditional elements in Chinese society and the Christian community. Western missionaries doubtless played leading roles in the Christian movement in China during this century. They spread the Gospel; planted and led the churches; founded schools, hospitals and other charities; and became deeply involved in the nation's modernization and reform movements. From the beginning, the largest segment of the missionary body in China was of Anglo-Saxony background.[2] Throughout the nineteenth century, missionaries to China were remarkably unified in their doctrinal outlook, their understanding of mission and church, and their mission strategies and methods. As James Alan Patterson summarizes, there existed across the world a "Protestant Missionary Consensus": first, evangelism and church planting as the priority of mission; second, "the doctrinal allegiance to the uniquely divine nature of Jesus Christ;" third, the willingness to define the social dimension of mission; and fourth, pragmatic ecumenism or cooperative mission efforts.[3] This consensus indeed reflected the theological orientation and ethos of evangelical unity in Great Britain and North America. Through the missionaries, this evangelical theology and ethos came to China and shaped the emerging native church. But the number of Chinese Protestants was still quite

---

2. According to Searle Bates, British missionaries accounted for 54 percent, and American 35 percent, of all Protestant missionaries in China in 1900. M. Searle Bates, "The Theology of American Missionaries in China, 1900–1950," in *The Missionary Enterprise in China and America*, ed. John K. Fairbank, Harvard Studies in American–East Asian Relations 6 (Cambridge: Harvard University Press, 1974), 136.

3. James Alan Patterson, "The Loss of a Protestant Missionary Consensus: Foreign Missions and the Fundamentalist-Modernist Conflict," in *Earthen Vessels: American Evangelicals and Foreign Missions, 1880–1980*, ed. Joel A. Carpenter and Wilbert R. Shenk (Grand Rapids: Eerdmans, 1986), 73–91.

small, and the native church's leadership ability and independence were still lacking or weak, even though the Chinese Christian community experienced significant growth in the nineteenth century.

The early twentieth century was a crucial period for Christianity in China. In the wake of the Boxer Rebellion in 1900, the social environment became quite receptive to new ideas from the West and Christianity. The decades after the 1911 Revolution witnessed the phenomenal growth of Protestant missionary forces and churches, as well as the explosion of mission-related higher educational and medical enterprises. In contrast to the previous century, the most significant change was perhaps the maturation and rise of the Chinese church. The church grew not only in quantity, but also in quality.[4] The social status and educational levels of believers were increasing. And the generations of Chinese church leaders—trained either domestically or abroad—began to take leadership roles in churches or church-related institutions, proving their capability to lead the churches independently and effectively. At church conferences and in the media, Chinese voices were heard frequently, and theological reflections by Chinese theologians were carried out intensely and systematically. The drive for indigenization was becoming a powerful trend, and more and more Chinese believers took initiative in establishing their own churches independent of missionary control. Even more dramatic was the revival movements—led by Chinese evangelists—that swept the country like a wildfire. Indeed, the days of missionary domination in the Chinese church were definitely gone.

The early twentieth century was also a time of unprecedented diversification and division within the Protestant missionary community and church in China. As Daniel Bays points out, the number of new denominational and independent faith missions significantly increased, and holiness teachings and the Pentecostal movement gained popularity.[5] Through publishing, guest speakers, and the arrival of a large number of young missionaries, liberal theology and the "social gospel" quickly began to powerfully impact the missionary circle.

---

4. In 1876, the number of Chinese Protestant church members stood at 13,035; in 1889, 37,287; in 1906, 178,251. D. MacGillivray, *A Century of Protestant Missions in China (1807–1907)* (Shanghai: The American Presbyterian Missions, 1907), 668.

5. Daniel H. Bays, "The Growth of Independent Christianity in China, 1900–1937," in *Christianity in China: From the Eighteenth Century to the Present*, ed. Daniel H. Bays (Stanford: Stanford University Press, 1996), 307.

The growing diversification increasingly challenged Christian unity in China. And the modernist-fundamentalist controversy finally shattered the so-called "Protestant missionary consensus" in the 1920s. Rooted in the nineteenth-century differences in mission strategy[6] and influenced and triggered by the controversy raging in North America, the conflict erupted as conservative missionaries rallied around the famous Bible Union of China, which was founded in 1920 and continued throughout the 1930s.[7] As a result, the missionary body in China became deeply polarized. On the one hand, relying on higher criticism of the Bible, liberals emphasized the humanity of Christ and immanence of God at the cost of their divinity and transcendence, respectively. In their attempt to re-interpret the Christian message according to China's social needs and cultural heritage, liberals focused on the ethical and social implications of the Gospel and regarded social transformation as the new goal of mission work. On the other hand, the fundamentalists or evangelicals staunchly defended infallible biblical authority and the supernatural aspects of the Gospel, and insisted on the central place of evangelism in mission work.

Within the Chinese church, the fundamentalist-modernist conflict was never as intense as among foreign missionaries, but the differences were nevertheless real and deep. And most churches were associated with one camp or the other. In the early decades of the twentieth century, a large number of Chinese Christians graduated from mission schools in China and seminaries or universities in North America, and began to take key positions in institutions such as Christian colleges, the National Christian Council, and the YMCA. With a liberal theological outlook and closer ties to the missionary establishment, they were most active among

---

6. J. Hudson Taylor (1832–1905) and Timothy Richard (1845–1919) were commonly considered the advocates of two different mission approaches: The former was theologically more conservative, focusing on evangelism among common folks, and the latter more progressive, aiming at the conversion of social elites. See Kenneth Scott Latourette, *A History of Christian Missions in China* (New York: Macmillan, 1929), 277; Paul A. Cohen, "Missionary Approaches: Hudson Taylor and Timothy Richard," in *Papers on China*, vol. 2 (Cambridge: East Asian Research Center, Harvard University, 1957), 29–62.

7. For a full account of the fundamentalist-modernist conflict among missionaries in China, please see Kevin Xiyi Yao, *The Fundamentalist Movement among Protestant Missionaries in China, 1920–1937* (Lanham, MD: University Press of America, 2003). In this period, the terms "conservative," "evangelical," and "fundamentalist" were largely interchangeable. So were the terms "modernist" and "liberal."

urban churches and institutions. Along with foreign missionary societies, they formed what Daniel Bays called the "Sino-foreign Protestant establishment."[8] Relatively few in number, liberals in the Chinese church were largely elites and exerted considerable influence within the church, even playing the role of church spokespersons to the general public. Optimistic about history and society, and critical of traditional evangelical mission models, they put social involvement and evangelism on equal footing.

If liberals in the Chinese church tended to be a vocal, elite minority, there existed a silent majority comprised of many grassroots urban and rural congregations within mission-related church structures, as well as within independent evangelical churches. Deeply shaped by the missionary movement of the nineteenth century, most of these churches were theologically quite conservative. Their teachings tended to be simple and biblical, and their ministries single-mindedly centered on spreading the Gospel and saving souls. By the 1920s, the overall conservative tendencies of most churches were further reinforced and sharpened by the rise of indigenous evangelical churches and the revival movement.

As Bays points out, the growth of numerous independent conservative groups was actually "the most important feature of this period" (1900–1937), even though it has been ignored by the Sino-foreign Protestant establishment and academia.[9] Some of the most prominent were the Assembly Hall (聚会处) or Little Flock (小群), Jesus Family (耶稣家庭), the True Jesus Church (真耶稣教会), the Spiritual Gifts Church (灵恩教会), and the Bethel Mission (伯特利布道团). These years also witnessed unprecedented waves of interdenominational evangelistic and revival movements initiated or led by Chinese Christians. From these movements emerged a generation of charismatic and influential Chinese church leaders, evangelists, and revivalists such as Wang Ming-dao (王明道), Watchman Nee (Ni Tuoshen, 倪柝声), John Sung (Song Shang-jie, 宋尚节), Ji Zhiwen (Andrew Gih, 计志文), Wang Zhai (Leland Wang, 王载), and Marcus Cheng (Chen Chong-gui, 陈崇桂). Theologically, these groups and individuals were influenced by various traditions such as holiness, reformed, premillenial, and Pentecostal. But they also had a lot in common: they were all staunch believers in infallible biblical authority and supernatural Christology, and empha-

8. Bays, "The Growth of Independent Christianity," 310.
9. Ibid., 308–10.

sized soul-saving evangelism instead of social and cultural involvement. Further, they were all hostile to liberal theology and liberal wings within the church. Wang Ming-dao, for example, was vocal and persistent in attacking modernism throughout his career, and he never hesitated to denounce liberals as the "false teachers or prophets."[10] What was upsetting for Chinese evangelicals was not only liberals' alleged denial and distortion of biblical teachings, but also their attempt to shift missionaries' focus from evangelism to social service and cultural witness. In Chinese evangelicals' minds, the social gospel and modernism were simply two sides of the same coin, and were without a doubt unbiblical and heretical. Consequently, to differentiate themselves from liberals, these evangelicals placed an almost exclusive emphasis on evangelism over against social involvements. The shunning of any social or political issues, or adoption of an apolitical attitude, became characteristic of the emerging Christian evangelical movement of the 1920s and 1930s. Understandably, Chinese evangelicals' contributions to the growth and character formation of the Chinese church were far greater and much more significant than their liberal counterparts. Even to this day, we can say that most Chinese Protestants across the world are evangelical, and that the liberal influence among them is negligible.

In sum, we can say that the Chinese evangelical movement was a fairly recent phenomenon as compared to the long history of the evangelical tradition in the West. And the indigenous evangelical churches in China never enjoyed a significant period of unity or consensus as their North American counterparts did prior to the fundamentalist-modernist division.[11] When the Chinese church became more independent in the early twentieth century, it immediately split into two exclusive, belligerent camps: fundamentalism and liberalism. Therefore, Chinese Protestants have little memory of historical unity. In the minds of Chinese evangelicals, the choice between evangelism and engagement of social concerns seemed to be an "either-or" from the very beginning. And the legacy they were left certainly contributed to later difficulties

---

10. See Wang Ming-dao, *Discernment of [the]Gospel* (真伪福音辨) (Hong Kong: Bellman House, 1987).

11. For more on the unity of evangelical Protestantism in America, see George M. Marsden, *Fundamentalism and American Culture: The Shaping of Twentieth-Century Evangelicalism, 1870–1925* (New York: Oxford University Press, 1980), 11.

encountered when Chinese evangelicals began to search for a new approach to social and political challenges.

Since the 1970s, the overseas Chinese church has reflected on this legacy. Many of the urban house churches in China today are, to some extent, following suit. In the ongoing discussion about Chinese evangelicals' approach to social engagement, we have seen much unfounded criticism and precarious dismissal of the legacy on the one hand, and a mere habitual reaffirmation of it on the other hand. What is lacking is a solid examination of what the legacy actually is. In the second part of this chapter, I aim to provide just that. In other words, I intend to recover precisely what the first generation of Chinese evangelicals believed about engaging social issues. To that end, I offer some evaluations of their words and stances in light of American evangelicals' experience and the contemporary context in which the Chinese church exists today.

As we know, the first half of the twentieth century was a turbulent era in Chinese history. As I have asserted in another work, "nationalism was the major driving force behind the social movements. For both ruling classes and the masses, the primary concern seemed to be the pursuit of political, economic, and military solutions for China's prolonged national crisis."[12] Not surprisingly, the church in China was constantly under pressure to prove that its message and work were relevant to the task of saving the country. Of course, liberals in the church were very eager to do just that and to adapt the Christian message to the urgent needs of the nation. But evangelical leaders and churches tried hard to continue to concentrate on spreading the Gospel and nurturing the churches. At a time when there was no urgent national crisis or nationwide patriotic movement underway, evangelicals could manage to shun political topics. However, as Japanese troops suddenly took over the northeastern provinces of China in 1931 and launched an all-out war against the country six years later, a hot debate about how believers should respond broke out and persisted within the Chinese Christian community. Such prominent evangelical figures as Wang Ming-dao and Watchman Nee found it impossible to continue to completely avoid political issues. As a result, a considerable amount of sermons and writings produced by Chinese evangelicals touched on society and politics and the proper Christian responses to them. They provide us with a rare and excellent opportu-

---

12. Kevin Xiyi Yao, *The Fundamentalist Movement among Protestant Missionaries in China*, 27.

nity to examine Chinese evangelicals' stance on social engagement in general. That is why I chose the Sino-Japanese War period (1931–1937) as the focus of the next part of this chapter.

II[13]

As mentioned previously, the theological thought of Chinese evangelicals in the early twentieth century was influenced by various theological traditions. These evangelicals' emphasis on sinful human nature and God's sovereignty appears to owe much to Calvinistic teachings. And their insistence on a dualistic worldview and the separation or conflict between the church and world can be traced back to Pietistic origins. The consequence is beyond doubt: Chinese evangelicals' view of society was very negative and pessimistic. The dominant position was that this world is the domain of the devil, full of sin, and inevitably worsening and sliding hopelessly toward final destruction. A new heaven and earth can only be established at the time of the second coming of Christ.

For Chinese evangelicals, the international and domestic turmoil of the 1930s only served to reconfirm their socio-historical view. This theme is almost everywhere in the writings by the evangelical authors of that era. The following words are quite typical and telling:

> If we think the world is getting more civilized and less sinful, we are wrong. In fact, the more civilized the world gets, the more sinful it becomes. This is because this world is not Jesus' kingdom, but under the rule of the devil. Thus, the so-called world civilization nowadays is not a genuine (spiritual) civilization, but rather a phony (material) civilization; under its cover of civilization are hidden many ferocious demons. We thought there is no crime worse than raping, robbing, and killing. But today massive killing of civilians is widespread... The deteriorating trend of the world is already revealed in the Bible, and should be familiar to us. Therefore, as we see how the Japanese warlords launched such a barbaric aggression upon us, we must know this is inevitable in

---

13. Most of the contents in this section is contained in my paper titled "Chinese Christians' Debate and Reflection on War and Peace after the '9.18.' Incident" ("九一八" 之后中国基督徒对战争与和平问题的思考与讨论) in Separation and Integration: Chinese Christians and the Rise of the Indigenous Church (离异与融会：中国基督徒与本色教会的兴起) (Shanghai: Shanghai People's, 2005), 57–88.

the world ... Taking a look at the past and present world, we can find this kind of evil and atrocity anywhere and anytime.[14]

In a sermon preached in 1940, Watchman Nee tried to make sense out of the many wars worldwide. According to him: "In this chaotic world today, the nations are fighting with each other, and wars and famines are everywhere. In the eyes of non-believers, the nations are fighting, because they hate each other; but in the eyes of God, they are actually united ... We must realize that wars are being manipulated by Satan. The truth is that the nations are not seeking to defeat each other, but to cause Christians to stumble, instead.[15] A dualistic worldview is clearly spelled out here. Behind all the occurrences in the world is ultimately a confrontation between God and Satan.

In such a world, Chinese evangelicals found their ultimate hope in their eschatology. Matthew 24:4–14 seemed to be the most helpful in interpreting the contemporary situation. With a firm belief in biblical prophecies and an expectation of the second coming, these evangelicals saw the signs of the coming doomsday: "'You will hear of wars and rumors of wars, but see to it that you are not alarmed. Such things must happen, but the end is still to come' (Matt 24:6) ... Today all these prophesized events are unfolding before us, and serve to strengthen our faith that his words will not fail. Nowadays the wars and rumors of wars are pouring into our ears and minds. And all the thundering of guns seems to urge us to prepare and wait for the coming of the glorious Lord."[16]

For these evangelical authors, there was nothing surprising in history, and everything was evolving according to what the Scriptures said. For the people living in a time of uncertainty and turmoil, this kind of belief could certainly be comforting and encouraging.

In Chinese evangelicals' reading of the signs of the time, the influence of premillennialism is evident. This is especially so in some of Wang Ming-dao's classical pieces. In the spring of 1936, Wang wrote an essay entitled "Can There Be Peace in the World?" In it, he expressed his view of society in this way: "The Scriptures tell us that this world is getting

---

14. "Christians Should Re-think Their Worldview at This Time of National Crisis" (基督徒在国难当中应整理的世界观念), True Light (真光) 36.11 (1937) 2.

15. Watchman Nee, "The World War and the Church" (世界争战与教会的关系), in Watchman Nee's Works (倪柝声文集) Second Collection 25:81–82.

16. Zhang Ting-rui (张庭瑞), "Christian Obligations in Wartime" (战乱中基督徒不可少的责任), True Light 2, no. 37 (February 1938) 5–6.

more and more corrupted. Consequently the peril and pain in society will increase day by day. When the world is completely corrupted, a massive disaster will come, which is God's punishment upon evil men, as well as the bitter fruit human sins produce. This teaching is being fully verified by what is going on in the world as we see it."[17]

Watchman Nee also made some classical statements about the end of the world. In 1936, he once preached about the appropriate Christian attitude Chinese Christians should have toward their own country and social issues. His point and argument are based on an interesting comparison of Christ's two comings:

> When Christ came to the world the first time, he mainly dealt with human sin, saved humans from sins, and gave them new life. When Christ comes again, he will solve all the social problems, and renew all political systems . . . His first coming only aimed to save us as individuals, instead of dealing with social issues. In other words, his first coming only solved spiritual problems, not material ones. That does not mean he had no intention to solve those national, social and international problems. Christ will come to solve all of them once for all.[18]

Needless to say, these Chinese evangelicals' view of history was definitely at odds with progressive or liberal viewpoints. In the minds of these evangelicals, there is simply no such thing as social progress, and this world is doomed. It is no wonder that they always categorically rejected liberals' optimistic views of history and society. In the same 1936 essay, Wang Ming-dao challenged the notions of "gradual and unstoppable progress of material civilization" and "improvement of human beliefs and morality."[19] According to him:

> It is a pity so many people nowadays are so ignorant! Treading the paths to peril, they dream about peace, and sing a song of peace. To fool themselves and others, they make up and advocate for "improvement of peace," "construction of a heavenly kingdom," "universal brotherhood," "world harmony," and so on. It is not a surprise that many non-believers are doing this. But surprisingly, many so-called Christians and preachers ignore the

17. Wang Ming-dao, "Can There Be Peace in the World?"(世界究竟能不能有和平呢) *Spiritual Food Quarterly* (灵食季刊) 37 (Spring 1936) 23.

18. Watchman Nee, "Christian Attitudes toward Nation and Society" (基督徒对国家社会的态度), in *Watchman Nee's Works*, Second Collection, 26:248, 250.

19. Wang, "Can There Be Peace in the World?" 24–25.

facts and God's words, and fool themselves and others by chanting the hypocritical slogans of peace along with others.... Sooner or later, as people in the world are dreaming and singing about peace, plagues will suddenly pour upon them.[20]

On the other hand, Wang did not completely deny a peaceful kingdom as the Christian ideal. In fact, he showed a great deal of enthusiasm for a world beating swords into plowshares, as spelled out in the second chapter of the book of Isaiah. In this "harmonious world" and "golden age," he said, "all peoples on the earth will turn to God, and worship Him and obey His teachings. There will be no more war and killing, and all the weapons will be destroyed."[21] However, apparently under the influence of premillennialism, Wang argued that this ideal world can be established only after the saints are taken away by Christ and plagues are poured onto the earth. Further, a new heaven and earth are by no means created by humankind, but will be set up and ruled by Christ after the judgment.[22] Wang's view directly contradicts the social gospel on two points. First, a peaceful and just world cannot be built on the basis of the existing society through step-by-step reform; it will come only when this world is destroyed. Second, a new world will be the result of God's work. Sinful human beings cannot accomplish this goal by themselves. Wang thus rejected liberals' preoccupation with social improvements as humanism "in contradiction with the biblical truths."[23]

To illustrate a similar point, Watchman Nee depicted the world as "an old, broken and useless big boat. What we can do is to save the passengers, and abandon the boat." Then he declared, "We believe there is no way to find the solutions for all social and national problems in today's world. The only way out is to simply give it up, and all the problems are going to be gone. When the new earth and heaven are established by the Lord, this old earth and heaven, along with all their problems, will all be taken care of. Therefore, we are not seeking to solve these problems, but to focus on saving individuals. Indeed, the salvations of individuals would somewhat affect society. Nevertheless, our purpose is not to save this world."[24]

20. Ibid., 26.
21. Ibid., 21–22.
22. Ibid., 30–31.
23. Ibid., 32–34.
24. Nee, "Christian Attitudes toward Nation and Society," 254–55.

Nee further exhorted that believers should not worry about social problems, for everything is under God's control. In his own words, "We saw that God has the solution for everything, and knows the steps to solve it. No one knows better than God . . . Thus you do not need to worry, and do not have to hastily come up with some ideas about what we should do next."[25] Obviously Nee was accusing liberals of playing the role of God. That is why he denounced the social gospel as "a dead end."[26]

Chinese evangelicals were staunch believers in God's rule in history. They believed that God's will can be discerned by what a nation is going through, as demonstrated by Israel's relationship with God recorded in the Old Testament. When a nation obeyed God and acted righteously, it would be blessed and protected by God. On the contrary, if a nation disobeyed God and did evil, it would taste the divine wrath. Based on such beliefs, these evangelical leaders often concluded that the fundamental cause behind the tremendous difficulties and hardships China was experiencing was their countrymen's immorality and disbelief in God; these led to his wrath and judgment. Wang Ming-dao made this point very clearly in the following statement: "We all know that our current ordeal is caused by our people's stubborn refusal to know and believe Jehovah, and by their immoral acts and sins . . . Once you defy God, all sins would be out of control . . . Under such a circumstance, how can we hope that our country has a bright and peaceful future?"[27] To make things even worse, some Chinese believers failed to maintain a holy life and acted just like non-believers. They were in more urgent need than non-believers for soul-searching. Not surprisingly, during those years, pleas for repentance such as the following were constantly made: "God's wrath is confronting the world and China. Is this because we Christians have not completely renewed ourselves? Whenever Israelites distanced themselves from God, national crisis would come. Shouldn't we be wakened by such a lesson?"[28]

25. Ibid., 250.

26. Ibid., 258.

27. Wang Ming-dao, "Why Do We Have So Many Ordeals?" (为什么我们接连遭遇这样多的祸患呢?), *Spiritual Food Quarterly* 86 (Summer 1948) 4.

28. Jiang Shu-ai (姜树蔼), "The Understanding and Endeavor Christians Should Have in the Midst of National Crisis" (国难声中基督徒应有的认识和努力), *True Light* 31.1 (1932) 48.

Therefore, in the eyes of Chinese evangelicals, the key to saving the country was neither armament nor cultural reconstruction, but full repentance and turning to God. The theological arguments went like this: "God is righteous as well as faithful. If you are willing to repent, he will immediately take back his wrath."[29] As China was drawn deeply into trouble, its people were told that "He will listen, but we must be willing to repent and pray first!"[30] This view was echoed by Wang Ming-dao: "If we want less peril in our country and more peace, our people must wholeheartedly repent, stay away from sin, and sincerely come to God. This is the only way out. The miserable fate of China cannot be changed by any other means."[31]

Furthermore, it was believed that repentance could facilitate an earlier coming of the kingdom of heaven. According to the thinking of Chinese evangelicals, all social problems were rooted in the downfall of individuals' souls and subsequent moral corruption. Therefore, instead of social and moral reform embraced by liberals, evangelicals tended to emphasize propagation of the Gospel and saving of souls as the ultimate solutions for social diseases. In the midst of a national crisis, this way of thinking still dominates Chinese evangelicals' thought and interpretation of social situations. So, a typical solution proposed by an evangelical author reads like this:

> The only way to fight the crime is to spread the gospel, because the gospel has real power: 1) it can make people open their eyes to their own sins and repent; 2) it can make people pursue goodness and righteousness; 3) it can make people love God and their neighbors; 4) it can unite all righteous people; 5) it can stop violence and atrocity; 6) it can bring the kingdom of heaven to the earth. Based on all these effects, it is fair to say that the propagation of the gospel can contribute to the national revival, strengthen the righteous forces, resist aggression, and punish crimes.[32]

Watchman Nee's elaboration on this point is even more systematic and noteworthy. According to him, "The job God wants us Christians

---

29. Wang Lang-sun (王兰荪), "Soul-Saving and Nation-Saving" (救灵运动与救国运动), *True Light* 31.5 (1932) 44.

30. Ibid., 45.

31. Wang, "Why Do We Have So Many Ordeals?" 5.

32. "Christians Should Re-think Their Worldview at This Time of National Crisis," 3.

to do today is just to save man from sin and obtain life from God,"[33] for all the problems in the world are caused by human sins,[34] Therefore, if sinful human nature is not dealt with, social evils cannot completely be eliminated. "There are many good 'isms.' But none of them can become reality, because they are carried out by sinful people."[35] Therefore, it is individuals' salvation that will eventually produce long-lasting social results. In Nee's own words, "After a man is saved, he would naturally contribute to society and help solve all national and social problems ... We do only one thing, namely saving people. As a result, the country and society would be naturally affected, even though it is done indirectly. The issue we focus on is a spiritual one, but the material would be affected. We care about individuals, but society also would be affected by us."[36]

In other words, Christians should not preoccupy themselves with social reform, but positive social contributions will be natural manifestations of Christian character. Nee believed it was the role of Christians to serve as "light" and "salt" in the world. After rejecting the idea that "we should make efforts to turn this world into a bright and clean one," he declared:

> We are the light. But that does not mean that we should go out to eliminate gambling, punish bad people, reform society, and so on. The true meaning is that the people there do not see the bad things in the first place. After Christians come, they open their eyes to the evil nature of these things, for everything is exposed in the light ... Salt can prevent the dead thing from smelling and rotting ... As the salt in the world, we can prevent the corrupted systems from smelling and rotting, instead of reform them.[37]

In a time of chaos and uncertainty, Nee repeatedly exhorted that "we should only try to be good Christians today rather than attempt to improve politics and society. All our hope is to wait for the second coming of the Lord. Once he comes, all problems will be resolved."[38] In the meantime, believers must be on alert against possible attacks launched by Satan through wars and other means. "In these days we must devote

33. Nee, "Christian Attitudes toward Nation and Society," 251.
34. Ibid., 250–51.
35. Ibid., 258.
36. Ibid., 252.
37. Ibid., 253–54.
38. Ibid, 263.

ourselves to prayers, instead of pursuing worldly pleasure . . . We pray that God keeps his children from stumbling, and the gospel is spread further."[39]

Some other Chinese evangelicals were even more enthusiastic than Nee about the social impact evangelism could produce. For them, spreading the Gospel and saving souls could significantly help solve the Sino-Japanese dispute and maintain peace, "because the promise of eternal life is a much better blessing for the Japanese than the occupation of three provinces. If Chinese all believe in the truth, peace will dawn on the entire country. This pursuit of truth for peace is more powerful than any political mobilization."[40] The conclusion is obvious: the Sino-Japanese dispute presented another situation that proved that evangelism must be the top priority. This truth is reflected in Jiang Shu-ai's statement: "The key to save the country and world is nothing but the propagation of the gospel. This important task is already on our shoulders, and we should be even more enthusiastic about it at this time of national crisis."[41]

As mentioned above, premillennialists tended to view the looming war as a sign of doomsday. Because they believed that the Gospel must be heard by all nations before the arrival of the king of peace, evangelism took on a growing urgency. As one writer points out, "before Christ comes again, the gospel must be brought to all nations as soon as possible, for spreading the gospel to the ends of the earth must take place before the end of the world and the dawning of God's kingdom. If we want His kingdom to come soon, we should make urgent efforts to spread the gospel."[42] The sinfulness of the world, the need for repentance, and the urgency of spreading the Gospel were all key themes of the Chinese church's fundamentalist-evangelical theology, and saving souls was considered the only true mission of believers in the world. The national crisis and anti-Japanese war served to strengthen Chinese evangelicals' commitment to these themes, as well as their confidence that they held the key to explaining and solving such situations. In the midst of a deepening national crisis, evangelicals and their liberal counterparts found themselves drifting further away from each other, and their controversy became more intensified. The former found the latter's

---

39. Nee, "The World War and the Church," 84.
40. Jiang, "The Understanding and Endeavor Christians Should Have," 45.
41. "Christians Should Re-think Their Worldview at This Time of National Crisis," 3.
42. Zhang, "Christian Obligations in Wartime," 6.

reliance on human efforts to achieve peace completely unacceptable. This sentiment is powerfully expressed in the following words:

> The League of Nations cannot achieve peace, and anti-war treaties cannot stop the violence around the world. All these are hypocritical. Only as the King of Heaven is coming can you find true peace. If we want the kingdom to come, there is no other way but the propagation of the gospel. The peaceful kingdom of heaven can be established only by His name. The false teachings of new theology are the plot of Satan. It spreads some half-truths to draw people away from God and rely on their own way. That only leads to defeat and the loss of eternal life. They are not the ambassadors of the gospel but the running dogs of Satan, and their words are in opposition to the Scriptures.[43]

Such words doubtless point to the dominant position and primary concerns of Chinese evangelicals in the midst of China's crisis in the 1930s. However, regarding the practical question of whether Chinese Christians should join their countrymen in defending their country, some little-known evangelical figures did demonstrate their patriotism quite directly. On the one hand, they unconditionally endorsed evangelicals' focus on "saving souls;" on the other hand, they called for a certain amount of attention to be paid to matters related to "the campaign of saving the country."[44] In their view, "preoccupation with 'saving the country' is doubtless wrong, but preoccupation with 'saving souls' is not better. In a time of thorough moral bankruptcy and national disaster, we have to make efforts on both fronts; neither one is dispensable . . . On the spiritual front we fight Satan . . . On the bodily front we resist evil Japanese robbers."[45] Someone went even further in broadening what it means to "spread the Gospel": "the so-called propagation of the gospel can be done not only in words but also by financial donations and other deeds; all kinds of services in this national crisis could be our opportunities to share the gospel."[46] Citing the examples of such biblical figures as David and Nehemiah, some evangelical authors clearly advocated for the Christians' right to take

---

43. Jiang, "The Understanding and Endeavor Christians Should Have," 46.

44. See Jiang, "The Understanding and Endeavor Christians Should Have," 49; Wang Lan-sun, 39.

45. Wang Lan-sun, 41; 46.

46. "Christians Should Re-think Their Worldview at This Time of National Crisis," 3.

up weapons to defend their own country.[47] By doing so, they showed their disagreement with the liberal camp's pacifist party.

III

Chinese evangelicals have always been aware that one of their major differences with their modernist counterparts was the concentration on preaching the Gospel and saving souls, instead of on social services and political reform. Even in a time of chaos and violence, the mainstream Chinese evangelical church never wavered on this point. On the contrary, the turbulent social environment compelled the Church to become more articulate about its social viewpoints. For the first time in the history of the Chinese church, a truly evangelical social theology was spelled out in a rather comprehensive and systematic way. It is correct to say that Chinese evangelicals never participated in social movements as consistently and ardently as their liberal counterparts. But it is incorrect to say that they did not have their own social theory. The dualism between Christ and the world, or between the sacred and secular; the belief in the sinful nature of the world and the fallenness of humanity; a fervent hope for the end of the world and the second coming; and the subsequent urgent need for aggressive evangelism and the lack of interest in direct social and political engagement are all characteristic of Chinese evangelicals' views on social engagement. Despite the great variety of groups and charismatic leaders within their family, Chinese evangelicals have demonstrated an amazing consensus in their approach to society and politics.[48]

After the anti-Japanese war was over, the polarization within the Chinese Protestant church persisted, and the dominance of evangelical theology in the church also continued. The promising period of church growth (1945–1949) was so short that Chinese evangelicals never at-

---

47. See Jiang, "The Understanding and Endeavor Christians Should Have," 44–45; Wang Lan-sun, 42; 44; Zhang, "Christian Obligations in Wartime," 5.

48. In his groundbreaking study of Marcus Cheng, Ying Fuk-tsang (邢福增) points out that Cheng failed to construct any theory of social concern out of the Chinese fundamentalist tradition, even though he was more open to social issues than most of his fellow fundamentalists. See Ying Fuk-tsang, *The Praxis and Predicament of a Chinese Fundamentalist: Chen Chong-gui (Marcus Cheng)'s Theological Thought and His Time* (中国基要主义者的实践与困境---陈崇桂的神学思想与时代) (Hong Kong: Alliance Bible Seminary, 2001), 166–67.

tempted to revise their approach to social engagement.⁴⁹ Moreover, the decline of fundamentalism and the birth of the contemporary neo-evangelical movement in North America apparently had very little impact upon the evangelical church in mainland China.

Throughout the 1950s and 1960s, the polarization within the Protestant church in mainland China was further complicated by the intervention of political forces. The emerging and powerful Three-Self Patriotic Movement (TSPM) was increasingly dominated by such liberal figures as Y. T. Wu (吴耀宗), and evangelical leaders either confronted the TSPM from the very beginning or were marginalized or expelled from the movement.⁵⁰ As the TSPM became the only legitimate national organ for the Protestant churches, the only choice for the churches in China was either to join the TSPM simply as a means to survive (even though most of the churches did not agree theologically) or to go underground. Under such a harsh environment, any creative, spontaneous theological re-thinking of heritage on the part of the evangelical churches was out of the question. This task was left to the overseas Chinese church and, later, to the emerging house church in the mainland in the wake of the Cultural Revolution (1966–1976).

Overseas Chinese churches are also spiritual descendants of the evangelical revivals of the 1920s and 1930s in China. Even to this day, their basic attitude toward society continues to be defined by the dualism so common among the first generation of Chinese evangelicals. After World War II, the awakening of social awareness and the sense of social

---

49. In the late 1940s, Chinese evangelicals' evangelistic efforts among college students were quite successful and resulted in an influx of young, college-educated believers in the church. See Leung Ka-lun (梁家麟), *By Faith They Did It: The Beijing Christian Student Association and the Chinese Christian Evangelistic Band* (他们是为了信仰---北京基督徒学生会与中华基督徒布道会); *Wen hua ji kan* 10 (Hong Kong: Alliance Bible Seminary, 2001). Given enough time, was it possible that these young believers would develop a new social awareness and thinking regarding the mission of the evangelical church in China?

50. See Ying Fuk-tsang, *Anti-Imperialism, Patriotism and the Spiritual Man: A Study on Watchman Nee and the "Little Flock"* 反帝. 爱国. 属灵人—倪柝声与基督徒聚会处研究 (Hong Kong: The Christian Study Centre on Chinese Religion and Culture, 2005), 190–205. Wang Ming-dao's celebrated rejection of the TSPM is quite telling, for he refused to join the TSPM on the ground that the movement was purely modernistic. See Ng Lee Ming (吴利明), *Christianity & Social Change in China* (基督教与中国社会变迁) (Hong Kong: Chinese Christian Literature Council, Ltd., 1990), 156–63; Philip L. Wickeri, *Seeking the Common Ground: Protestant Christianity, the Three-Self Movement, and China's United Front* (Maryknoll, NY: Orbis, 1988), 164–70.

responsibility played a major role in the international evangelical movement. The reversal of "the Great Reversal" of the 1920s was embodied in numerous denominational declarations and actions, inter-denominational conferences, and influential international fellowship such as the Lausanne Movement. Amid these circumstances, a movement was also initiated in the overseas Chinese church to reflect on its own theological tradition and to gain a new social consciousness. Voices were frequently and repeatedly raised criticizing the dualism of the sacred versus the worldly, and the consequent lack of social and cultural responsibilities on the part of the Chinese evangelical church both past and present. And the call was constantly made to mobilize overseas Chinese evangelicals for a new mission to society and culture. A prominent case is the "Chinese Movement of World Evangelization," begun by a group of Chinese participants in the Lausanne Conference in 1974. Two years later, this Movement issued a declaration stating: "The fundamental task of the church is to preach the gospel and save souls. However, in order to demonstrate God's love to the world, the church needs to devote herself to loving witness and making more significant social impact."[51] After more than three decades, this move toward a greater social concern has achieved significant success, resulting in more and deeper cultural and social involvements on the part of at least some segments of the overseas Chinese Protestant community.

During the same period, mainland China experienced the turmoil of the Cultural Revolution, and religious life was completely suppressed most of the time. It was not until the late 1970s and early 1980s that the Chinese Communist Party and government restored their religious policy and correspondent controlling structure. Consequently, the TSPM was also resurrected, and a new China Christian Council was founded. For the past three decades, the churches under the TSPM structure have experienced steady and considerable growth. Indeed, just as in the 1950s, almost all of the church leaders and theologians with liberal theological views can still be found only within the TSPM. But the movement as a whole, as Leung Ka-lun observes, has shifted somewhat toward evangelical theology,[52] whereas the liberals are now much less vocal.

---

51. Timothy Loi-wai Lam (林來慰), *A Historical Study of the CCCOWE Movement (1976-1986)* 华福运动纵横谈——个历史研究 *(1976-1986)*(Hong Kong: Chinese Coordination Centre of World Evangelism, 1990), 109.

52. See Leung Ka-lun, *The Rural Churches of Mainland China since 1978* (改革开放以来的中国农村教会) (Hong Kong: Alliance Bible Seminary, 1999), 366–73.

And the majority of congregations associated with the TSPM remain loyal to the evangelical or fundamentalist tradition formed before 1949. Furthermore, the churches under the TSPM appear to be more political or to have greater social concern than their spiritual predecessors, as their leaders keep calling for increased patriotism and contributions to the country's modernization campaign. However, such emphases seem to owe more to the political pressure the churches face than to a particular strain of theological thinking, even though top church leaders such as Bishop Ding Guang-xun (丁光训) do try to justify the TSPM's social stance with rather liberal theologizing.

For the past three decades or so, the growth of house churches has been even more impressive than that of churches within the TSPM.[53] In the 1980s, most house churches were found in the rural areas and largely consisted of marginal social groups such as peasants, the elderly, women, and the poorly educated. These churches were thus in no position to challenge the TSPM churches in size and social status. But in the 1990s, the spread of the house church movement in urban areas dramatically changed the landscape of Protestantism in China. Ultimately, the TSPM has been overshadowed by the rise of urban house churches and the conversion of a large number of intellectuals, professionals, and college students, who have mostly joined the house churches. Theologically, the house church movement is predominantly evangelical, and its basic doctrinal stands are consistent with those held by the generation before 1949, despite the fact that many of the churches started spontaneously and did not have any direct link with this older generation.

In a book published in 1993, Alan Hunter and Kim-kwong Chan depicted the political stance of the house church as follows: "In our experience the home meetings are not politicized. Those who attend seek a satisfying spiritual life and tend to favour a strict separation of religion and politics, often typical of theologically conservative, pietistic traditions; engagement in politics may be seen as liberalism and unspiritual. They are often apolitical, poorly educated, devout believers following a long tradition of lay leadership and indigenous patterns of religious

---

53. The "house church" in China is still a controversial term debated by scholars, and its definitions are numerous. (See Leung Ka-lun, *The Rural Churches of Mainland China since 1978*, 53–62.) In an effort to make the term meaningful for this study, I contend that the house church's most defining characteristic is its lack of association with the TSPM structure. I do acknowledge, however, that the relationship between the house church and the TSPM is not necessarily hostile, and that mutual respect between them is in fact quite common.

organization. A few have objections to particular TSPM pastors, but usually on personal rather than political grounds."[54]

This is certainly an accurate portrayal of the mainstream house church movement in the 1980s. What characterized Chinese evangelical thought before 1949 once again became a part of popular teaching in the house churches of the 1980s. This approach to the world and politics was demonstrated powerfully in the house churches' standing aside from the student democracy movement in 1989. Some observers tend to explain house churches' disinterest in politics as the result of the fear of persecution and an attempt toward self-protection.[55] Without dismissing such practical factors entirely, I would argue that the house churches' overall theological orientation was more influential. Ironically, one of the accusations some prominent house church figures brought against the TSPM leaders was precisely that they had become too "political" by cooperating with the government.[56] Satisfied with their obedience to the secular authority in accordance with the instruction of Romans 13, the house churches rejected attempts to control the churches through the TSPM and other channels. So, at least in the minds of the house church members, the nature of their resistance was spiritual, not political.

The newly growing house churches in China's urban areas share an overall theological outlook with the churches of the 1980s. In their loyalty to biblical authority, emphasis on personal spiritual growth, and enthusiasm for mission, members demonstrate that they are also the genuine heirs of Chinese evangelical tradition. On the other hand, it cannot be denied that some of these churches also exhibit some significant new features. In addition to a new openness to intellectual life and theological education, strong social and cultural concerns definitely distinguish these churches from the old generations and churches of the 1980s. A process similar to what occurred in overseas Chinese churches has finally begun in the mainland churches: a critical reflection on their own heritage and a deliberate identification with such international evangelical movements as the Lausanne Movement. As a result, the dominance of old attitudes toward culture, society, and politics has been giving way

---

54. Alan Hunter and Kim-kwong Chan, *Protestantism in Contemporary China* Cambridge Studies in Ideology and Religion (Cambridge: Cambridge University Press, 1993), 85.

55. See Tony Lambert, *The Resurrection of the Chinese Church* (Wheaton, IL: Shaw, 1994), 215-6

56. Leung Ka-lun, *The Rural Churches of Mainland China since 1978*, 372-73.

to a diversification of stances regarding these arenas. According to a very insightful article penned by a mainland author, at least three basic approaches can be identified in the Chinese church today.[57]

First is the separatist approach. Having the longest history, this type of approach is the theological offspring of Wang Ming-dao and his generation. Like most of the house churches of the 1980s, churches loyal to this approach hold fast to their pietistic and separatist stance and show no interest in cultural and political issues. However, unlike the 1980s, the 1990s witnessed the declining influence of these churches within the house church movement. And the mushrooming urban house churches and their new social and cultural consciousness have been on the rise, replacing the separatist groups as the mainstream of the house church movement.[58]

These young urban churches' unprecedented interests in social and cultural issues are beyond question. And evidence shows that their social awareness is linked to the surging popularity of Reformed theology in urban house churches in recent years. In contrast to the pietistic tradition that deeply influenced the theological thinking and worldview of Chinese evangelical leaders prior to 1949, the Reformed theology's emphasis on God's universal sovereignty and providence certainly encourage the churches to pay greater attention to society and culture. Moreover, whereas the older generation was attracted more by the Calvinistic stress on human sin and divine authority, the contemporary urban house churches seem to be drawn more by the Calvinistic ecclesiology with its intellectual and cultural implications.

However, as the above cited author points out, once the social awareness of the house churches is translated into concrete approaches to society and culture, two distinctive approaches begin to emerge. The first group of the house churches and believers has a strong tendency toward human rights activism, understanding the church's prophetic roles in highly political terms and tying the human rights agenda closely to the church's mission and calling. For this group, to live out one's Christian faith is to defend religious freedom, fight for social justice, and push for political reform in China. As staunch critics of the Chinese government, members appear somewhat anti-communist and tend to be

---

57. Sun Ming-yi (孙明义), "Understanding the Urban House Churches in China" (认识中国城市家庭教会). Online: http://Christiantimes.org.hk/.

58. Ibid.

highly critical and confrontational in their dealings with authority. These groups are usually small in size and number, consisting mainly of some well-known individuals who had been actively involved in human rights and the democratic movement before they became Christians. But the popularity and celebrity status they enjoyed among overseas churches and human rights groups in recent years are disproportionate to their numbers. And yet they are often considered the spokespersons of the house churches in China.[59]

The mainstream urban house churches in China today deliberately try to strike a middle ground between the separatist and political activist extremes. On the one hand, these churches make efforts to step out of the shadow of the apolitical tradition and total disengagement from culture and society, instead embracing their roles as the "city on a hill" and "light of the world." On the other hand, they distance themselves from the political activists' approach by emphasizing the unique nature and mandate of the church. Learning from history, they sense the danger of politicizing the Gospel via an activist approach and refuse to identify the church with any political organization that would downgrade the church into a mere instrument of a particular political agenda. For them, the politicization of the church is not only unbiblical, but also puts it at risk of being viewed as a political and cultural threat to the government and country, thus potentially becoming trapped and victimized in international political conflicts.[60]

These churches do not necessarily oppose all of the basic values and visions of Christian human rights activists. They do, however, differ in how to implement and manifest such values. For these churches, instead of becoming directly involved in the political struggle for human rights, their main business in social involvement is to teach the fundamental values or guiding principles of genuine Christian social and cultural thought by lecturing, publishing, and other means. They also illustrate these principles and values through charitable activities and social services. Rather than self-isolation, they seek to engage authority, society, and culture; rather than confrontation, they seek to initiate a sincere dialogue and constructive interaction with authority. Sharing the vision of a

---

59. Ibid.

60. Given the Chinese people's painful memory of the historical ties between Christianity and Western colonialism, this concern is well grounded.

democratic and free China, they definitely prefer reform over revolution as the best way to reach that goal.⁶¹

Given the long history of apolitical stances of Chinese evangelical churches, the current diversification of the churches' attitude toward society and the growing social concerns of the urban house churches are nothing less than a breakthrough. There is no doubt that Chinese evangelical churches are at a critical point: they are re-thinking and re-examining their heritage, and trying to integrate a newly-found social awareness into the traditional focus on evangelism. Given the fact that the Chinese church has never before had anything close to such an integration as have its American counterparts, its attempt is certainly not an easy task. But a consensus appears to be emerging: a loyalty to the church's unique mission should enhance, and not contradict, a sense of social and cultural responsibility.

Needless to say, the fast growth and tremendous vitality of the church in China are attracting more and more attention from the Christian community and observers around the world. However, as Daniel Bays points out, the study of the church in contemporary China has been and still is unusually polarized and controversial.⁶² In my view, there seems to be much bias, misunderstanding, and oversimplification of Christianity in China today on the part of overseas supporters of both house churches and the TSPM for various reasons. And the current trend in the United States is that, as Bays asserts, ". . . for the past two decades the advantage in the contest for public opinion on the correct image of the church in China has been with those defending the unregistered church groups and attacking the Chinese state, its policies, and the TSPM."⁶³ Of all the voices supporting the house church, one of the most troubling focuses on a handful of Christian human rights activists, and views the house church simply as a part of the larger human rights cause in China. For some overseas churches, the most meaningful support they can offer is to support the house churches in their confrontation of Chinese authority and to defend their rights against persecution. To do so, some of these

---

61. See Sun Ming-yi (孙明义), "Understanding the Urban House Churches in China" (认识中国城市家庭教会). Online: http://Christiantimes.org.hk/.

62. Daniel H. Bays, "Western Public Discourse on the Nature of the Church and the Future of Christianity in China" (a paper presented at the conference celebrating the 200th anniversary of Rev. Robert Morrison's arrival in China at the University of Hong Kong on April 26–27, 2007), 1.

63. Ibid., 7.

overseas groups are not afraid to cooperate with the U.S. government and other political forces.⁶⁴ This tendency is especially strong in certain segments of the evangelical camp in America. And the growth of the evangelical churches in China is even interpreted in geopolitical terms, perceived as a good fit to U.S. global strategy and as a benefit to the whole world in the long run.

A good example is the popular book *Jesus in Beijing* by David Aikman. In this work, Aikman acknowledges that "China's house church Christians are uniformly patriotic and cautious . . . They want to see religious and political freedom come to China, but in an evolutionary, reformist process, not through political violence against the authorities."⁶⁵ However, the overall orientation of the book still rests largely on a rather political theme: "how Christianity is transforming China and changing the global balance of power." With a rather euphoric prediction of China's Christianization, the author is quite certain that China's democratization will be facilitated to a great extent by the growth of the Christian community and its expanding influence in the society. Further, he envisions a future pro-West and pro-Israel superpower that will stand together with America in the fight against terrorism.⁶⁶

In my view, Aikman's viewpoints and approach are theologically questionable, supported by weak evidence, and harmful to the church in China.⁶⁷ Looking back at the history of and recent developments in China's evangelical churches, I wonder whether Aikman tends to examine the church in China through the lens of a certain segment of the

---

64. See Sun Ming-yi, "Understanding the Urban House Churches in China," 2. Bays notes that religious freedom has become increasingly prominent since 1989 in human rights campaigns targeting China, and he attributes this trend to the conversion of a significant number of Chinese democracy activists. (Bays, "Western Public Discourse on the Nature of the Church and the Future of Christianity in China," 5–6).

65. David Aikman, *Jesus in Beijing: How Christianity Is Transforming China and Changing the Global Balance of Power* (Washington, DC: Regnery, 2003), 289.

66. Ibid., chapter 15.

67. As Sun Ming-yi argues, history has proven that the problems of the church cannot be solved through political means. And to tie the church's mission with human rights is to confuse its mission with a political agenda, thereby burdening the church with an unnecessary obligation. (Sun, "Understanding the Urban House Churches," 4) Leung Ka-lun points out that this kind of approach would involve the church in an ideological struggle, vindicating the Communist Party's suspicion that the Christian community is part of a Western conspiracy against China and thus leading to more hostility against the Chinese church. Leung, *The Rural Churches of Mainland China since 1978*, 436.

American evangelical movement, thus projecting certain agendas of the American church onto the Chinese church. In his classical study of American fundamentalism, George Marsden points out that "within fundamentalism we find a strikingly paradoxical tendency to identify sometimes with the 'establishment' and sometimes with the 'outsiders.' During the development of fundamentalism its adherents wavered between these two opposing self-images."[68] Marsden's analysis is very helpful in understanding American evangelicals' changing attitude toward culture and society. When evangelicals in America become identified with the "establishment," they tend to envision a "Christendom" with a Christian dominance in cultural, political, and social life, and press for a greater Christian influence and agenda in the public arena. This "establishment" mentality has been very much embodied in the Christian right in American politics since the 1980s. Moreover, many supporters of the house churches in China are associated with this movement. It is therefore no wonder that they would cheer a few Chinese Christians' efforts to link their faith with human rights and democracy, and to look at the growth of Christianity in China through the lens of Christendom and even as an American global campaign for human rights.

But the history of Chinese evangelical thought shows almost no trace of Christendom or "establishment thinking." On the contrary, the dominant theme of the Chinese evangelical theological tradition is its pietistic emphasis on the tension and separation between the church and world, which reminds us of the "outsider" image in American evangelical history. The result was the classical evangelical apolitical stance. In contemporary China, this position still commands the loyalty of a significant number of churches under both the TSPM and house church structures. Even among the emerging urban house churches, it is still quite influential. In their critical reflection on their heritage and exploration of a new approach to society and culture, the mainstream urban house churches have no intention of rejecting the theology of Wang Ming-dao and Watchman Nee entirely. Rather, they attempt to integrate the pietistic insistence on the uniqueness of the church with the Calvinistic emphasis on the universal sovereignty of God. They also exhibit a deep commitment to spiritual growth and a fresh openness to Christian witness in social and cultural life. And they are resisting any attempt to hijack the church for the sake of ideology or political agenda.

68. George Marsden, *Fundamentalism and American Culture*, 6–7.

Unlike the churches in America, Chinese Christians have always been a minority in Chinese society in terms of both population percentage and social influence. Whereas it may be legitimate to boldly predict that the number and influence of Christians will significantly increase in the next several decades, we must realize that it is perhaps unrealistic to expect China to someday become a new "Christendom" or "Christian nation."[69]

Indeed, the church in China is rapidly changing and acquiring new features. But the question can and should be asked whether the model of "Christendom" is a good or desirable path for the church in China to take in the future. This is a very critical question, as Chinese churches are exploring their future direction at this very moment, and different visions are competing for their attention. And the "Christendom" thinking has apparently already found its way into the theological discourse of the house church movement As a result, a vague concept of "Christian nation" or "Christian culture" is constantly used without any careful circumscription and is being pursued as the final goal of the church's mission.[70] However, in my opinion, a vision of a Christian community with a prophetic voice and loving witness in a not-so-friendly world may be more akin to the Chinese churches' evangelical heritage, more relevant to their context and status, and more beneficial to their future. In any case, as we support the Chinese church in it endeavor, let us fully take its history and context into account, also keeping in mind that the final decision must be left to the Chinese Christians.

---

69. The notion of "Christendom" or of a "Christian nation" is theologically debatable. And so is its desirability and feasibility.

70. The United States of America has often been regarded as the model of a "Christian nation" by many Chinese. See Ge Yu (于歌) : *The Essence of America—A Nation and Its Diplomacy Dominated by Protestant Christianity* (美国的本质—基督新教支配的国家和外交) (Beijing: The Press of Contemporary China, 2006).

5

The Old Testament in Its Cultural Context

Implications of "Contextual Criticism" for Chinese and North American Christian Identity

K. Lawson Younger Jr.

INTRODUCTION

CHRISTIANS ALL OVER THE world struggle with issues of identity within the various different cultures in which they find themselves. Some Christians identify themselves through "Christian" tradition, which may or may not actually be Christian. No matter what culture Christians are in, they ultimately should derive their identity from the Bible. But this presents an ongoing problem. The Bible (whether Old or New Testament) was written in different cultural settings than the one Christians are in today. There are, of course, varying degrees of difference, but all cultures are different from those of biblical times. In the case of the Old Testament, the distance between the biblical cultures and the modern cultures can be quite pronounced. This is not simply a chronological distance. While this is the most obvious difference, it may not be the most outstanding difference.

Many people view the Bible as a product of Western culture. This is true of people all over the world, even in North America. While the Bible has had an undeniable impact on the development of Western civilization, the Bible itself is not a product of the West. To some, it may seem that I am stating the obvious; but to many, it will come as a surprise. In the case of the Old Testament, it is an utterly ancient Near Eastern cultural product! Written in Hebrew, with small portions in Aramaic, it is a collection of West Semitic linguistic texts, produced, chiefly in the Fertile Crescent with its unique environments, during the Iron Age and in the material cultures of that period. Put simply, it is an ancient Near Eastern textual artifact! Even the New Testament manifests a deep cultural connection with the Near East, more so than one might typically think. A very large percentage of the text of the New Testament was written inside of "Asia," primarily by Jewish Palestinian believers. Therefore, it is quite erroneous to view the Bible as a Western product, or Christianity as originating in the West.

Since the Old Testament is "an ancient Near Eastern textual artifact," it requires an effort on our part to understand the cultures that produced it. Texts are one of the manifestations or expressions of culture. Therefore, they require a cultural hermeneutic that discerns the matrix out of which they arose. If any of us wrote an essay in our first language and culture, we would hope that someone in the future translating it into their language and culture would make an effort to understand the cultural and linguistic context in which we produced our text. We would hope that they would not confuse our figures of speech as literal, would not disregard our rhetorical devices, and would not misappropriate a cultural item, especially something that is completely foreign or missing in their culture. Furthermore, the Old Testament manifests, at a number of places, overwhelming cultural dissimilarities from that of its neighbors. In other words, there are many instances where the Old Testament writers were writing to an audience that they assumed would know the cultural, literary, and historical context, and that this audience would immediately perceive both the similarities and differences!

There are two further issues. First, cultures are not entirely monolithic. During any specific time period, a culture manifests porosity and hybridity and thus cannot be defined in purely essentialist terms (i.e., as consisting of distinctive traits *per se*).[1] Second, because of its lengthy

---

1. John Storey, *Cultural Theory and Popular Culture: An Introduction*, 4th ed. (Athens: University of Georgia Press, 2006); E. Y. Sung, "Culture and Hermeneutics," in *Dictionary for Theological Interpretation of the Bible*, ed. Kevin J. Vanhoozer (Grand Rapids: Baker Academic, 2005), 150–55. Clifford Geertz, *The Interpretation of Cultures: Selected Essays*, Harper Torchbooks (New York: Basic, 1973), 89–90, defines culture as "an historically transmitted pattern of meanings embodied in symbols, a system of inherited conceptions expressed in symbolic forms by means of which men [sic] communicate, perpetuate, and develop their knowledge about and attitudes toward life."

time period, the Old Testament reflects there are multiple cultural contexts in the Old Testament. For example, Israel's culture in the wilderness in the late second millennium is different from that of the patriarchs in the earlier second millennium; and both of these cultures are different from Israel in the land before the united monarchy, which is also different from that of Israel during the divided monarchy, and the exile and the post-exilic contexts (all of which are located in different periods of the first millennium). One must also add to this, geographic distinctions within the borders of Israel. This can be seen, for instance, in the differences between the Cisjordanian and Transjordanian regions, or between the northern and southern regions. These differences are manifested in many things, like dialect, but much more. Let me give a diachronic example. In Ruth 4:7–8, the removal of a sandal for the purpose of finalizing a business transaction is described as a dated cultural phenomenon. The biblical writer gives an explanation of this practice because it is no longer a cultural phenomenon in the later Old Testament context. Thus, the Old Testament itself is not a monolithic culture, but evinces multiple cultural contexts. Yet, at the same time, there are features encountered in all periods and geographic regions that are common to Israel, and not to its neighbors (e.g., Israel's aniconic tradition[2]). Hence, within the multiple cultural contexts, there was a kind of *koine* Israelite culture.

In this chapter, I will suggest that a crucial element in the proper exegesis of any biblical passage is the exercise of a thoroughgoing "contextual criticism." Furthermore, I will argue that the use of such criticism is fundamental to the proper development of Christian identity in any culture. In other words, solid contextual exegesis is a first step. If the Old Testament is going to be used to inform Christian identity in *any* modern cultural context, it must start with a meticulous probe into the Old Testament's cultural contexts.

In certain ways, I am not suggesting anything new. The importance of context to the interpretation of Scripture has been observed by many Christians throughout church history, though obviously more so at particular times than others. The notion of the historical, grammatical hermeneutic is rooted in the concept of context. Moreover, at the beginning of the twenty-first century, there exists a wealth of data to enhance a well-developed "contextual criticism" due to the incredible discoveries

---

2. See Richard S. Hess, *Israelite Religions: An Archaeological and Biblical Survey* (Grand Rapids: Baker Academic, 2007).

made in the last two hundred years of study of the Near East. At no other time in the history of the church has the amount and quality of this material, which informs the interpreter about the ancient context of Scripture, been so great. As one scholar has recently and rightly noted, due to widespread excavation and scientific advances, "the biblical world is better understood and more easily accessible than at any other time since the biblical period itself."[3]

Yet, it is truly ironic that both in the academy and the church there is a growing disinterest in the context of the biblical texts, and a growing interest in what the text means to individual readers or particular communities. In a number of circles today, the quest for "the original context" is a highly neglected—if not totally neglected—part of exegesis. So whenever I mention "culture" or "cultural exegesis," I am using these terms to refer to the ancient contexts. This is different from the way many scholars are using the term "cultural exegesis." They use it to refer to the exegesis of modern cultures. While the understanding of modern cultures is an important step in forming "Christian identity," it will fail if it is not grounded in a painstaking effort to ascertain the ancient cultural contexts. In fact, such an approach can run the risk of violating the very integrity of the biblical texts. In a nutshell, I am saying that doing the theology of the Old Testament starts with a scrupulous assessment of the "original context," that is, a thoroughgoing "contextual criticism."

NON-CONTEXTUAL EXEGESIS AND ITS RESULTS

In the Academy

There are many factors behind the growing disinterest in the context of the Bible. Certainly not all secular scholars are disinterested in contextual study; a significant number are engaged in it. However, in general, over the last few decades, many scholars have resisted any comparative study. In the case of the academic study of the Bible, the growing disinterest in the context of the Old Testament is the result of three important factors.

---

3. John M. Monson, "The Value of Context in Studying Scripture: Original Context as a Framework for Biblical Interpretation" (paper presented at the Wheaton College Faith and Learning Paper, September 2003); John M. Monson, "Contextual Criticism as a Framework for Biblical Interpretation," in *Israel: Ancient Kingdom or Late Invention?*, ed. Daniel I. Block (Nashville: B. & H. Academic Group, 2008), 25–55.

The first (and perhaps primary) factor is the hermeneutical shift to reader-oriented interpretations. In these systems, the hard-core commitment to the indeterminacy of meaning and the multi-valency of texts has resulted in the removal of the biblical text from its context, and its deconstruction to suit the ideological presuppositions of the reader. This approach puts the reader rather one-sidedly in control of the literature, conforming it to the categories and interests of current ideology without regard to the categories and interests of ancient literature.[4] The problem lies in an *imbalance* between the triad of author, text, and reader, with a grossly overstated role for the reader, since the production of meaning is seen to be in the absolute power of the reader.[5] Rather than allowing the literature of ancient Israel to address us on its own terms—however remote from ours (whether in China or North America)—it too easily makes of biblical literature a reflection of our own concerns at the beginning of the twentieth-first century, whether secular or theological.[6] Thus, among biblical scholars who employ such readings, there is little interest in comparative analyses with ancient Near Eastern texts.

While some of the different reading strategies employed today have provided new and valuable insights[7] to greater or lesser degrees,

---

4. For some "common sense" discussion, see Adele Berlin, "A Search for a New Biblical Hermeneutics: Preliminary Observations," in *The Study of the Ancient Near East in the Twenty-First Century*, ed. Jerrold S. Cooper and Glenn M. Schwartz (Winona Lake, IN: Eisenbrauns, 1996), 195–207.

5. A. K. M. Adam, *What Is Postmodern Biblical Criticism?* Guides to Biblical Scholarship. Old Testament Series. (Minneapolis: Fortress, 1995), states, "If in postmodern accounts there is neither a unified, totalized reader, nor a unified, autonomous text, then no more is there an 'author'; postmodern interpretations are, in a word, 'unauthorized'... For postmodern readers, 'the author' is a fragmented, contested range of possible identities; the modern, unified, unambiguous author who authorizes only particular, correct interpretations, no longer exists." See also George Aichele et al., *The Postmodern Bible: The Bible and Culture Collective* (New Haven: Yale University Press, 1995).

6. Simon B. Parker, *Stories in Scripture and Inscriptions: Comparative Studies on Narratives in Northwest Semitic Inscriptions and the Hebrew Bible* (New York: Oxford University Press, 1997), 4. Two things come to mind here. First, there is an amazing similarity between the reader-oriented readings (e.g., that of Derrida) and the rabbinic interpreters of the first centuries BC and AD, neither of whom appear to have any concern for context or history. Second, such ahistorical readings as advocated by Adam (see footnote 2 above) are, astoundingly, ignored by ancient Near Eastern specialists, who are dealing with actual ancient textual artifacts for which some modern ideological reading is rightly considered utterly useless in a historically driven endeavor.

7. I am thus not arguing that we go backwards.

these reader-oriented approaches are fundamentally ahistorical.[8] There can be little doubt that the ancient authors designed their rhetoric and conventions to create a certain impression on the reader or hearer, and that intended impression is lessened or confused by a modern reader's ignorance of the ancient rhetorical devices and presuppositions that these texts employ. Some apprehension of the ancient culture and social environment that such rhetoric and conventions presupposed and addressed—in which the composer made his or her choices—is essential for fulfilling the role of "implied reader."[9] While the reader plays a role in the interpretive process, author and text (hence "original context") are vital components. There was an author and a context; there was and is a text; and there were, are, and will be readers.

The second factor is the trend within scholarship to date all biblical materials to the Persian or Hellenistic periods. Some of this has been driven by the post-modernist hermeneutic, but some has been derived from a more extreme form of traditional historical criticism, particularly in Germany. Among these scholars, there is a conviction that the text originates from such a late date that it is no more than a retrojection back upon the past. In short, they believe it is a fiction made up by later writers for their ideological purposes. For example, these scholars argue that the book of Joshua has no value in the historical reconstruction of ancient Israelite history: it says absolutely nothing about the origins of Israel in the land. Rather, the book is seen as an ideological retrojection from a later period—either as early as the reign of Josiah or as late as the Hasmonaean period.[10] Another example can be seen in the argument that the *herem* is a fictional, post-exilic concept. Never mind that the

---

8. Some even violate the integrity of the text; see, for example, J. Cheryl Exum, "Feminist Criticism: Whose Interests Are Being Served?" in *Judges and Method: New Approaches in Biblical Studies*, ed. Gale A. Yee (Minneapolis: Fortress, 1995), 83–88. Her interpretation ends up being the opposite of what the text actually says!

9. Otherwise, it is like studying Gregorian chants through the filter of rap music.

10. See, for example, Nadav Na'aman, "The 'Conquest of Canaan' in the Book of Joshua and in History," in *From Nomadism to Monarchy: Archaeological and Historical Aspects of Early Israel*, ed. I. Finkelstein and N. Na'aman (Jerusalem: Israel Exploration Society, 1994), 218–81; Thomas C. Römer, "Transformations in Deuteronomistic and Biblical Historiography: On 'Book-Finding' and Other Literary Strategies," *ZAW* 109 (1997) 1–11; John Strange, "The Book of Joshua: A Hasmonaean Manifesto?" in *History and Traditions of Early Israel: Studies Presented to Eduard Nielsen, May 8th 1993*, ed. André Lemaire and Benedikt Otzen; VTSup 50 (Leiden: Brill, 1993), 136–41.

root *ḥerem* (חרם) actually occurs in Moabite (ninth century) and Old South Arabic (eighth century) inscriptions.[11]

Obviously this has impacted how certain scholars view the relevance of the ancient Near Eastern data. Let me be clear. I am not arguing for a return to the "traditional" historical-critical method. While one can learn from some of the observations of those practicing it, I believe that it is insufficient as a literary method.

A third factor is a narrowing of the role of the Old Testament scholar to the canon. Such is seen in Brevard Childs' canonical approach. Though there are many positives to his approach, not the least of which is the emphasis on a synchronic interpretation, ignoring the original historical context produces insufficient interpretation. As with reader-oriented interpretations, there is a danger of becoming ahistorical.[12] Childs may have been reacting to some scholars who overstressed the parallels between the Old Testament and the ancient Near East, what has been termed "parallelomania."[13] However, this reaction has led to the downplaying of the data to the point of ignoring clear, informative correlations, producing a type of "parallelophobia."[14]

In this light, William W. Hallo's work[15] in proposing a balanced approach—a "contextual method"—that seeks to observe both com-

---

11. See Lauren A. S. Monroe, "Israelite, Moabite and Sabaean War-*ḥērem* Traditions and the Forging of National Identity: Reconsidering the Sabaean Text RES 3945 in Light of Biblical and Moabite Evidence," *VT* 57 (2007) 318–41; K. Lawson Younger, "The *Ḥerem* in Light of Recent Study," in *In Search of Philip R. Davies: Whose Festschrift Is It Anyway?* ed. John Rogerson and Duncan Burns (Edinburgh: T. & T. Clark, forthcoming).

12. Childs largely ignores the context of the biblical authors and those who shaped the canon. See the critique of J. J. M. Roberts ["The Ancient Near Eastern Environment," in *The Hebrew Bible and Its Modern Interpreters*, ed. Douglas A. Knight and Gene M. Tucker; Centennial Publications / SBL (Philadelphia: Fortress, 1985), 96]. Monson, "The Value of Context," rightly notes that, "This approach is very popular among conservative scholars in part because it relieves them of the need to explain their high view of Scripture to the skeptical academy."

13. A term coined by Samuel Sandmel, "Parallelomania," *JBL* 81 (1962) 1–13. For an example of parallelomania in practice, see Mitchell Dahood, *Psalms*, 3 vols., AB 16–17A (Garden City, NY: Doubleday, 1966–1970).

14. See Robert Ratner and Bruce Zuckerman, "'A Kid in Milk?' New Photographs of *KTU* 1.23, Line 14," *HUCA* 57 (1986) 15–60. For further discussion, see K. Lawson Younger, *Ancient Conquest Accounts: A Study of Ancient Near Eastern and Biblical History Writing*, JSOTSup 98 (Sheffield: JSOT Press, 1990).

15. "Biblical History in Its Near Eastern Setting: The Contextual Approach," in *Essays on the Comparative Method*, ed. C. D. Evans et al.; Scripture in Context 1,

parisons as well as contrasts in the literature of the ancient Near East and the Hebrew Bible is paramount. The literature of the ancient Near East was produced not only out of a particular culture, but also out of a larger literary tradition. Therefore, comparison with other similar literature within that tradition—that which serves the same purpose, uses the same structure, or refers to the same subject—reveals certain aspects of a text that might otherwise remain hidden.[16] A counterbalance to speculation and conjecture is thus provided, as are the genre "expectations" necessary to read the biblical text competently.[17]

In the Church

As far as the church is concerned, there are a number of interrelated factors that negatively impact the contextual study of the Scriptures. First, some believe that since the Bible is an inspired communication from God to us, it must be comprehensible on its own, without having to read the literature of cultures that Israel—indeed God—condemned. They feel an anxiety about discovering the Bible's human dimension or historical rootedness, which, in their view, might lessen the divine character of the message.[18] Hence, the text is all that is needed for interpretation.[19]

PittTMS 34 (Pittsburgh: Pickwick Publications, 1980), 1–12; "Compare and Contrast: The Contextual Approach to Biblical Literature," in *More Essays on the Comparative Method*, ed. W. W. Hallo et al.; Scripture in Context 2 (Winona Lake, IN: Eisenbrauns, 1983), 1–30; chapter 2: "The Contextual Approach," in William W. Hallo, *The Book of the People*, BJS 225 (Atlanta: Scholars, 1991).

16. Parker, *Stories in Scripture and Inscriptions*, states: "A just comparison gives due weight to both commonalities and differences and seeks to explain both—as respectively part of the common culture Israel shared with its neighbors and antecedents, or as part of the particular culture or sub-culture of the individual work—or indeed of the creativity of its author(s)."

17. K. Lawson Younger, "The 'Contextual Method': Some West Semitic Reflections," in *The Context of Scripture*, volume 2, *Monumental Compositions from the Biblical World*, ed. W. W. Hallo and K. L. Younger Jr. (Leiden: Brill, 2000), xxxvii.

18. Simon B. Parker, "The Ancient Near Eastern Literary Background of the Old Testament," in *The New Interpreter's Bible*, ed. L. E. Keck (Nashville: Abingdon, 1994), 1:229.

19. John H. Walton, *Ancient Near Eastern Thought and the Old Testament: Introducing the Conceptual World of the Hebrew Bible* (Grand Rapids: Baker Academic, 2006), 36, has recently summed up this view: "God has inscripturated his revelation through the use of human authors and language, but the theological meaning of the text is located in the canon, not bound up in the authors' limitations, humanity, and culture. For this group, a careful study of the text is all that is necessary to glean the truth of God's

But being the inspired word of God does not negate the Old Testament from being a human literary product, an ancient Near Eastern textual artifact! The authors of Scripture were not only divinely inspired, but also historically and culturally bound.

Second, a commitment to a misunderstanding of the perspicuity of Scripture causes some to see contextual study as a threat. Since a high level of training in specialized fields is necessary to do comparative studies, they feel that scholars are trying to take the Bible out of their hands. They feel that such study is elitist and throws them right back into dependence on a few, as the medieval Roman Catholic church looked to the authority of the magisterium for interpretation.[20] Individualism leads them to disdain any hint that they cannot be self-sufficient interpreters.[21]

But this is clearly a misunderstanding of the reformers' teaching about the perspicuity of Scripture. They certainly did not believe that everything in Scripture was accessible and understandable to everyone.[22] Their efforts to root their exegesis in the original languages speak against a simplistic view of perspicuity, and argue in favor of utilizing all the data with which God provides us in order to understand his word.[23] The concept of the perspicuity of Scripture affirms that the basic teachings and content of Scripture can be understood because of God's revelation. There is no secret, mysterious revelation embedded in the Scriptures,

---

Word. In a related way, it is not uncommon for traditional interpreters to believe that the divine authorship of Scripture is mitigated if the human input into the text is used to arrive at an interpretation. Inspiration, in their view, lifts the text above its human element."

20. There is a common misconception that interpretation was in the hands of the clergy. But, technically, authority did not reside in the clergy per se, but in the teaching authority of the church, specifically the magisterium.

21. Walton, *Ancient Near Eastern Thought*, 36.

22. Luther states: "I certainly grant that many passages in the Scriptures are obscure and hard to elucidate, but that is due, not to the exalted nature of their subject, but to our own linguistic and grammatical ignorance; and it does not in any way prevent our knowing all the contents of Scripture." J. I. Packer and O. R. Johnston, *Martin Luther on "The Bondage of the Will": A New Translation of "De Servo Arbitrio" (1525), Martin Luther's Reply to Erasmus of Rotterdam* (Westwood, NJ: Revell, 1957), 71.

23. Although he worked with a theological rubric, Calvin employed in his thoroughgoing exegesis every resource available in his day, especially primary languages; see Paul T. Fuhrmann, "Calvin, the Expositor of Scripture," *Interpretation* 6 (1952) 188–209. It seems likely that the exegetes of the Reformation period would have exploited the *realia* (i.e., material cultural evidence) and comparative literature to their fullest potential had they been available to them in that day (Monson, "The Value of Context").

and they can be comprehended without special knowledge of its interpretation via the magisterium.[24]

Third, some believe that inspiration means that there is another level of meaning in a text beyond what it says and that it is this deeper theological meaning that is what God intends to say. Thus, the interpretation is driven by a theological concept/concern/doctrine that trumps the simple, straightforward (literal, if you like) meaning of a text. In this situation, a "theological reading of Scripture" becomes no more than a reading into a text of a preconceived theological concept (which may or may not be actually derived from or based on any biblical text). One of the greatest challenges the church faces in every time period is the imposition of preconceived theological systems upon the text, thereby not allowing the text to speak for itself. Augustine's sermon on David and Goliath is a prime example. Augustine refers to David's five pebbles (1 Sam 17:40) as the five books of Moses, the chosen stone (1 Sam 17:49) symbolizing the unity of those who fulfill the law through love.[25] While one might find Augustine's theology far more satisfying than that of Pelagius, such theological imposition is just that—theological imposition! It is not exegesis of the text in its original context! Such readings, no matter how wonderful their devotional points may be, *rob* the biblical text of its message—a message that might play a significant role in the life of the interpreter and the church.[26] Therefore, hermeneutical rigor demands a contextual approach. If there is no validation process for the

---

24. Paul Althaus, *The Theology of Martin Luther*, trans. R. C. Schultz (Philadelphia: Fortress, 1966), 77, notes: "The Roman assertion that the Scripture must be interpreted by the teaching office of the church is based on the presupposition that the Scripture is an obscure book."

25. *The Works of Saint Augustine: A Translation for the 21st Century*. Vol. 2, *Sermons on the Old Testament, 20–50*, trans. E. Hill; ed. J. E. Rotelle (Brooklyn, NY: New City, 1990), 137–53, esp. 139.

26. It is important to remember that while the hermeneutics of the Middle Ages can be characterized as "a precritical approach that could acknowledge spiritual senses of the text beyond the literal sense," that of the Reformation can be characterized as "a precritical approach that strove to locate spiritual meaning entirely in the literal sense"; Richard A. Muller, "Biblical Interpretation in the Era of the Reformation: The View from the Middle Ages," in *Biblical Interpretation in the Era of the Reformation: Essays Presented to David C. Steinmetz in Honor of His Sixtieth Birthday*, ed. R. A. Muller and J. L. Thompson (Grand Rapids: Eerdmans, 1996), 14. Muller also points out that it is important to remember that "precritical" does not mean "uncritical."

production of meaning, then we cannot really establish the meaning of any text.[27]

Fourth, for some Christians, there is an intentional dependency on the interpretations of those who have preceded them. Tradition and the creeds are regarded as foundational to doctrine as the biblical text itself. How could God leave all of those generations without the wherewithal to read his Word accurately? If the likes of Augustine or Calvin were hampered or even crippled by the lack of cultural studies, and could perhaps even have misinterpreted passages because of their ignorance of ancient culture, the fear that Christian doctrine might be exposed as a house of cards would seem too real and threatening. Thankfully, faith is built on God's word, not "tradition."

Fifth, far and away, the factor that drives Christian complacency with respect to incorporating context in everyday Bible study is the overriding focus that makes the Bible speak to the existential needs and emotional concerns of believers in the church. I coin this "pietistic existentialism," and it is prevalent in the evangelical community today. Actually, it is a false "pietism" because it is rooted in existentialism, and it is really a newer permutation of older devotional-type readings that ignored context. So, whereas the Bible continues to be under assault in the academy, in the Church the historical and cultural context of Scripture is severely underutilized. Sadly, archaeological and linguistic material that elucidates the biblical text is often displaced by the urgent quest for "relevance" and "personal religious experience," often labeled "application" or "contemporary significance." American pragmatism fuels this, causing many to want "instant spiritual results," quick fixes to the problems of their self-absorbed lives. There is simply no time for the reading—let alone the serious study—of Scripture, with its concomitant mediation. And most certainly there is no time for struggling to understand the original context.

The North American evangelical church has, in large measure, failed in its seminaries to train men and women to attain reading competency in assessing the original context of a passage. We do very well at teaching the biblical languages, at least the grammar and vocabulary glosses; we don't do so well in contextual matters. Due to the recent positive

---

27. See Kevin J. Vanhoozer, *Is There a Meaning in This Text? The Bible, the Reader, and the Morality of Literary Knowledge* (Grand Rapids: Zondervan, 1998); Vanhoozer, *First Theology: God, Scripture, and Hermeneutics* (Downers Grove, IL: InterVarsity, 2002).

impact of Christian anthropologists and missiologists, many seminaries are rightly adopting some type of cultural studies curriculum so that their graduates can minister in the multicultural environment of today. I commend this. But virtually no seminary has a core required course in the study of the original cultural contexts of the Bible. Thus, the original context is still quite underutilized.

In light of the fact that "the biblical world is better understood and more easily accessible than at any other time since the biblical period itself," it is truly ironic that in the academic study of the Bible, the text is viewed with great skepticism or serves as a pretext for promoting the reader's ideology. But it is even more ironic that there is such a disregard for the contextual study of the Bible among Christians.[28] I find myself in many ways more understanding of the academic revisionism of my secular scholar friends than I am of Christians who lack the willingness to work at understanding the original context of a passage. I am sometimes overwhelmed by the complacency regarding (or in some cases outright opposition to) the integration of this *God-given data, God-given data*! If, in fact, God has revealed Himself in space and time in his word, it is incumbent on us to understand that revelation in the context in which he revealed it; particularly when he has given us the means to do so!

Dangers Posed by Agenda-Driven Contextual Study

The "contextual criticism" that I am advocating is not the "medicine" that will cure all of the church's woes throughout the world. It is essential to proper interpretation, but there are dangers if the "medicine" is not taken properly.

Unfortunately, there are individuals who bring an agenda to their comparative study. Thus, those who seek to disprove the Bible will misuse or misrepresent the ancient Near Eastern data. Frequently hiding under the guise of scholarship, upon close inspection and assessment, their arguments are seen to be no more than special pleading. But there are also Christians who are driven by an agenda to prove the Bible who misuse this data. Very often those who would be apologists lack the appropriate training in the various disciplines necessary to do this work. So their work is frequently characterized by misinterpreted data, out-

---

28. Perhaps sixteen centuries of theological study in the West have conditioned the Christian community to interpret Scripture apart from its original context.

of-date or disproven arguments, and/or neglect or ignorance of data that would mitigate their polemics. All of this results in nothing more than special pleading. There is a need in the church for apologists, but not of this sort.[29]

Thus, whether secular or confessional, the data is made to say either more than it says or less than it says in order to persuade others to embrace a particular position. These excesses cloud the evidence and make the work harder. Yet, these excesses are just that—excesses. They stress the need for more careful scholarship.

CONTEXTUAL CRITICISM

If a crucial element in the proper exegesis of any biblical passage is the exercise of a thorough-going "Contextual Criticism," what is "Contextual Criticism?" "Contextual Criticism" is the methodology of establishing the "original context" through the analysis of three environments: 1) the Literary (Textual) Environment; 2) the Material Cultural (archaeological) Environment; and 3) the Geographic Environment. Contextual Criticism endeavors to ascertain the milieu in which the text of Scripture was produced in all aspects of its complexity. In order to properly understand a biblical text's original context, these three environments need to be studied and assessed.

The epistemological issues for assessing this data have been discussed at great length, particularly over the last thirty years, so that scholars can now apply a sound methodology.[30] This is especially the case with the literary materials. But many of the principles apply to the data of both the material cultural environment and the geographic environment.

Literary (Textual) Environment

The Hebrew Bible is a textual artifact, or, better, it is a collection of textual artifacts made up of various genres that are attested in the ancient

---

29. This brings to mind a saying of William F. Albright, *Archaeology of Palestine and the Bible* (New York: Revell, 1932), 133: "The Bible can stand by itself; it has suffered more in many respects from its well-intentioned friends than from its honest foes."

30. Hallo, "Biblical History"; Hallo, "Compare and Contrast"; Hallo, *The Book of the People*; Meir Malul, *The Comparative Method in Ancient Near Eastern and Biblical Legal Studies*, AOAT 227 (Neukirchen-Vluyn: Neukirchener, 1990); Younger, "The 'Contextual Method'"; Walton, *Ancient Near Eastern Thought*.

Near Eastern literary record.[31] Thus, through a thorough employment of a comparative and contrastive methodology (i.e., what William Hallo[32] has termed the "contextual method"), it is possible to silhouette the biblical texts against their literary background.[33] When comparing or contrasting the biblical texts with ancient Near Eastern texts, the issue that must always be at the fore is the matter of propinquity.[34] The texts must undergo a thorough assessment along the lines of chronological, linguistic, geographic, and cultural propinquity.[35] "When we study an ancient text, we cannot make words mean whatever we want them to, or assume that they meant the same to the ancient audience that they do to a modern audience. Language itself is a cultural convention, and since the Bible and other ancient documents use language to communicate, they are bound to a culture. As interpreters, we must adapt to the language/culture matrix of the ancient world as we study the Old Testament."[36]

Therefore, propinquity must be assessed in all cases: whether it is in the evaluation of borrowing, literary dependence, and possibilities of influence, or in the act of ascertaining "the cognitive environment"[37] or "conceptual world" of the biblical text. Texts are only one manifestation of culture and, therefore, they demand an engagement with other cultural expressions and the environment out of which they grew.[38]

One example of how the literary (textual) environment can silhouette the biblical texts is found in a genre that is extremely common in the ancient Near East, but rarely studied by biblical scholars. This is the

---

31. Tremper Longman III, "Israelite Genres in Their Ancient Near Eastern Context," in *The Changing Face of Form Criticism for the Twenty-First Century*, ed. Marvin A. Sweeney and Ehud Ben Zvi (Grand Rapids: Eerdmans, 2003), 177–95.

32. Hallo, "Biblical History"; Hallo, "Compare and Contrast"; Hallo, *The Book of the People*.

33. Richard S. Hess, "Ancient Near Eastern Studies," in *Interpreting the Old Testament: A Guide for Exegesis*, ed. Craig C. Broyles (Grand Rapids: Baker Academic, 2001), 201–20.

34. Dennis Pardee, "Review of *Scripture in Context: Essays on the Comparative Method*," *JNES* 44 (1985) 220–22; Younger, "The 'Contextual Method.'"

35. Younger, "The 'Contextual Method.'"

36. Walton, *Ancient Near Eastern Thought*, 20.

37. Ibid., 21 argues that propinquity matters more in the case of literary questions and less with regard to larger cultural concepts or worldviews. But in my opinion, propinquity must always be at the forefront so that cautious, deliberate consideration of all the data takes place.

38. See Monson, "Contextual Criticism," 28.

genre of "Ration Lists."[39] These texts are attested throughout the third, second, and first millennia, all over the ancient Near East, in many different languages and cultures (including epigraphic Hebrew). So there is no doubt of their propinquity. Since in the ancient world, a very large portion of the population lived on a subsistence level, the rationing of food (especially grains for the making of bread) was vital to one's very survival.

During the second half of the Third Millennium, standard rations were developed for three basic commodities: barley (ŠE) (*hordeum vulgare*), oil (Ì), and wool (SÍG).[40] Included in these Ration Lists were an extensive range of professions from shepherds to weavers, agricultural workers to brewers, and even slaves. They included men, women, and children, and varied according to age and status.[41]

These Ration Lists give the portions in the Sumerian capacity measure of the SÌLA or the Akkadian *qû* (Neo-Assyrian *qa*).[42] This measure varied somewhat during different periods and locations, but it roughly equaled 1 liter, usually of barley,[43] and as Marvin Powell[44] has noted, the ancient norm for a daily food ration throughout the entire history of Mesopotamia seems to have been widely regarded as approximately 1 SÌLA or *qû* (i.e.> 1 liter).[45] As is known scientifically today, adult males consuming 1 liter (2,700 calories) and adult females consuming 0.83 liters (2,160 calories) have a sufficient energy intake, especially if allowances are made for smaller size and hotter climate.[46] Hence, the 1 SÌLA/*qû*/liter allocation—sometimes referred to as one loaf of bread—can be

---

39. For a more detailed discussion of the ration data and the implications of the ephah, see K. Lawson Younger, "Two Comparative Notes on the Book of Ruth," *JANES* 26 (1998) 121–25.

40. Ignace J. Gelb, "The Ancient Mesopotamian Ration System," *JNES* 24 (1965) 230–38.

41. Rosemary Ellison, "Diet in Mesopotamia: The Evidence of the Barley Ration Texts (c. 3000–1400 BC)," *Iraq* 43 (1981) 37.

42. *CAD* Q 288–91. Or in West Semitic texts in the vocabulary of dry measurements

43. The variance for these Mesopotamian measures seems to lie between 0.83 and 1.02 liters.

44. Marvin A. Powell, "Masse und Gewichte," *RlA* 7 (1987–90) 457–517; "Weights and Measures."

45. Also see Gelb, "The Ancient Mesopotamian Ration System"; and "Measures of Dry and Liquid Capacity," *JAOS* 102 (1982) 585–90.

46. Ellison, "Diet in Mesopotamia," 38–39.

considered the minimum-survival daily nutritional dosage.⁴⁷ Such ration recipients had a diet that contained adequate energy intake,⁴⁸ but could be accompanied by a marked nutritional imbalance over an extended period of time. The iron content could perhaps be low for girls and women, but adequate for men. The most serious deficiencies are vitamins A and C, and these must be made up elsewhere. Insufficient vitamin C can cause scurvy (one form of leprosy).⁴⁹ The lack of vitamin A can produce blindness.⁵⁰ This may have been a major factor in a number of the cases of blindness in the ancient Near East, as it is today in some third-world contexts.⁵¹ An understanding of this ration data is helpful in assessing information recorded in a number of biblical texts.

Ruth 2:17 states: "So Ruth gleaned in the field until evening; and she threshed what she had gleaned; and it was about an ephah of barley." The text stresses the large quantity of grain that Ruth threshed⁵² from her gleanings in the field of Boaz: k^e'ēpāh $ś^{e'}$ōrîm (כְּאֵיפָה שְׂעֹרִים) "about an

---

47. F. M. Fales, "Grain Reserves, Daily Rations and the Size of the Assyrian Army: A Quantitative Study," *SAAB* 4 (1990) 29.

48. Marten Stol, "Private Life in Ancient Mesopotamia," in *CANE* 1 (1995) 496. This statement is clearly based on Ellison 1981:43. While one can technically survive on the 1 SÍLA/*qû*/liter ration, a frequent daily average ration in Mesopotamia for males was a 2 SÍLA/*qû*/liter ration.

49. Ellison ("Diet in Mesopotamia," 39) notes that scurvy that developed during the winter months might be cleared up when the green vegetables appeared.

50. Technically, the deficiency of vitamin A is the main cause of *xerophthalmia* ("severe drying of the eye surface through failure to produce tears"; also known as *Keratoconjunctivitis sicca*) and *keratomalacia* ("drying and ulceration of the cornea") — conditions that, if not halted, produce permanent blindness. Mesopotamian medicine called the symptoms *Sinlurma* (*si-lu-ur-ma-a*), and the *āšipu* typically recommended eating liver, a known source of high levels of vitamin A. See JoAnn Scurlock and Burton R. Andersen, *Diagnoses in Assyrian and Babylonian Medicine: Ancient Sources, Translations, and Modern Medical Analyses* (Urbana: University of Illinois Press, 2005), 158, 195.

51. It is possible that the frequent use of the phrase IGI.NU.DU8 "blind," usually taken to refer to prisoners of war who had been deliberately blinded, may refer to people who have been blinded or partially blinded by vitamin A deficiency. See Ellison, "Diet in Mesopotamia," 39–42 and "Some Thoughts on the Diet of Mesopotamia from c. 3000–600 BC," *Iraq* 45 (1983) 149.

52. In order to thresh small quantities, the stalks and ears of the grain were beaten with a stick (cf. Judg 6:11 and Isa 28:27). For such threshing techniques, see Oded Borowski, *Agriculture in Iron Age Israel* (Winona Lake, IN: Eisenbrauns, 1987), 63.

ephah of barley."[53] Commentators, with the exception of Sasson,[54] usually give some kind of conversion figure for an *ephah* and end at that. Nielsen in her commentary concludes: "Of course, the important thing is not to find out exactly the actual weight but to be overwhelmed by Boaz's generosity to Ruth."[55] While the text is obviously giving this data in order to demonstrate Boaz's ḥesed toward the two widows, what would be the practical, real-life implications? Certainly this datum about the significant amount of grain gleaned by Ruth is not given to the reader in order "to add to her list of virtues that she was as strong as an ox."[56] It must have had some tangible, utilitarian value.

An ephah was one-tenth of a *ḥomer*. The *ḥomer* was the amount that one donkey could carry, roughly 90 kgs, fixing the assload of barley at ca. 150 liters or the assload of wheat at ca. 120 liters. Even allowing for uncertainties and upward adjustment by redefinition of norms, the "natural" assload can hardly have exceeded 200 liters. Because of diachronic and political circumstances, it seems likely that there were a number of *ḥomer* norms in the pre-exilic period. However, the probable parameters of the pre-exilic dry measures from smallest to greatest were: *omer* → *ephah* → *ḥomer* ≈ 1–2 liter → 10–20 liters → 100–200 liters respectively.[57]

---

53. Shemaryahu Talmon's suggestion, "The New Hebrew Letter from the Seventh Century B.C. in Historical Perspective," *BASOR* 176 (1964) 33) and followed by Daniel I. Block, *Judges, Ruth*, NAC 6 (Nashville: Broadman & Holman, 1999), 670, that the preposition *ke* before *'epāh* may be an example of *kaph veritatis* indicating exactitude is based on a supposed usage in the phrase *kymm* in the Meṣad Ḥashavyahu (Yavneh Yam) ostracon (*KAI* 200, line 5). But its use in that inscription is not certain. See J. Renz, *Handbuch der Althebräischen Epigraphik*, 2 vols. (Darmstadt: Wissenschaftliche Buchgesellschaft, 1995), 1:325n3.

54. Jack M. Sasson, *Ruth: A New Translation with a Philological Commentary and a Formalist-Folklorist Interpretation*, Johns Hopkins Near Eastern Studies (Baltimore: Johns Hopkins University Press, 1979), 57; *Ruth: A New Translation with a Philological Commentary and a Formalist-Folkorist Interpretation*, 2nd ed., Biblical Seminar 10 (Sheffield: JOST Press, 1989).

55. Kirsten Nielsen, *Ruth, A Commentary*, OTL (Louisville: Westminster John Knox, 1997), 61–62.

56. Edward F. Campbell, *Ruth*, AB 7 (Garden City, NY: Doubleday, 1975), 104.

57. The even larger capacity measure for an ephah that is sometimes listed in commentaries (i.e., 36.4 liters) is a measure based upon much later sources and would produce a homer (364 liters) that no donkey could carry! See the detailed discussion of Marvin A. Powell, "Weights and Measures," in *ABD* 6 (1992) 897–908. It may be that early Hebrew norms for the *ḥomer* may not have been very different from the con-

Since the ancient norm for a daily food ration was approximately 1 liter,[58] if Ruth's ephah equaled about 10–20 liters of barley, she had threshed enough for the two women to eat for a little more than a week. In Ruth 2:23, it states that Ruth continued to glean in Boaz's fields "until the barley and wheat harvests were finished." According to Deuteronomy 16:9–12 and the Gezer Calendar,[59] the time period from the beginning of the barley harvest to the end of the wheat harvest was normally seven to eight weeks, concluding at Pentecost. If Ruth averaged the same amount each day (i.e., one ephah—remember that on this first day she gleaned half a day on the edges of the field, where she would have gleaned less) and if she worked the entire seven to eight weeks, she would have gleaned an amount of barley and wheat that would have fed the two women, at the minimum rate, for approximately two-thirds of a year, or, at the maximum rate, for more than an entire year. Thus, the ancient readers would have perceived the import of this gleaning detail in Ruth 2:17 as heightening the generosity of Boaz toward the two widows on a scale greater than what modern readers have even begun to perceive. In other words, they would have calculated this datum to realize that Boaz was insuring that the two widows would survive to the next harvest!

Material Cultural (Archaeological) Environment

The material cultural environment includes analyses of such things as the artistic record (iconography, images, and reliefs), the architectural record (houses, palaces, defensive walls, and gates), the ceramic typological record (pottery assemblages), and the record of technologies. It is impossible to discuss in detail how much the archaeological data has

---

temporary Mesopotamian *homer*. Thus, Mesopotamian *qû* → *sūtu* → *imēru* ≈ *omer* → *ephah* → *homer* ≈ 1 liter → 10 liters → 100 liters respectively. The NIV text note states that the ephah is "probably about 3/5 bushel (about 22 liters)." This seems to be too high in light of recent research.

58. Powell, "Weights and Measures," 904. E.g., one SÎLA (Sum.) or *qû* (Akk.) throughout the entire history of Mesopotamia. For a full discussion, see L. Milano, "Food and Diet in Pre-Classical Syria," in *Production and Consumption in the Ancient Near East: A Collection of Essays*, ed. C. Zaccagnini et al. (Budapest: Chaire d'Egyptologie de l'Université Eötovos Loránd de Budapest, 1989), 201–71; and Fales, "Grain Reserves."

59. According to this extrabiblical Hebrew inscription (lines 4–5), a month was devoted to harvesting barley and a month was devoted to harvesting wheat. See the discussion and bibliography in Daniel Sivan, "The Gezer Calendar and Northwest Semitic Linguistics," *IEJ* 48 (1998) 101–5; and Borowski, *Agriculture in Iron Age Israel*, 31–44.

illuminated the Old Testament.⁶⁰ I will briefly discuss one passage and list a few further items.

In Isaiah 20:1, one reads: "In the year that the commander-in-chief, who was sent by King Sargon of Assyria, came to Ashdod and fought against it and took it." The following verses (2–6) are a prophecy of God's future judgment on Egypt and Cush based on the event in verse 1. Thus, the contemporary event that Isaiah chose to use to make his point about God's judgment on Egypt and Cush was the fall of Ashdod. Isaiah relied on his readers' knowledge about this contemporaneous event, assuming that all of them would know exactly what he was talking about.

However, prior to the discovery and decipherment of cuneiform, biblical scholars knew nothing about Sargon (of course, not realizing that he was, in fact, Sargon II). Since his name was not preserved in classical sources, upon which prior to the discovery and decipherment of cuneiform documents biblical scholars were entirely dependent, commentaries up to 1860 usually treated Sargon as an alias for one of the better-known Assyrian rulers mentioned in 2 Kings and Isaiah.⁶¹

Today, however, on account of the Assyrian royal inscriptions, we know that the fall of Ashdod took place in 712/711 BC; that the *turtānu*, "the commander-in-chief," led the campaign because Sargon II stayed in Assyria since he was building a new capital city;⁶² that the Ashdodite king, named Yamani, had sent messengers to Egypt and Cush (actually Cush

---

60. Israel Finkelstein and Neil Asher Silberman, *The Bible Unearthed: Archaeology's New Vision of Ancient Israel and the Origin of Its Sacred Texts* (New York: Free Press, 2001); Thomas W. Davis, *Shifting Sands: The Rise and Fall of Biblical Archaeology* (Oxford: Oxford University Press, 2004).

61. Furthermore, virtually all biblical scholars considered Pul to be an Assyrian king who was distinct from and ruled earlier than Tiglath-pileser (III). See Steven W. Holloway, *Aššur Is King! Aššur Is King! Religion in the Exercise of Power in the Neo-Assyrian Empire*, Culture and History in the Ancient Near East 10 (Leiden: Brill, 2002). In fact, without a knowledge of the accession/non-accession regnal dating systems from the ancient Near Eastern inscriptional record, the chronology of the northern and southern kingdoms in the book of Kings would be hopelessly confused.

62. Some of the laborers on this building project were deported Israelites, as clearly indicated in a Neo-Assyrian letter. See K. Lawson Younger, "'Give Us Our Daily Bread'—Everyday Life for the Israelite Deportees," in *Life and Culture in the Ancient Near East*, ed. Richard E. Averbeck et al. (Bethesda, MD: CDL, 2003), 276–77; Simo Parpola, "The Construction of Dūr-Šarrukin in the Assyrian Royal Correspondence," in *Khorsabad, le palais de Sargon II, roi d'Assyrie: Actes du colloque organisé au musée du Louvre par le Service culturel les 21 et 22 janvier 1994*, ed. Annie Caubet, Louvre conférences et colloques (Paris: La documentation Française, 1995), 47–77.

was in control of Egypt); that the Assyrians inflicted severe punishment on the Ashdodites for their rebellion, as revealed by archaeological evidence of a mass grave with the remains of approximately 3,000 humans, many beheaded (a common Assyrian practice with rebels); that many of the surviving Ashdodites were deported naked to Assyria, which Isaiah then personally illustrated; that while Yamani, the ruler of Ashdod, escaped to Egypt, six years later the Cushite king of Egypt, Shebitku, extradited him to Sargon.[63] Thus, we know precisely what Isaiah's readers were assumed to know about the fall of Ashdod and what the intended significance of the prophecy was: the type of judgment visited upon a small neighboring city-state by Sargon II, a well-known king of the day, will come upon the "mighty" empire of Egypt and Cush in which many Judahites were wrongly trusting for deliverance. If Egypt and Cush could not "save" a small city-state like Ashdod from destruction and, in fact, could not "save" themselves from it, what hope would Judah have in trusting in Egypt and Cush to "save" them? Thus, God's people (in any age) shouldn't trust worldly powers to "save" them!

Further items are: 1) biblical persons are attested in reliefs (such as the Black Obelisk portraying Jehu), in steles (e.g., the Tell Dan Stele or the Merenptah Stele with the first extra-biblical mention of Israel), and in seals (such as the seal of Yaazaniah); 2) images of deities (such as El and Baal) combined with textual material like the myths (e.g., from Ugarit) and the *Mīs Pî* ritual (describing the magical process of the image becoming the deity) provide insight into numerous passages; 3) liver models provide great visual insight into the divinatory nature of sacrifice in the ancient Near East (in large measure contrastive to Old Testament sacrifice); 4) architecture of the Iron Age house illuminates various passages (like Judges 11, where Jephthah vowed to sacrifice the first thing out of the door of his house as a burnt offering); 5) weights provide data about the Old Testament economy, among other things; 6) jewelry can demonstrate graphically the apotropaic aspects of life for those uncommitted to Yahweh; and much more.

---

63. K. Lawson Younger, "Recent Study on the Inscriptions of Sargon II: Implications for Biblical Studies," in *Mesopotamia and the Bible: Comparative Explorations*, ed. Mark Chavalas and K. Lawson Younger, JSOTSup 341 (Sheffield: Sheffield Academic, 2002), 312–18.

Geographic Environment

This is the physical setting of the Old Testament. It includes areas of study like geology, ecology, hydrology (i.e., water regimes), meteorology (i.e., climate), and cartography (particularly toponymic study). It would also include things like natural resources, topography, fauna and flora, agriculture, settlement patterns, building materials, lifestyles dictated by geographic concerns (e.g., nomadic or urban life), and highways and trade routes. Thus, for example, through the archaeological work of James Hoffmeier of Trinity Evangelical Divinity School, the toponymic issues of the route of the Exodus are being clarified.[64]

In the case of hydrology and meteorology, the land of Israel is a dry farming zone. That is, it is completely dependent on sufficient rainfall for agricultural activities. Natural or artificial irrigation is not possible like the riverine regimes of Egypt or Mesopotamia. The limit for rain-fed arable farming is roughly the 8 inch (200 mm) per annum level. In Palestine, rainfall can occur from roughly the beginning of October to the end of March, give or take a few weeks. It does not rain from roughly the end of March to the beginning of October, give or take a few weeks. Therefore, if in a given year there is not sufficient rainfall during the winter months, drought and famine can quickly follow. It should thus be no surprise that the most important deity of the Canaanites was Baal, the god of the storm. Hydrology was an important factor in every aspect of life, including religion (cf. the blessings and curses of Deuteronomy 28).

In addition, there is another common, important meteorological phenomenon: *ḥamsîn*. This is the Arabic name for the hot, dry wind that blows in from the desert, typically from March through June. In Israel, it blows from the East, bringing dust from the Arabian desert with oppressive heat and increasing the temperature many degrees in very little time so that it feels like one is in an oven.[65] The biblical term for a *ḥamsîn* is *rûaḥ qādîm* (רוּחַ קָדִים), "an east wind" (cf. Jonah 4:8).

---

64. James K. Hoffmeier, *Israel in Egypt: The Evidence for the Authenticity of the Exodus Tradition* (New York: Oxford University Press, 1997); Hoffmeier *Ancient Israel in Sinai: The Evidence for the Authenticity of the Wilderness Tradition* (New York: Oxford University Press, 2005).

65. The phenomenon of *ḥamsîn* (sometimes spelled in English as "Khamsin") is experienced throughout the Near East. The term *ḥamsîn* is derived from the Arabic word for "fifty." It is typically a southerly wind that blows from the Sahara across Egypt in the spring, usually from March through May. Like in Israel, Jordan experiences this phenomenon from the East. It is also experienced in Iraq and Syria.

While this is an extremely brief discussion of Israel's meteorology and hydrology, the facts presented here inform many passages in the Scriptures. One example is Psalm 1. Commentators on this wonderful wisdom psalm have done a good job explaining the parallelism and structure of the poetry, analyses that are due in large measure to the archaeological discovery of the Ugaritic texts. They also explain the similes: the blessed man is "like a tree planted by streams of water"; the wicked are "like chaff that the wind blows away." But most commentators have not applied the geographic environment to the interpretation. The simile of being "like a tree planted by streams of water" had a powerful original context because the original readers knew experientially the meteorological phenomena of the region. No rainfall occurs from April to October in most years. *Ḥamsîn* occurs almost every year. A tree without a significant source of water will likely not survive the summers, much less the *ḥamsîns* and droughts. The blessed man not only survives the summers, but even the *ḥamsîns* and droughts of life, prospering and bearing his fruit in season! The wicked, on the other hand, are likened to the chaff that the ordinary, everyday wind (*rûaḥ* [רוּחַ]) blows away. Importantly, it is simply the *rûaḥ* (רוּחַ), not the *rûaḥ qādîm* (רוּחַ קָדִים), the *ḥamsîn*. In other words, the perishing of the wicked is not the reults of the *ḥamsîn* (the extraordinary harsh wind), but the ordinary, everyday wind that can blow away chaff. Therefore, a contextual reading that is sensitive to the geographic environment greatly enriches the theological teaching of this psalm (as well as many other passages).

CONCLUSION

These three environments (literary, material cultural, and geographic) form an inseparable triad, which together define the original context of a text. They are not mutually exclusive, but interrelated. Moreover, there is no particular order to the analysis of these environments. It is, for example, not necessary to study the literary environment before analyzing the geographic environment. Rather, all three environments contribute to the total package: namely the establishment of the "original context" (as best as that can be accomplished in light of what has been discovered within these different environments). There is great value in reading the biblical text in the context of its physical setting through geography, its material cultural context through archaeology, and its literary context through comparative/contrastive literary analysis with the ancient Near

Eastern literature. This triad provides the "original context" that, when conjoined with the actual linguistic, textual context of the biblical text, generates the "intended" meaning. Through such a process of reading, the full power of the biblical text is enlivened by the Holy Spirit, who utilizes the "original" message of Scripture in the hearts of humans in order to bring glory to the Lord Jesus Christ. God has allowed us to live in a time period when, through contextual criticism, we can ascertain the intended meaning of a large percentage of the biblical texts. Therefore, to ignore this highly significant information is to be irresponsible. It is a poor stewardship of what God has given us.

The original context can offer a restraint on some of the far-out readings of Scripture. It can serve as an external control to reign in ideological misuses and methodological excesses, from the reductionistic readings of biblical criticism to the purely existential, mystical, and devotional approaches of Scripture that many Christians continue to embrace today. Whenever the context is missing, a text can be interpreted in any number of ways that move beyond the confines of what its context would support. Context can demonstrate that many readings of a given text bear no semblance to the intent of the original author for his or her implied audience.

Will Christians continue to interpret the Bible without concern for the "original context"? Of course they will. Will God continue to do great works in spite of this? Of course he will. Will God hold believers accountable for poor interpretations and their results? Of course he will.

We need to be responsible readers. We need to know what the genres of antiquity did and did not do, and to develop reading competencies for Old Testament literature. We need to gain evaluative skills for handling the archaeological material. And we need to gain a thorough awareness of the geographic setting of the Bible. Through dependence on the Holy Spirit, we can apply wisdom to these matters and formulate better interpretations and understandings of the Hebrew Bible. And by gaining the necessary competencies and applying wisdom in the exegesis of our target culture, we can formulate the kind of Christian identity that God wants us to be formulating.

The good news is that God has acted in "human history," revealing himself in his word. He has sent his son, who died and rose again as a mighty act in "human history." And no matter what the culture is (whether in China or North America), according to Ephesians 1, God is now acting in "human history" establishing Christian identity "in Christ."

6

"Holy War" and the Universal God

Reading the Old Testament Holy War Texts in a Biblical-Theological and Postcolonial Setting

TREMPER LONGMAN III

THE "DIVINE WARRIOR" WITH its background in "holy war" is one of the most stirring themes in the Old Testament, but also one of the most difficult for a modern Christian to understand and appreciate. The battle of Jericho, for instance, is a magnificent display of divine power as the walls of this powerful Canaanite city-state come tumbling down so that the Israelites can defeat it without even raising a single siege ramp. On the other hand, if, as I believe we can safely presume, Joshua followed the requirements of *herem* (Deut 20:16–18) on this occasion, this victory would have been followed by the summary execution of every man, woman, and child in the city (see Josh 6:18–21).

Indeed, reading the account of the Conquest raises ethical questions. What are the moral grounds for Israel to enter into territory occupied by the Canaanites, engage them in battle, kill them, and take their land. Are the Israelites engaged in genocide for the purpose of colonization?

Today, Christians who believe that a book like Joshua is more than an historical account of the past have additional questions to consider. As the Word of God, what continuing relevance does this book have as canon, as "standard of faith and practice," today? In the history of interpretation, these holy war traditions have been used to justify warfare in the Christian era. In the post-Constantine era, Church Fathers cited the book of Joshua as justification for military action against Muslims in the

Holy Land. The exact opposite approach can also be observed in the history of tradition. Rather than embracing Joshua as a model for modern warfare, the book, along with the rest of the Old Testament, was declared irrelevant by others (Marcion). While the orthodox church condemned the decanonization of the Old Testament, on a practical level many people and even theologians[1] have effectively done just that.

In order to answer these and other questions, we must first come to a full understanding of the Old Testament's view of holy war. We will see that even in the Old Testament, the institution is not static. However, to address the question of whether holy war is a Christian concept will require our study of the New Testament as well.[2]

HOLY WAR IN THE OLD TESTAMENT

Rather than beginning with the actual accounts of battles in the Old Testament, we will start by turning to the Deuteronomic texts that legislate holy war: Deuteronomy 7 and 20. The basic premise of holy war is that God will fight for his people; he will be their divine warrior. As Israel enters Canaan, they are militarily inferior to their foes. Israel left Egypt after years of servitude. Because of their sin, they spent forty years in the wilderness. In the wilderness, they would not have the opportunity to make or collect weapons. On a human level, they were completely vulnerable. As they reflect on their weakness, though, they are to remember the power of God. God is the one who will win the victory (Deut 7:17–26). For that reason, it does not even matter how many people are in the army. If a man was newly married, just planted a vineyard, built a house, or is just plain frightened, they can stay back from the battle (20:5–9).

Since God is the one who won the victory for the Israelites, all the plunder and the prisoners of war belong to him. They are *ḥerem*, "devoted to God," which effectively means that there are no prisoners really;

---

1. See C. S. Cowles, "The Case for Radical Discontinuity," in *Show Them No Mercy: Four Views on God and Canaanite Genocide*, ed. Stanley N. Gundry, Counterpoints (Grand Rapids: Zondervan, 2003), 13–44. See below for more on his thought on this matter.

2. For my previous work on the theme of holy war, see Tremper Longman III and Daniel G. Reid, *God Is a Warrior*, Studies in Old Testament Biblical Theology (Grand Rapids: Zondervan, 1995), and "The Case for Spiritual Continuity," in *Show Them No Mercy*, 159–87.

the survivors are killed.³ Of course, the legislation makes a distinction between those outside the promised land and those within, with the former having the option of surrender and, even in the case of a battle, sparing the lives of the women and children (20:10–18).

These texts from Deuteronomy provide a rationale for *ḥerem* in the purity of Israel. If the Canaanites were allowed to survive, they would lure Israel away from the true worship of Yahweh toward idolatry (7:25–28; 20:18).

While the laws of Deuteronomy help us begin to develop an understanding of holy war, the historical books go further in providing us with more information about its actual practice. As we examine the various battle reports found in the Old Testament, we realize that warfare is worship in ancient Israel. After all, the Ark of the Covenant, the most potent symbol of the presence of God,⁴ is with the army and attended by the priests. The Ark takes pride of place in the battle of Jericho. The instructions for this battle (Josh 7:2–5) feature the Ark circling the city's walls once a day for six days, being led by seven priests blowing trumpets. On the climactic seventh day, the Ark circles the city seven times. On the seventh time, the priests are to sound a long blast on their horns and then the people are to shout. At that moment, the walls fell down and the people took the city. In this scenario, the people provided service to the Lord in the presence of the Lord—in other words, they worshipped him.

Since warfare is worship, the army must be spiritually prepared to go to battle. Indeed, they must be as spiritually prepared to go on the battlefield as they would be to enter the holy sanctuary. Thus, they must be ritually pure. Such a concern motivates the mass circumcision and observance of the Passover on the eve of the battle of Jericho (Josh 5:1–12). It may even explain the excuse that Uriah the Hittite gives for why he does not sleep with Bathsheba as David expected he would. How could Uriah become ritually unclean by an emission of semen (Lev 15:15–18) when the "ark and Israel and Judah are staying in tents" on the battlefield in Rabbah (2 Sam 11:11)?

---

3. See Philip D. Stern, *The Biblical Ḥerem: A Window on Israel's Religious Experience*, BJS 211 (Atlanta: Scholars, 1991) for a detailed discussion.

4. Marten H. Woudstra, *The Ark of the Covenant from Conquest to Kingship*, International Library of Philosophy and Theology, Biblical and Theological Studies, (Philadelphia: Presbyterian and Reformed, 1965).

In addition, there are indications that sacrifices were necessary before the battle, also demonstrating the ceremonial nature of holy war. While such a practice was probably *de rigueur* before holy wars, we read about it in the text when it fomented trouble for Saul (1 Sam 13). The king knows that he has to offer sacrifices before battle, but the one divinely authorized to oversee the ritual, the priest Samuel, is late. In the meantime, Saul's troops were deserting him. Saul rashly performed the ritual himself, thus bringing on himself not only Samuel's wrath, but also God's. After all, as we observed in Deuteronomy 20, if troops are frightened, they should go home. As we will see below, it does not matter how many soldiers are in the army.

Of course, Israel cannot presume that every battle they might want to enter is a holy war. God had to make his will known to his war leader. Sometimes the divine authorization for war comes when God himself appears to the war leader (Josh 5:13–15), but on other occasions the war leader has to make an inquiry of the Lord. Such is the case in 1 Samuel 23:1–6, where David is presented with a situation: the Philistine plundering of the Judean city of Keilah. Rather than just marching off into battle, David asks God concerning his will in the matter. Verse 6 indirectly reveals the means of inquiry ("Now Abiathar son of Ahimelech had brought the ephod down with him when he fled to David at Keilah"), since the high priest carried the oracular Urim and Thummim (Exod 28:29–30).

The religious nature of holy war is also clear in the execution of the battle. In the first place, as mentioned previously, the Ark of the Covenant (when it existed) was taken onto the battlefield. Thus, the army was accompanied by priests. 2 Chronicles 20:20–30 gives us a rare peak at the march into battle. After a stirring sermon, by King Jehoshaphat, the Levitical singers took their appointed place at the head of the army as they advanced toward the enemy. Earlier, the Israelites on their march in the wilderness were also pictured as an army on the march with the Ark at their head. Moses would begin each day's journey with these words:

> Rise up, O LORD!
> May your enemies be scattered;
> may your foes flee before you. (Num 10:35)

With God present with them in battle, there was no need for large numbers of troops or sophisticated weapons. Indeed, such were discouraged in order to keep Israel from attributing victory to their own resources rather than to God. The classic illustration of this characteristic of holy war is the story of Gideon, whom God made whittle down his army from thirty-two thousand to three hundred (Judg 7:1–12). Strikingly, the single combat of David and Goliath also exemplifies this principle of holy war. In the one corner is Goliath, a professional soldier armed to the teeth (1 Sam 7:4–7). In the other corner is David, a naïve, young man, who is not even in the army. He has no armor and his only weapon is a slingshot. Even so, the battle is indeed unfair—but in David's favor. David makes this clear when he says to Goliath, "You come against me with sword and spear and javelin, but I come against you in the name of the LORD Almighty, the God of the armies of Israel, whom you have defied. This day the LORD will hand you over to me, and I'll strike you down and cut off your head. Today I will give the carcasses of the Philistine army to the birds of the air and the beasts of the earth, and the whole world will know that there is a God in Israel. All those gathered here will know that it is not by sword or spear that the LORD saves, for the battle is the LORD's, and he will give all of you into our hands" (1 Sam 17:45–47).

It is of interest to note that though God is the divine warrior and wins the battle, that this does not relieve Israel of their responsibility to enter and participate in the battle. David, for instance, must confront Goliath and throw the sling that kills the giant. God does not instruct him to deliver his stirring speech and then step back a hundred yards so he can throw lightening down on Goliath from heaven. Similarly, Israel's army must march around the city for days while the priests carry the Ark and blow trumpets before the wall comes tumbling down. God wins the victory, but Israel must exert itself in battle. I have always been struck by the analogy that exists here with our salvation (an analogy that may not be at all coincidental, as we will see below). In Phil 2:12b–13, Paul expresses the two-sided nature of salvation in this way: ". . . work out your salvation with fear and trembling, for it is God who works in you to will and to act according to his good purpose."

In terms of outcome, of course, there is no doubt if it is truly a holy war. God wins the battle for his people. And the people's first response should be praise. It is remarkable just how many holy war victory songs there are in the Old Testament. One of the first and most memorable is the Song of the Sea in Exodus 15, which also marks the first time God is explicitly called a divine warrior in Scripture. Moses led the Israelites in this song on the occasion of the defeat of Pharaoh's chariot troops and the rescue of the defenseless Israelites at the Re(e)d Sea. It appropriately begins:

> I will sing to the LORD,
>   for he is highly exalted.
> The horse and its rider
>   he has hurled into the sea.
> The LORD is my strength and my song,
>   he has become my salvation.
> He is my God, and I will praise him,
>   my father's God, and I will exalt him.
> The LORD is a warrior (*'ish milhama*);
>   the LORD is his name.
> Pharaoh's chariots and his army
>   he has hurled into the sea.
> The best of Pharaoh's officers
>   are drowned in the Red Sea.
> The deep waters have covered them;
>   they sank to the depths like a stone. (Exod 15:1–5)

A second example comes from the historical books, the song of Deborah (Judg 5) that rejoices over God's victory over the Midianites. While the song has some negative comments to make about certain tribes, its praise of Yahweh as their victor is unalloyed:

> O LORD, when you went out from Seir,
>   when you marched from the land of Edom,
> The earth shook, the heavens poured,
>   the clouds poured down water.
> The mountains quaked before the LORD,
>   the One of Sinai,
>   before the LORD, the God of Israel.
> So may all your enemies perish, O LORD!
>   But may they who love you be like the sun
>   when it rises in its strength. (Judg 5:4–5, 31)

This poem illustrates another characteristic of holy war that we have not considered as of yet. God will often utilize the force of his creation to execute his warfare against his enemies. Notice Judges 5:20–21:

> From the heavens the stars fought,
>   from their courses they fought against Sisera.
> The river Kishon swept them away,
>   the age-old river, the river Kishon.
>   March on, my soul; be strong!

These are stirring examples of holy war hymns that celebrate specific victories. In the psalms, we have a significant number of psalms whose original setting is clearly holy war. Some of these are songs sung in anticipation of a battle (e.g., Ps 7, with the characteristic call for God to "rise up"). Others find their setting in the midst of battle (Ps 91), but here we are interested in those songs that were sung after victory.[5]

The conclusion to Psalm 24 (vv. 7–10) makes it clear that this was the setting of this well-known hymn:

> Lift up your heads, O you gates;
>   be lifted up, you ancient doors,
>   that the king of glory may come in.
> Who is this King of glory?
>   The LORD strong and mighty,
>   the LORD mighty in battle.
> Lift up your heads, O you gates;
>   lift them up, you ancient doors,
>   that the king of glory may come in.
> Who is he, this King of glory!
>   The LORD Almighty—
>   he is the king of glory.

This interchange almost certainly took place between two priests, one stationed at the top of the gate in the city of Jerusalem and the other accompanying the Ark of the Covenant at the head of the army returning from a successful holy war. The first priest asks the question to which everyone knew the answer, but which allowed for the celebration of God specifically as the LORD Almighty (*Yhwh seba'ot*, better, "Lord of Hosts," his heavenly army). He is, after all, "mighty in battle."

Again, a number of psalms find their setting here. The difference between such psalms and songs such as Exodus 15 and Judges 5 is that the psalms are historically non-specific. This is typical of psalms in general; they are not embedded in any particular event. They are worded in such a way that they can be used and reused for similar though not necessarily identical situations.

Along with the praise, holy war, at least within the land of Canaan, concluded with the execution of the *ḥerem*, which we described above as turning over to God all of the plunder and all of the prisoners of

---

5. Tremper Longman III, "Psalm 98: A Divine Warrior Victory Song," *JETS* 27 (1984) 267–74, which identifies about a third of the Psalter as related to the waging of holy war.

war. While in the lands outside of Canaan, the women and children were not put to death, within the land of Canaan the entire population was to be killed. There were no prisoners in holy war within the land of Canaan itself.

Deuteronomy 20 legislates this practice. The historical accounts of battles, such as the battle of Jericho, do not dwell on the subject, though they do clearly indicate that *herem* was performed in the aftermath of the battle: "They completely destroyed everything in it with their swords—men and women, young and old, cattle, sheep, goats, and donkeys" (Josh 7:21). Only Rahab, who had come over to Israel's side, was spared.

When Israel does not perform *herem*, it becomes a problem for Israel. Of course, at Jericho, Achan stole some of the plunder, thus leading to Israel's defeat at Ai (see below). In 1 Samuel 15, Saul has not fully executed *herem*. He has not offered up all of the sheep to the Lord, nor has he executed King Agag.[6]

This picture of Holy War raises the question of genocide. The Old Testament historical books describe the divinely authorized destruction of whole peoples by another group with the result that they displaced them from their homeland. Is this any different from other imperialistic attempts to colonize another people's land? Indeed, the picture is complicated when we realize that these texts have been used to justify the genocidal and imperialistic impulses of Christians through the centuries.

I will resist the temptation to present an immediate answer to this important question. Rather, we must first look at the development of the institution/theme of holy war through Scripture, particularly into the New Testament, before we consider the ethics of Old Testament holy war and the question of any possible post-Old Testament justification for holy war.

As I have studied the themes of holy war and the divine warrior over the past three decades, I believe I can explain it best under five topic headings. Before I do so, though, I first want to express my opinion that these are not five different strategies, but five phases of God's overarching and consistent strategy for defeating evil.

---

6. Nor apparently others, since the Amalekites (Agagites) remain a threat to Israel down to the time of the conflict between Mordecai, son of Kish (and thus a descendant of Saul), and Haman the Agagite. See the insightful analysis by Karen H. Jobes, *Esther*, NIVAC (Grand Rapids: Zondervan, 1999).

THE FIVE PHASES OF HOLY WAR

The first phase of holy war is found in the Old Testament. Indeed, as we have described the nature of holy war we have used examples from this phase: God fights his (and Israel's) flesh and blood enemies. Thus, the battle against Egypt at the Sea, the Amalekites in Exodus 17, the Canaanites city-states in Joshua, the wars against the foreign oppressors in the book of Judges, and many, many accounts of battles down through the period of the Old Testament are all illustrative of this phase.

Since we have already devoted so much attention to the first phase already, we will proceed to phase two: God fights against Israel. Throughout the history of Israel there are accounts of battles where God fights against Israel. At the time of the judge Eli, his wicked sons Hophni and Phinehas were leading the army against the Philistines (1 Sam 4). In the first battle, the Philistines defeat Israel. It is at this point that Hophni and Phinehas think to bring the Ark of the Covenant onto the battlefield. The context of their decision, however, makes it clear that they decide this not as a matter of faith. They appear to believe that the Ark was almost a magical amulet. So in the next phase of the battle against the Philistines, Israel again suffers defeat in spite of the presence of the ark. Of course, Israel's defeat is not the result God's inability to save. He proves this over the first few days that the Ark is housed in the temple of Dagon. On the first morning, the Philistines discover Dagon's statue prostrate before the Ark. On the second morning, after they had settled the statue back into place, they again discover Dagon again on the floor— only this time with severed head and hands (1 Sam 5:1–5).

A second example of what has been called "reverse holy war" takes place during the Conquest. After defeating Jericho, likely the most powerful of the city-states, Joshua sends troops against Ai (in Hebrew "Ruin"), the very name of which connotes weakness. Even so, Israel is easily defeated. Why? God willed it due to Achan's breach of the laws of holy war (Joshua 7).

The most striking example of God appearing as a warrior who fights against Israel takes place toward the end of the Old Testament period, when God allows Babylon to defeat Judah. Actually, he does not simply allow the defeat of Judah, he himself accomplishes it. That is the perspective of the book of Lamentations as it bemoans the destruction of Jerusalem:[7]

> He [Yahweh] bends his bow against his people,
> > as though he were their enemy.
> His strength is used against them
> > to kill their finest youth.
> His fury is poured out like fire
> > on beautiful Jerusalem.
> Yes, the Lord has vanquished Israel
> > like an enemy.
> He has destroyed her palaces
> > and demolished her fortresses.
> He has brought unending sorrow and tears
> > upon beautiful Jerusalem. (2:4–5)

Of course, God has abandoned and turned hostile toward his people because they have abandoned him. During many of the times when the kings have betrayed Yahweh, the divine warrior wages war on behalf of his faithful prophets. A good example of this is found in 2 Kings 6 when the Aramaeans surround the city in which Elisha and his prophetic colleagues lived. In response to the fear of his servant, Elisha prayed that God might open his eyes with the result that "when he [the servant] looked up, he saw that the hillside around Elisha was filled with horses and chariots of fire" (v. 17), in other words, the heavenly army.

Though the divine warrior defeated Jerusalem, this event is not the end of the story for Israel. In the exilic and post-exilic period, God commissioned prophets to bring a message of hope in the midst of Israel's oppression. Daniel, Zechariah, and Malachi are examples of prophets who speak of the future coming of the divine warrior who will rescue his people from their oppressors.

In the vision recorded in chapter 7, for instance, Daniel sees four beasts emerging from a chaotic sea.[8] By this time (whether sixth century or second century BC), the sea and its monsters were well established symbols for evil and chaos. The hybrid nature of the first beast and third beasts, as well as the non-organic description of the fourth beast (with its iron teeth and claws), adds additional darkness to the symbolism.

---

7. See Tremper Longman III, *Jeremiah, Lamentations*, NIBC Old Testament Series 14 (Peabody, MA: Hendrickson, 2008) 336–38.

8. For a full discussion and bibliography, see Tremper Longman III, *Daniel*, NIVAC (Grand Rapids: Zondervan, 1999), 174–98.

The interpreting angel tells Daniel that these beasts represent evil human kingdoms, the ones that oppress the people of God (7:17). The second half of the vision, though, moves from beasts that represent evil human kingdoms to human figures who represent the divine realm. One "like a son of man" rides the cloud into the presence of the Ancient of Days. Interestingly, both figures represent God, a point not lost on the New Testament writers who associated the human-like figure riding the divine war chariot with Jesus Christ (Matt 24:30; Mark 13:26, etc.). According to this vision, then, God the warrior will come and will defeat the forces of evil.

A similar message is found in Zechariah 14, which begins with a description of the enemies of God's people looting and abusing the people of Jerusalem. The tide turns, though, in v. 3: "Then the LORD will go out and fight against those nations as he has fought in times past." The rest of the chapter describes the Lord's victory over his enemies.

Our final example is from Malachi 4, the final chapter of the Christian canon of the Old Testament. Here the prophet proclaims, "The day of judgment is coming burning like a furnace. On that day, the arrogant and the wicked will be burned up like straw. They will be consumed—roots, branches, and all" (4:1).

It is with this note of expectation of future divine intrusion that the Old Testament comes to a close. Of course, intertestamental literature develops this theme further, and there might be some benefit to describing the use of this theme in the period between the Testaments. For my purpose, though, it is best to go right to the New Testament and listen to the first voice that speaks. John the Baptist there prepares the way for Jesus with the following words:

> You brood of snakes! Who warned you to flee God's coming wrath? Prove by the way you live that you have repented of your sins and turned to God. Don't just say to each other, "We're safe, for we are descendants of Abraham." That means nothing, for I tell you, God can create children of Abraham from these very stones. Even now the ax of God's judgment is poised, ready to sever the roots of the trees. Yes, every tree that does not produce good fruit will be chopped down and thrown into the fire. I baptize with water those who repent of their sins and turn to God. But someone is coming soon who is greater than I am—so much greater that I'm not worthy even to be his slave and carry his sandals. He will baptize you with the Holy Spirit and with fire. He

is ready to separate the chaff from the wheat with his winnowing fork. Then he will clean up the threshing area, gathering the wheat into his barn but burning he chaff with never-ending fire. (Matt 3:7–12)

Notice just how similar John's words are to the late prophets of the Old Testament. He expects the Messiah's return to result in the violent judgment of God's enemies.

That John held this expectation is underlined by his surprise at the course of Jesus' earthly ministry. After he baptized Jesus, John was thrown in jail. While in jail, he receives what are to him disturbing reports about Jesus' activities. John hears that he Jesus is healing the sick, preaching the good news to the poor, and exorcising demons. Where is the burning with fire and the chopping down of the rotten wood! Confused, John sends two of his disciples to Jesus with the probing question, "Are you the Messiah we've been expecting or should we keep looking for someone else?" (Matt 11:3). Jesus tells them to go back and report to John that he is healing the sick and preaching the Good News.

What, precisely, is Jesus telling John? Reading between the lines, he is saying, in essence, "John, I am the divine warrior you were expecting. However, I have intensified and heightened the warfare so it is directed, not against flesh and blood enemies, but rather the spiritual powers and authorities." And this enemy is not defeated by killing, but rather by dying.

When Jesus was arrested in the Garden of Gethsemane, Peter took violent steps to protect him. He pulled out his sword and succeeded in cutting off the high priest's servant's ear (Matt 26:51). Jesus turned to him and said, "Put away your sword. Those who use the sword will die by the sword. Don't you realize that I could ask my Father for thousands of angels to protect us (a reference to the heavenly army), and he would send them instantly? But if I did, how would the Scriptures be fulfilled that describe what must happen now?"

"What must happen now" of course is a reference to Christ's crucifixion, resurrection, and ascension by which he defeated Satan and the spiritual powers and principalities. Accordingly, Paul could use military language in order to describe these great redemptive events. In Col 2:13–15, we read: "You were dead because of your sins and because your sinful nature was not yet cut away. Then God made you alive with Christ, for he forgave all our sins. He canceled the record of the charges against us and took it away by nailing it to the cross. In this way, he disarmed the spiritual rulers and authorities. He shamed them publicly by his victory over them on the cross." Christ's death and resurrection could be described as a military victory followed by a parade in which the prisoners of war were led through the streets and thus shamed. The latter metaphor is used to describe the ascension in Eph 4:7–8:

> However, he has given each one of us a special gift through the generosity of Christ. That is why the Scriptures say:
>
> When he ascended to the heights,
>   he led a crowd of captives
>   and gave gifts to his people.

Paul here quotes Ps 68:18 in reference to his ascension. Psalm 68 itself is a battle psalm praising Yahweh as divine warrior, but here being applied to Christ.

Of course, Jesus' words and actions, as well as Paul's interpretation of them, raises the question as to whether John the Baptist was wrong in his initial understanding of what Christ came to do. Jesus himself seems to correct John's misapprehension of his work after all. Upon close reflection and broader scriptural context, we hesitate to make that judgment. John is a prophet after all, and prophet's often did not understand the full import of their divinely given message. Jesus' earthly ministry was to focus the attack on spiritual powers. But Jesus also announced his return and described it in ways that suggest violence against both spiritual and physical enemies of God.

In Mark 13:26, for instance, Jesus states that "everyone will see the Son of Man coming on the clouds with great power and glory," a quote from Daniel 7:13. The vehicular cloud is the divine war chariot, and Daniel 7 describes the Son of Man as having defeated the forces of evil human kingdoms represented by hybrid sea monsters.

The book of Revelation develops the theme of God's culminating battle against his human and spiritual enemies most fully. Revelation 19:11–21 is illustrative:

> Then I saw heaven opened, and a white horse was standing there. Its rider was named Faithful and True, for he judges fairly and wages a righteous war. His eyes were like flames of fire, and on his head were many crowns. A name was written on him that no one understood except himself. He wore a robe dipped in blood,

and his title was the Word of God. The armies of heaven, dressed in the finest of pure white linen, followed him on white horses. From his mouth came a sharp sword to strike down the nations. He will rule them with an iron rod. He will release the fierce wrath of God, the Almighty, like juice flowing from a winepress. On his robe at his thigh was written this title: King of all kings and Lord of all lords.

Thus, redemptive history ends with a final judgment described in holy war terms. Evil is once and for all defeated.

Now with the entire scope of the biblical theology of holy war and the divine warrior laid out, we can now turn to the questions with which we opened this essay, questions concerning the significance and continuing relevance of this theme today.

REFLECTING ON THE ETHICS OF HOLY WAR

The church today occupies the space between the first and second comings of Christ. Thus, the people of God as the people of God may not take up physical weapons in the execution of holy war. While this leads Mennonite writers on holy war toward a pacifist position,[9] in my mind it does not settle the question of whether Christians can rightfully participate in military service as citizens of a nation state. That is a different topic for another paper. What is clear to me, though, is that holy war texts in the Old Testament provide no justification for warfare in the present redemptive era. We should, in the words of Moonjang Lee, "exercise the hermeneutics of suspicion on the texts used to justify the colonial powers."[10] It is proper to reject unconditionally any past or present use of the Old Testament holy wars for the purpose of warfare, especially those that justified the actions of the colonial powers, such as the Crusades, or the Western wars that displaced the Indian nations of America.

However, even so, such a view should not, in my opinion, lead modern Christian readers of the Old Testament to adopt the view that the holy wars of the Old Testament are somehow sub-Christian or morally

---

9. See Vernard Eller, *War and Peace from Genesis to Revelation* (1981; reprinted, Eugene, OR: Wipf and Stock Publishers, 2003); and Millard Lind, *Yahweh Is a Warrior*, A Christian Peace Shelf Selection (Scottdale, PA: Herald, 1980).

10. Moonjang Lee, "Asian Biblical Interpretation," in *Dictionary for Theological Interpretation of the Bible*, ed. Kevin J. Vanhoozer et al. (Grand Rapids: Baker Academic, 2005), 68–69.

wrong. Recently such a view was argued by C. S. Cowles, a theologian from Point Loma Nazarene University.[11] He believes that Christ's ethic in the gospels ("turn the other cheek") is the standard by which Old Testament ethics should be judged, and he contends that as it turns out, the two are at odds with each other. "Moses' genocidal commands make a mockery of God's justice, not to mention his holiness and love."[12] Of course, the biblical text tells us that Moses is not the originator of these commands; they ultimately come from God. Even so, Cowles in effect renders the Old Testament subcanonical, emulating the error of the Marcionites.

Such an approach to the issue of Old Testament holy war suffers from an even more egregious mistake, its selective use of the New Testament. In the first place, based on Jesus' general approval of the Old Testament, "there are no grounds for reckoning that Jesus disapproved of the story in Joshua."[13] As we observed from our survey above, the New Testament does not speak merely of the present spiritual warfare, but also of the future final battle against evil that will mark the end of all human and spiritual enemies of God. Cowles, like Marcion before him, operates with a very selective and limited canon, culled only from the portions of the New Testament that are aligned with his own moral standards.

As a matter of fact, in my opinion the best way to understand Old Testament *ḥerem* warfare is as an intrusion of consummation ethics.[14] That is, as an act of judgment against the Canaanites whose sin is cited as the reason for their defeat (as early as Genesis 15:16). But, as we say above (under the discussion of "phase two"), God also fought against Israel. These wars, too, may be viewed as acts of divine judgment. As Goldingay puts it, "When Israel behaves like the Canaanites, Yhwh treats it like the Canaanites."[15]

---

11. Cowles, "The Case."

12. Ibid., 18.

13. John Goldingay, *Israel's Gospel*, Old Testament Theology 1 (Downers Grove, IL: InterVarsity, 2003), 490.

14. An approach first suggested to me by Meredith G. Kline, *The Structure of Biblical Authority* (Grand Rapids: Eerdmans, 1972).

15. Goldingay, *Israel's Gospel*, 479.

Against Cowles and others who want to relegate the Old Testament to secondary status,[16] I reaffirm the traditional Christian affirmation that the whole of the Bible, both Old and New Testaments, is the canon of the church. We should not disown the actions of Joshua, but we should also not imitate them today. There is both continuity and discontinuity between the Old and New Testaments. Today we are engaged in spiritual holy war, and that is a war which is directed toward the spiritual powers and authorities (Eph 6:12). Swords and spears will not work against these enemies, which is why God has equipped us with the more powerful armor and weapons of truth, God's righteousness, peace, faith, and salvation (Eph 6:13–17). Furthermore, this warfare is not waged just against evil "out there" (2 Cor 10:3–6), but also against that in our own hearts and minds (Rom 7:14–25).[17]

---

16. I greatly appreciate Goldingay's analysis of holy war, and he always affirms the canonical status and significance of the Old Testament texts. However, I would take exception to his view that "the ḥerem was always a theological principle rather than a practice. It constituted an assertion that Israel must not allow itself to be led astray by the traditional religion of the land" (*Israel's Gospel*, 500). The problem with his view is twofold. First, as we saw with Jericho, there are occasions, according to the text, where Israelites did perform ḥerem. Second, when they did not, it was a result of their sin. L. Daniel Hawk also critiques Old Testament ḥerem in a way that judges it sub-Christian and relates it to "stories of dispossession, colonization, and ethnic cleansing"; *Joshua*, Berit Olam (Collegeville, MN: Liturgical, 2001), xii–xiii.

17. For a popular exposition of what it means to engage in spiritual holy war today, see Dan B. Allender and Tremper Longman III, *Bold Love* (Colorado Springs: NavPress, 1993).

7

"Holy War" and the Universal God

Reading the New Testament Conquest Accounts in a Post-Colonial Setting

David W. Pao

"HOLY WAR" AND MODERN MISSIONARY MOVEMENTS

THE CELEBRATION OF THE 200th anniversary of the first Protestant missionary's arrival in China provides us with an opportunity to consider various topics related to the impact of the missionary movements, the development of Western evangelicalism and global Christianity, the relationship between biblical confession of faith and indigenous religions, and the reading of the Bible in various cultural contexts. At the intersection of these various considerations, one often finds the symbol of the Holy War. This symbol points to various periods of our history that many people find disturbing. For those who consider themselves to have been manipulated by such a War's powerful and oppressive forces, this symbol can evoke a deep sense of anger and resentment. Many who are outside the Christian movement also employ this symbol in an effort to reduce the power of the Gospel to the political and economic agendas of particular nation states.

In historical terms, from the time of the Crusades in the Middle Ages to the perceived struggles between "Christian" nations and "Muslim" states in our contemporary era, the "Holy War" remains a powerful symbol.¹ In such contexts, religions are often considered to be instruments of the marginalized, but also irrational forces that fuel continuous military conflicts between groups with competing ideologies.²

In discussions of the history of Christianity in China, modern missionary movements that "coincided with," if not "were aided by," the expansion of Western colonial powers have been regarded as versions of such "Holy War." This is particularly true in the case of the spread of Christianity on Chinese soils. Western missionaries began to have a significant presence in China only after the nation was forced to open itself to European forces in the late 1850s. These missionaries were considered instruments of Western imperialism as they sought to impose a foreign ideology upon the Chinese nationals.³ The earliest response was therefore that Christianity was anti-Confucian. Although numerous charges were made against the Christianity of the Westerners in the following decades, the one constant was that the missionaries sought to denationalize the converts, as evidenced by the Westerners being "slow to acknowledge the Chinese as equals in culture and character."⁴

The situation in Hong Kong in particular provides a clear window into such issues because of its unique history as a British colony, and because of the challenges presented to the local Chinese churches in the postcolonial setting following the turnover to Mainland China in 1997. Within weeks after Hong Kong was ceded to the British in 1841, eight Protestant missionaries arrived there, and, according to the report of one of these missionaries published on February 18, 1841 in the *Canton*

---

1. See, for example, the discussion in Karen Armstrong, *Holy War: The Crusades and Their Impact on Today's World*, 2nd ed. (New York: Anchor, 2001) and Peter Partner, *God of Battles: Holy Wars of Christianity and Islam* (Princeton: Princeton University Press, 1998).

2. Mark Juergensmeyer, *Terror in the Mind of God: The Global Rise of Religious Violence*, updated ed., Comparative Studies in Religion and Society 13 (Berkeley: University of California Press, 2001); Lee Harris, *The Suicide of Reason: Radical Islam's Threat to the Englightenment* (New York: Basic Books, 2007). See also a more nuanced discussion in William T. Cavanaugh, "Does Religion Cause Violence?" *HDB* 35 (2007) 22–35.

3. See Hsieh Hsing-yao, "How Did Imperialism Use Religion for Aggression on China? A Historical Survey of Missionary Work in China," in *Religious Policy and Practice in Communist China: A Documentary History*, ed. Donald E. MacInnis (London: Hodder & Stoughton, 1972), 133–37.

4. Carl T. Smith, "The Adaptation of the Protestant Church to a Chinese and Colonial Situation," *Ching Feng* 26 (1983) 76.

Register, the hope of this little village lay in the civilization and the religion that was brought by the presence of the British troops:

> It...may form a substantial foundation, in the providence of God, on which to establish, under the auspices of the flag which now waves upon its summits, the true principles of commerce, justice, and the Christian religion, where protected these may flourish untrammeled, until this nation be enlightened and saved.[5]

Even after a century and a half of relatively peaceful rule by the British government in Hong Kong, many local Christians continued to see the church as maintaining and supporting the British role as a colonizing power.[6] To many, the link between the "sword" of the colonizers and the "gospel" that they brought remained an obstacle for continuing the mission of the local church. Moreover, in the post-1997 context, the church faced, and continues to face, the challenge of proclaiming the good news in a context where the authenticity of the message is tested without the support of a "Christian" government.

These historical and contemporary concerns force us to return to the fundamental texts containing the roots of both the Gospel message and the idea of divine warfare. This chapter contends that a proper reading of selected conquest narratives in the biblical material will provide a proper perspective for the examination of these related issues as we consider the power of the Gospel message and its claims for submission and obedience.

CONQUEST NARRATIVES IN THE NEW TESTAMENT

The significance of the "divine warrior" motif in the Old Testament requires no further demonstration.[7] In this chapter, we will thus focus

---

5. Quoted in Kate Lowe, "The Beliefs, Aspirations and Methods of the First Missionaries in British Hong Kong, 1841–5," in *Missions and Missionaries*, ed. Pieter N. Holtrop and Hugh McLeod, Studies in Church History, Subsidia 13 (New York: Boydell, 2000), 52.

6. See Kwok Nai Wang, "Christian Churches in Hong Kong under Colonial Rule," *Tripod* 98 (1997) 28–42.

7. See Gerhard von Rad, *Holy War in Ancient Israel*, trans. Marva J. Dawn (Grand Rapids: Eerdmans, 1991); Frank M. Cross, *Canaanite Myth and Hebrew Epic* (Cambridge: Harvard University Press, 1973), 112–44; Paul D. Hanson, *The Dawn of Apocalyptic* (Philadelphia: Fortress, 1975), 292–334; Millard C. Lind, *Yahweh Is a Warrior: The Theology of Warfare in Ancient Israel* (Scottdale, PA: Herald, 1980); Sa-Moon Kang, *Divine War in the Old Testament and in the Ancient Near East*, BZAW 177 (Berlin: de

instead on the significance of such a motif in the New Testament. While others have studied the use of this Old Testament motif in the New Testament,[8] my focus here will be on the rhetorical and theological function of the New Testament conquest narratives in their own historical and cultural contexts. Though these conquest narratives do draw from the Old Testament traditions, they are also situated in the first-century Roman world in which Roman imperial claims occupy a significant place in both texts[9] and images.[10] Within this context, divine warfare in the New Testament takes on added significance. Not only do these conquest narratives aim at providing the fulfillment for Old Testament promises, they also offer a model for discussing the claims of power and the critique of such claims within a wider salvation-historical framework.

Although some have claimed that divine warfare ceased to be an important motif in the New Testament,[11] most would recognize the presence of this motif in numerous New Testament passages. These include the portrayal of the ministry of Jesus as defeating the power of Satan in both historical (Matt 12:28; Luke 11:21–22) and cosmic terms (Luke 10:18; cf. Col 2:15); within this framework, divine warfare also becomes a metaphor for discipleship (Luke 14:31–32) and missions (Matt 28:16–20).[12] In his epistles, Paul often employs military imagery in describing the role and mission of the followers of Christ (Rom 13:12; 1 Cor 9:7; 2 Cor 6:7; Phil 2:25; 1 Thess 5:8; 1 Tim 1:18; 2 Tim 2:3, 4;

Gruyter, 1989); Tremper Longman III and Daniel G. Reid, *God Is a Warrior*, Studies in Old Testament Biblical Theology (Grand Rapids: Zondervan, 1995), 31–88.

8. See, for example, Tremper Longman III, "The Divine Warrior: The New Testament Use of an Old Testament Motif," *WTJ* 44 (1982) 290–307.

9. J K. Newman, *Augustus and the New Poetry,* Collection Latomus 88 (Brussels: Berchem, 1967).

10. Niels Hannestad, *Roman Art and Imperial Policy*, trans. P. J. Crabb (Aarhus, Denmark: Aarhus University Press, 1988); Paul Zanker, *The Power of Images in the Age of Augustus,* trans. Alan Shapiro, Jerome Lectures, 16th series (Ann Arbor: University of Michigan Press, 1990).

11. Rolf P. Knierim, "On the Subject of War in Old Testament and Biblical Theology," *HBT* 16 (1994) 17, suggests, for example, that divine warfare "is no longer an essential issue because the end of history is already determined by the eschatological presence of Jesus Christ and the eschatological existence of his church." This, however, is to ignore the continuous struggles between God and Satan on the historical plane in this period between the "already" and "not-yet."

12. Matt 28:16–20 should thus be considered in light of the presence of the Exodus/Conquest motif in this pericope; cf. Kenton L. Sparks, "Gospel as Conquest: Mosaic Typology in Matthew 28:16–20," *CBQ* 68 (2006) 651–63.

Phlm 2). More extensively, one finds the autobiographical description of Paul himself as a soldier in the eschatological battle against the evil one (2 Cor 10:3–6).[13] Beyond these examples of military imagery, one also finds literal references to battles of the past (Heb 11:34), as well as to the wars and turmoil that will appear before the end of times (Matt 24:6; Mark 13:7; Luke 21:9; cf. 2 Thess 2:7). It should also be noted that terms such as "day of the Lord" (cf. 1 Cor 1:8; 5:5; 2 Cor 1:14; Phil 1:6, 10; 2:16) and concepts such as the cloud-riding Son of Man (Matt 26:64; Mark 13:26; 14:62; Luke 21:27, 36; cf. Matt 16:27; 24:27; 25:31; Mark 8:38) draw from Old Testament traditions of divine warfare.[14]

Without denying the significance of these metaphors and allusions, we will focus in this chapter on three New Testament texts in which the conquest motif can be considered as one of the main *leitmotifs*, or even organizing principles. These three texts will serve as our foundational bases from which various issues related to the reading of the conquest narratives in a post-colonial setting can be examined. These three texts interact in different ways and to different degrees with the Old Testament divine warfare traditions, but they all provide provocative examples of conquest narratives that address issues surrounding the dawn of a new era in salvation history.

The first example appears in the form of a historical narrative that depicts the conquest of the Gospel message in the Acts of the Apostles. In this conquest account, the emphases on the victory (and deliverance) of the people of God and the defeat of their enemies become prominent. This emphasis on conquest is well articulated in the summary statement in Acts 19:20, "So the Word of the Lord grew mightily (κατὰ κράτος) and prevailed."[15] Here, the employment of the unique phrase κατὰ κράτος ("mightily") should not be overlooked. In ancient Greek literature, this phrase usually appears in military conquest accounts.[16] Although "mightily" only appears in Acts 19:20 in the Lukan narrative,

---

13. For those who deny the Pauline authorship of Ephesians, 2 Cor 10 "contains the most extensive military imagery in Paul's letters"; Brian K. Peterson, "Conquest, Control, and the Cross," *Int* 52 (1998) 259.

14. Longman, "The Divine Warrior," 292–97.

15. In this chapter, all English biblical quotations are taken from the New Revised Standard Version (NRSV) unless otherwise noted.

16. See, for example, Menander, *Per.* 407; *Dio Chrys.* 26 [43], 11; *Inscriptiones Graecae* XII 5, 444, 103; *The Tebtunis Papyri* I-III 27, 83; and the discussion in W. Michaelis, "Κράτος," in *TDNT* 3 (1965) 905–10.

the fact that this verse is the third of a group of three similarly worded and strategically located summary statements in this travel narrative testifies to the significance of this conquest motif for the entire narrative (cf. Acts 6:7; 12:24). Moreover, 19:20, which functions as the climax of these summary statements, also corresponds to the programmatic statement in 1:8 that emphasizes the importance of "power" in the subsequent episodes.

Traveling can be considered as a constant symbol of military conquest accounts, and such traveling as an act of mapping a territory can "concretely reveal and assert lines of power and linguistic impositions."[17] It is within this conquest paradigm that individual episodes in the travel narrative in Acts should be examined. For example, the numerous instances of the confrontation between the Word of God (and its messengers) with the political or religious leaders of various cities and regions can thus be understood as military conflict in which the Word of God is always portrayed as the victor. Not only can the travel narrative be understood as a conquest narrative, it should also be understood against the background of the Exodus tradition as developed and transformed in the Book of Isaiah.[18] The use of the Exodus tradition in Isaiah has long been recognized by scholars,[19] and the act of conquest is considered as the central element of this New Exodus.[20] In this New Exodus narrative, one finds the fulfillment of God's promises as He again calls a people and gives them an identity as they seek to serve Him in the unfolding of His

---

17. See Susan Gallagher VanZanten, "Mapping the Hybrid World: Three Postcolonial Motifs," *Semeia* 75 (1996) 233.

18. For a detailed defense of this hypothesis, see David W. Pao, *Acts and the Isaianic New Exodus*, WUNT 2/130 (Tübingen: Mohr/Siebeck, 2000).

19. See, for example, Bernhard W. Anderson, "Exodus Typology in Second Isaiah," in *Israel's Prophetic Heritage: Essays in Honor of James Muilenburg*, ed. Bernhard W. Anderson and Walter J. Harrelson (New York: Harper, 1962), 177–95; and John E. Hamlin, "Deutero-Isaiah's Reinterpretation of the Exodus in the Babylonian Twilight," *Proceedings: Eastern Great Lakes and Midwest Biblical Societies* 11 (1991) 75–80; and Samuel E. Loewenstamm, *The Evolution of the Exodus Tradition*, trans. Baruch J. Schwartz, Publication of the Perry Foundation for Biblical Research in the Hebrew University of Jerusalem (Jerusalem: Magnes, 1992).

20. Cross, *Canaanite Myth and Hebrew Epic*, 99–111, sees the conquest of the divine warrior as central to both the early Exodus tradition and the one developed in Isaiah. Lind (*Yahweh Is a Warrior*, 47) likewise argues that "the exodus and wilderness period is the time of holy war 'par excellence.'"

eternal purpose. This Lukan New Exodus account will provide a valuable text as we examine New Testament conquest narratives.

The second example can be found in Ephesians where Paul describes the involvement of God's people in the victory of God's own battle through Christ. Ephesians 6:10-20 provides the most explicit and extensive use of the divine warrior motif in the Pauline Epistles. Christians are called to "[p]ut on the whole armor of God, so that [they] may be able to stand against the wiles of the devil" (Eph 6:11). Few would deny the significance of this passage in discussions of divine warfare in Paul, but the motif of divine warfare can also be traced back to the earlier sections of this epistle where Paul describes the Lordship of Jesus (1:20-23) and the conflict between God and Satan through the work of Christ on the cross (2:1-22).[21] Moreover, the detailed description of this "armor of God" in 6:14-17 is also based on the earlier sections in which Paul described the power of the Gospel message.[22] Not to be missed is the fact that the imagery of the armor of God is drawn from the imagery of the divine warrior in Isaiah 11 and 59.[23] One is not able to discuss the implications of the New Testament's use of the conquest motif without drawing upon the resources provided by Paul in this significant epistle.

Finally, in addition to being a traditional symbol in historical narratives and epistles, the conquest motif also plays a prominent role in the New Testament apocalyptic portrayal of the end times. In Revelation, the climax in the depiction of the struggle between God and Evil appears in chapter 19 where the rider of the white horse "judges and makes war" (Rev 19:11). He is followed by "the armies of heaven" (19:14) as they fight against and destroy "the beast and the kings of the earth" (19:19). The portrayal of the eschatological battle is not limited to Revelation 19, however. Already in chapter six, one finds the depiction of eschatological judgment in the appearance of the four horsemen who will bring war and chaos to humankind (6:1-8). This chaos ultimately leads to the "battle on the great day of God the Almighty" (16:14). This conquest nar-

---

21. See, for example, Timothy G. Gombis, "Ephesians 2 as a Narrative of Divine Warfare," *JSNT* 26 (2004) 403-18.

22. See, for example, Markus Barth, *Ephesians 4-6*, AB 34A (Garden City, NY: Doubleday, 1974), 793-800.

23. See Thorsten Moritz, *A Profound Mystery: The Use of the Old Testament in Ephesians*, NovTSup 85 (Leiden: Brill, 1996), 178-212; and Thomas R. Yoder Neufeld, *Put on the Armour of God: The Divine Warrior from Isaiah to Ephesians*, JSNTSup 140 (Sheffield: Sheffield Academic, 1997), 131-45.

rative is significant not only because it presents the most explicit critique of Roman imperialism in the New Testament text, but also because it portrays the final battle between God and the Evil One.

CONQUEST, POWER, AND SUBVERSION

In light of the significance of the divine warfare motif in Acts, Ephesians, and Revelation, it seems appropriate to address issues associated with the reading of New Testament conquest narratives in a postcolonial setting by interacting with these three books. Without attempting to cover all relevant concerns, this section will deal with four common themes in these books as they relate to the question at hand.

God and His Word as the Ultimate Warrior

In the New Testament conquest narratives, a clear emphasis is placed on the role of God as the active and victorious Warrior. His followers are called to witness, acknowledge, and participate in such victorious acts, but the decisive battle belongs to the act of God both in and beyond history. In Acts, although Peter, Stephen, Philip, and Paul are often considered to be the main characters, it is the Word of God that functions as the subject of this conquest narrative. Similarly, in his discussion of Lukan theology, François Bovon notes that "the Book of Acts does not recount primarily the history of either the church or the Holy Spirit. It situates in the foreground the diffusion of the Word of God."[24] Not only is this diffusion of the Word of God a focus in Acts, but the book's travel narrative and the movement of the Word of God can also be further correlated. It is worth noting that through the numerous (circular) travels of the apostles,[25] one can almost trace the linear journey of "the Word of God/the Lord" all the way from Jerusalem to Rome.[26] This linear journey is made possible by the fact that after "conquering" a city, the Word

---

24. François Bovon, *Luke the Theologian: Fifty-Five Years of Research (1950–2005)*, trans. Ken McKinney, 2nd rev. ed. (Waco: Baylor University Press, 2006), 457. See also Daniel Marguerat, *The First Christian Historian: Writing the 'Acts of the Apostles,'* trans. Ken McKinney et al., SNTSMS 121 (Cambridge: Cambridge University Press, 2002), 254.

25. Cf. Rom 15:19.

26. See Acts 4:31; 6:2, 7; 8:14, 25; 11:1; 12:24; 13:5, 7, 44, 46, 48, 49; 15:35, 36; 16:32; 17:13; 18:11; 19:10, 20; 20:35; cf. Acts 28:31.

of God never returns to that city.²⁷ Such linear movement is consistent with our reading of Acts as a conquest narrative of the Word in that a conquered city does not need to be conquered again.²⁸

Attributing conquests to the Word assumes that the Word is an active being who is able to work as an instrument of God's will in history. First, the three summary statements in Acts all point to the "growth" of the Word (Acts 6:7; 12:24; 19:20). This itself highlights the significance of this Word of God as a living being. This Word is one that was sent by God to the sons of Israel (10:36; 13:26), and the relationship between Jesus and the Word is reflected in the fact that the apostles are called to be "servants of the Word" (Luke 1:2). The clearest indication that Luke presents the Word as an active agent of God can be found in Acts 13:48, where the Gentiles who heard the message "praised the Word of the Lord." This phrase assumes that these Gentiles regarded the Word as a powerful manifestation of God's own work.²⁹ Finally, at the end of Paul's journey, Paul commends the Ephesian elders to "God and to the Word of his grace," as this Word is able "to build up and to give the inheritance among all who are sanctified" (lit., 20:32). Again, one finds the parallel between the Lord and His Word. Moreover, the phrase "the Word of his grace" may be rendered as "the powerful Word," as the word "grace" in the Lukan writings often points to the power of God (6:8; 14:3; cf. Luke 4:22).³⁰

The fact that the subject of this conquest narrative is the Word of God has several important implications for our study. First, while the Word is the victorious and glorious Word, the church is the one that suffers in the hands of the enemies of the Word. This motif therefore points to the coexistence of the theology of glory and the theology of suffering in the same narrative. First, the Word is the powerful Word, but this power does not inherently and completely rest on individuals who preach this Word. Second, this understanding of the Word also allows

27. In other words, although the apostles may have visited a particular city two or three times, the term "Word of God" consistently appears in connection with only one of the visits.

28. See Pao, *Acts and the Isaianic New Exodus*, 147-80.

29. Elsewhere in the Lukan writings, the object of the act of praising is always either God (Luke 2:20; 5:25, 26; 7:16; 13:13; 17:15; 18:43; 23:47; Acts 4:21; 11:18; 21:20) or Jesus (Luke 4:15; Acts 3:13).

30. See M. Cambe, "La χάρις chez saint Luc," *RB* 70 (1963) 193-207; and John Nolland, "Words of Grace (Luke 4:22)," *Bib* 84 (1984) 44-60.

for the failure of the apostles. The ability of the Word to conquer the world does not depend on the moral perfection of its agents. Finally, human agents cannot claim to "possess" this Word. Therefore, these agents cannot claim to have conquered the world through their own power or initiative.

The subject of the divine warfare in Ephesians is likewise primarily God and His Word. Whereas believers are called to "[p]ut on the whole armor of God" (Eph 6:11) in the final section of this epistle, Paul earlier emphasizes that "God put this power to work in Christ when he raised him from the dead and seated him at his right hand in the heavenly places, far above all rule and authority and power and dominion, not only in this age but also in the age to come" (1:20–21). Paul reminds believers that their participation in the victory of Christ "is not [their] own doing; it is the gift of God" (2:8).

This focus on the central role of God through Christ is reflected in the ways Paul portrays believers' involvement in divine warfare in Ephesians 6:10–20. First, believers are not mainly called to gain more ground on behalf of God. They are primarily called, rather, to hold onto the ground won by God Himself, as they are charged to "withstand" and "stand firm" (6:13; cf. 6:14).[31] More importantly, unlike the Jewish contemporaries who envision the eschatological battle as being fought with human enemies,[32] Paul emphasizes that "our struggle is not against enemies of flesh and blood but against the rulers, against the authorities, against the cosmic powers of this present darkness, against the spiritual forces of evil in the heavenly places" (6:12).[33] These are precisely the en-

---

31. Robert A. Guelich, "Spiritual Warfare: Jesus, Paul and Peretti," *Pneuma* 13 (1991) 46; Moritz, *A Profound Mystery*, 199–201; Neufeld, *'Put on the Armour of God,'* 135–36. Moritz further suggests that the metaphor adopted here is not that of active warfare, but of Roman arena fighting (cf. 1 Cor 15:32; 2 Tim 4:17) in which "[t]he only possible way to avoid death was repeatedly to excel in bravery and to withstand the opponent, animal or human, long enough to impress the audience which might then cheer for a pardon" (208).

32. One can point to the acts of the political revolutionaries and popular prophetic movements in the time of Jesus, as they attempted to overthrow those who oppressed Israel; cf. Richard Horsley, *Jesus and the Spiral of Violence: Popular Jewish Resistance in Roman Palestine* (San Francisco: Harper & Row, 1987), 59–145. One can also point to the ideology of the Qumran sect as foreshadowing the eschatological battle between the followers of the Righteous One and those who oppose them.

33. Tremper Longman III, "The Case for Spiritual Continuity," in *Show Them No Mercy: Four Views on God and Canaanite Genocide*, ed. C. S. Cowles et al. (Grand

emies that had already been conquered by God through Jesus' death on the cross (1:20-21; 2:14).³⁴ Finally, the fact that the cross became the symbol of victory is also significant in that it is through weakness and humiliation that the power and glory of God are manifested. Elsewhere, Paul also "boasts" of his weaknesses and struggles (2 Cor 11:21-29) as he trusts in the God who is able to reveal His power despite human inadequacies. This is, after all, the same Gospel that is contained in the Word that the apostles preached.

This same focus on the centrality of the death of Christ as the critical turning point in the struggle between God and Satan can be found in the book of Revelation. In the first part of his heavenly vision, John introduces the one who is able to control history as "the Lamb that was slaughtered" (Rev 5:12; cf. 5:6, 9; 13:8). In Jewish apocalyptic traditions, we encounter the lamb-figure that serves as a military and royal symbol (cf. *1 En.* 89:45-46; 90:6-19; *T. Jos.* 19:8).³⁵ In Revelation, this is the supreme Ruler who has the authority to open the seals of the scroll (5:8; 6:1). He is the "Lord of lords and King of kings" (17:14), and He alone deserves to be the supreme object of worship (5:8, 12; 7:9, 10). Such a ruler is naturally understood as the leader of the people of God (7:17), and He is identified as "the Lion of the tribe of Judah, the Root of David" (5:5). This Lamb as the Conqueror is most clearly portrayed in 17:14, where John asserts that God's enemies "will make war on the Lamb, and the Lamb will conquer them." It is striking, therefore, to see that this Lamb was a "slaughtered" Lamb, but it is precisely because of his death that this Lamb could be the supreme Ruler and Conqueror. Moreover, because of his death, this Conqueror is able to deliver those who follow him: "for you were slaughtered and by your blood you ransomed for God saints from every tribe and language and people and nation" (5:9).

Rapids: Zondervan, 2003), 179-81, sees this as the fourth phase of the biblical presentation of divine warfare, as believers are not called to be involved in physical warfare but to participate in the spiritual battle as initiated by Jesus himself.

34. In 2 Cor 10:3, Paul also notes that "we do not wage war according to human standards."

35. See Norman Hillyer, "The Lamb in the Apocalypse," *EvQ* 39 (1967) 229. This is not to deny, however, the significance of the Passover Lamb tradition (cf. C. K. Barrett, "The Lamb of God," *NTS* 1 [1954-55] 210-18), especially in light of the significance of the Exodus tradition in the entire book of Revelation; cf. Massey H. Shepherd, *The Paschal Liturgy and the Apocalypse* (Richmond: John Knox, 1960), 77-97.

When we arrive at the climactic battle in Revelation 19, the one who is identified as sitting on the white horse is "The Word of God" (ὁ λόγος τοῦ θεοῦ, 19:13). While this Word is closely related to the Lamb in this climactic end of the book (cf. 19:7, 9; 21:9, 14, 22, 23; 22:1, 3), this Word is better understood as the Gospel that focuses on the slaughtered Lamb.[36] As in Acts, this Word of God is able to conquer the world as it points to the decisive victory of God via His work through Jesus. This not only draws attention to the unique and significant work of Jesus on the cross, but this Gospel message also redefines power in that believers are to imitate Jesus in their sufferings. Through their sufferings, they will also be able to conquer and overcome the evil force (2:7, 11, 17, 26; 3:5, 12, 21; 12:11; 15:2; 21:7).

New Testament conquest narratives consistently affirm that God is the ultimate warrior, and that He is the one who has won the decisive battle through Christ. Followers of Christ can participate in this victory not through the assertion of power, but through the acceptance and proclamation of the Gospel of the cross. Through this Gospel, one finds the redefinition of power and victory, as suffering and humiliation become the ultimate weapon through which the sovereignty of God can be affirmed.

Theological and Political Imperialism

These three conquest accounts draw attention to God as the ultimate victor, and to him as the one and only Lord of all. It is tempting, however, to see this theological claim as a veiled expression of nationalism when members of a people group claim to have the right to impose their ideology and sovereign rights on an inferior people group. In the words of one who understood himself to be the victim of such acts of theological and political oppression:

> To call upon Jesus as Lord suddenly began to strike me as a classic example of the colonized participating in our own oppression. To call upon Jesus as Lord is to concede the conquest as final and to become complicit in our own death, that is, the ongoing

---

36. Jan Fekkes III, *Isaiah and Prophetic Traditions in the Book of Revelation: Visionary Antecedents and Their Development*, JSNTSup 93 (Sheffield: JSOT Press, 1994), 196–98, has demonstrated that Rev 19:13, 15 allude to the portrayal of Yahweh the warrior in Isaiah 63:2–3. The powerful "Word of God" in 19:13 may also stem from the Isaianic tradition (cf. Isa 40:8; 55:11); cf. Pao, *Acts and the Isaianic New Exodus*, 179.

genocidal death of our peoples. It is an act of the colonized mind blindly reciting words that the colonizer has taught us which violate our own cultures but bring great comfort to the lordly colonizer and his missionaries.[37]

In these three New Testament conquest narratives, one does find an unwavering insistence on the theological claim that Jesus is Lord, but these narratives are equally insistent in their refusal to translate this claim into a mere ethnic or national assertion.

In Acts, the Lordship of Jesus is repeatedly affirmed. To the "entire house of Israel," he is "both Lord and Messiah" (Acts 2:36). To the Gentiles, he is also the "Lord of all" (10:36) because he has been raised from the dead and became the judge of both Jews and Gentiles (17:31). In light of such claims, one is therefore not surprised to find one of the most absolute and particularistic claims in the New Testament texts: "There is salvation in no one else, for there is no other name under heaven given among mortals by which we must be saved" (4:12).[38]

Luke is, however, equally emphatic when he argues that the Gentiles are not simply to be incorporated into the Jewish race. Already in Acts 1:8, the mission to the Gentiles became the focus of the mission in Acts. This is also the focus of Paul's mission (Acts 9:15; 22:15; 26:17–18). Luke further makes two related arguments establishing that the Gentile converts are not simply a dependent sect within Jewish Christianity. First, Luke provides a critique of Jewish election theology by suggesting that God is an impartial God: "I truly understand that God shows no partiality, but in every nation anyone who fears him and does what is right is acceptable to him" (10:34–35). Second, building on the impartiality of God, Luke further emphasizes that Jews and Gentiles are equal in status: "in cleansing their hearts by faith he has made no distinction between them and us" (15:9; cf. 11:12). These two arguments move beyond the confines of contemporary Judaism in asserting that a new era in the history of salvation has begun. In redefining the people of God, this

---

37. George Tinker, "Jesus, Corn Mother, and Conquest: Christology and Colonialism," in *Native American Religious Identity*, ed. Jace Weaver (Maryknoll, NY: Orbis, 1998), 139.

38. Since Peter in his earlier speech drew upon Joel 2:28–32 (Acts 2:17–21), here he may also be alluding to Joel: "You shall know that I am in the midst of Israel, and that I, the Lord, am your God and there is no other" (Joel 2:27). In the wider context of Acts, however, this became a statement that reaches beyond the confines of Israel.

community would be defined by their faith in Christ and not by their cultural and historical heritage.[39]

Both the universal Lordship of God/Christ and the unity of Jews and Gentiles are at the center of Paul's concern in Ephesians. As noted, the power of God through Christ is already established at the beginning of his argument (Eph 1:20–23). This power is manifested in the creation of one people through Christ's death on the cross: "in his flesh he has made both groups into one and has broken down the dividing wall" (2:14). The unity of Jews and Gentiles is the mystery that had been hidden for ages: "the Gentiles have become fellow heirs, members of the same body, and sharers in the promise in Christ Jesus through the gospel" (3:6).

Not only does Paul focus on the unity of Jews and Gentiles, he also regards harmony between the two to be an essential instrument for the divine warfare to which believers are called in Ephesians 6:10–17. In so doing, Paul strikingly subverts the idea of conquest and warfare. Moving beyond destruction and division, the Gospel of peace became the instrument through which victory could be achieved. Several important items in this armor point to the peace that was accomplished by Christ on the cross. "The belt of truth" (6:14) points to "the word of truth, the gospel of your salvation" (1:13), and "the breastplate of righteousness" (6:14) refers to the accomplishment of Jesus on the cross.[40] The "shoes" are explicitly identified as the readiness to "proclaim the gospel of peace" (6:15), and this Gospel of peace points to the power of the cross (2:14). The "shield of faith" (6:16) refers to our faith in Christ's work (3:12), and "the helmet of salvation" (6:17) points back to the Gospel of Jesus Christ (1:13). Finally, the "sword of the Spirit" (6:17) likewise references Paul's call for "the unity of the Spirit in the bond of peace" (4:3). In short, these weapons all aim to maintain the peace that was accomplished by Christ

---

39. Throughout his writings, one finds Luke wrestling with the identity of God's people through striking uses of the metaphors of family and meals. See David W. Pao, "Family and Table-Fellowship in the Writings of Luke," in *This Side of Heaven: Race, Ethnicity, and Christian Faith*, ed. Robert J. Priest and Alvaro L. Nieves (Oxford: Oxford University Press, 2007), 181–93.

40. This "righteousness" is best understood as primarily the act of God rather than a human virtuous act (cf. 4:24); Moritz, *A Profound Mystery*, 202–3. This, however, does not deny the significance of human obedience in light of such divine acts; see David Wenkel, "The 'Breastplate of Righteousness' in Ephesians 6:14: Imputation or Virtue?" *TynBul* 58 (2007) 275–87.

when his death on the cross broke down the barriers between Jews and Gentiles.[41]

This understanding of warfare as the maintenance of eschatological peace is further supported by three observations. First, in Ephesians 4, Paul had already adopted military metaphors in describing the accomplishment of Christ: "When he ascended on high he made captivity itself a captive; he gave gifts to his people" (4:8; cf. Ps 68:18). Significantly, he identifies these gifts as the existence of "one body and one Spirit . . . one Lord, one faith, one baptism, one God and Father of all" (4:4–6). Second, in an earlier reference to the battle against "the devil" (4:27), Paul focuses on living in peace rather than in anger (4:26–30). Again, the way of peace became the weapon against the evil one. Finally, in concluding his discussion of the armor of God, Paul points to the act of prayer, especially prayer for his mission "to make known with boldness the mystery of the gospel" (6:19). Paul earlier identified this "mystery of the gospel" as the creation of the one body in Christ (3:1–6). This conclusion therefore reinforces the significance of such weapons as ones that subvert the status and power of their bearers for the sake of this Gospel of peace. Not only is "peace" the goal of divine warfare, "peace" is itself the instrument of such warfare because of the earlier victory by God through Christ in the cross event.[42]

In the Book of Revelation, one again finds the affirmation that as God (Rev 1:4, 8; 4:8; 11:17; 16:5; 21:6) is the Lord of history, Jesus is also worthy of such honor (1:17; 22:13). Because of this claim, salvation belongs only "to our God who is seated on the throne, and to the Lamb" (7:10). This conquest narrative likewise does not privilege a particular ethnic or social group as the superior victor. Unlike Jewish apocalypses that portray the Jews against the Gentiles, the only criterion that divides humanity is their faith in the one God and the one Lord. All nations that oppose God will be struck down (19:15), but those who are "faithful until death" will receive "the crown of life" (2:10). At the end of times, in Jerusalem "[t]he nations will walk by its light, and the kings of the earth will bring their glory into it" (21:24).

41. This does not, of course, deny the significance of human obedience, but human acts cannot be considered apart from both Christ's death on the cross and the gospel of peace that this event produced.

42. To achieve "peace" is often the claim of the colonizers, as evidenced by Roman imperial propaganda, but here "peace" became the instrument through which humans can play a part in this divine warfare.

The distinction between theological and political claims can be seen in the focus on the power of death and suffering.[43] The followers of Christ "have conquered him [the Dragon] by the blood of the Lamb and by the word of their testimony, for they did not cling to life even in the face of death" (12:11). In the midst of this conquest narrative, the critique of the use of the power and strength of this world is striking: "If you are to be taken captive, into captivity you go; if you kill with the sword, with the sword you must be killed" (13:10). Being captured and the refusal to use the sword then became the ultimate weapon through which the ultimate war can be won. Again, not only does the author resist transferring the strong and clear theological claim into political and national claims, he subverts the utility of physical power by focusing on the power of being faithful to the slaughtered Lamb.

A proper reading of these conquest narratives makes it obvious that a distinction must be made between theological and political imperialism. In terms of theological claims, it is difficult to avoid this conclusion:

> Christianity is an inherently imperial religion in the sense that it claims that the revealed truth of God was incarnated uniquely in the person of Jesus Christ, that all men and women are called to respond in repentance and faith to that revelation, and that the kingdom of God inaugurated in the coming of Christ makes absolute demands upon all people and all cultures.[44]

Such imperialism should not, however, be confused with political imperialism in which the ideology of one particular ethnic or political people group is imposed upon another group through political and military forces. Diversity in theological beliefs should therefore not be considered as the necessary means through which political peace can be achieved.[45]

---

43. This ultimately is derived from the metaphor of the "slaughtered Lamb"; see the discussion in section above (God and His Word as the Ultimate Warrior).

44. Brian Stanley, *The Bible and the Flag: Protestant Missions and British Imperialism in the Nineteenth and Twentieth Centuries* (Leicester, UK: Apollos, 1990), 184.

45. Contrast, therefore, the claims of United Nations Secretary-General Kofi Annan in his speech given during his reception of the Nobel Peace Prize in 2001: "even amidst continuing ethnic conflict around the world, there is a growing understanding that human diversity is both the reality that makes dialogue necessary, and the very basis for that dialogue." See the discussion in the following study, from which the above quotation was taken: Kenneth R. Chase, "Christian Discourse and the Humility of Peace," in *Must Christianity Be Violent? Reflections on History, Practice, and Theology*, ed. Kenneth R. Chase and Alan Jacobs (Grand Rapids: Brazos, 2003), 119–34.

In light of this distinction between theological and political imperialism, yet another distinction needs to be made. New Testament conquest narratives have often been read through the lens of later Christian traditions that pave the way for the ideology behind the Crusades of the Middle Ages. Historians have reminded us that "the adoption of holy war in the crusading movement of the late eleventh and early twelfth centuries broke a long tradition of refraining from bloodshed in Christ's name."[46] Moreover, the reconceptualization of the relationship between the State and the Church in the fourth century is also far removed from the traditions of the Holy War in the biblical material.[47] In short, while recognizing the danger of misreading biblical conquest narratives, a reduction of theological claims to the political aspirations of those in power is equally irresponsible.

Writing from the Margin

The recognition of the distinction between theological and political imperialism leads to a critical realization that although the conquest motif is a prominent one in the New Testament texts, these texts were all written from the margin. In a sense, then, one can argue that this motif becomes a rhetorical strategy whereby the power of the cross can be articulated within the creation of a symbolic universe that remains unconvincing to those who have yet to receive the Gospel message. It is not mere rhetoric, however, because the reality of the power of the cross and the resurrection is one confession that cannot be compromised. In terms of social location, though, the realization that these conquest narratives were generated from those who were without power allows one to read these narratives as anti-imperial claims.

Without addressing the complex issues regarding Luke's view of the Roman Empire,[48] two points seem to be clear: Luke was writing from the

---

46. Partner, *God of Battles*, xviii.

47. Joseph H. Lynch ("The First Crusade: Some Theological and Historical Context," in Chase and Jacobs, *Must Christianity Be Violent?*, 31–32) notes that "[i]n the eleventh century, the military profession, traditionally regarded by church leaders as utterly sinful and secular, was reconceptualized, indeed 'Christianized,' that is, integrated into a Christian ethical structure and given a morally positive purpose." He also suggests that this process of reconceptualization can be further traced back to the post-Constantinian period (32–35).

48. See, for example, the survey in Steve Walton, "The State They Were In: Luke's View of the Roman Empire," in *Rome in the Bible and the Early Church*, ed. Peter Oakes (Grand Rapids: Baker Academic, 2002), 2–12.

margin, and he is introducing a kingdom that surpasses that of Rome. The fact that Luke was writing from the margin is evident by the fact that Christianity in the first century was simply a marginal sect in the wider Roman Empire. To the Jews, the Christians simply belonged to "the sect of the Nazarenes" (Acts 24:5), and they persuaded people "to worship God in ways that are contrary to the law" (18:13). The Romans also considered the Christians to be a sect within Judaism, although they may have differed from other Jews concerning "questions about words and names and . . . law" (18:15). Their dispute was also over matters "about their own religion and about a certain Jesus" (25:19).

Although Christians were considered to be a sect that began in the outlying regions far from the center of power, Luke portrays this sect as one that challenged the imperial claims of Rome. At the beginning of his account, Luke presents Jesus as the "Savior" (Luke 2:11) who will bring "good news" (2:10) as He ushers in the era of "peace" on earth (2:14). These terms remind the audience of the Roman propaganda in which Augustus the "Savior" is the one introducing the "good news" as he establishes the Roman "peace."[49] By using these same terms, Luke is declaring that Jesus is the one who will usher in the eternal kingdom. Although Christians were not "acting contrary to the decrees of the emperor" as the Jews claimed, it is not entirely false that they say that "there is another king named Jesus" (Acts 17:7). It is not surprising, therefore, that Luke concludes his work by noting that Paul was "proclaiming the kingdom of God" at the center of the Roman Empire (28:31). Noting that Luke is describing a marginal sect that was challenging the claims of the Roman imperial power, this conquest narrative should be considered as a critique of the dominant power of the time. Rather than being politically imperialistic, this narrative actually provides fuel for a postcolonial reading properly defined.

In Ephesians, the challenge to the dominant power takes on a different form. While Paul also emphasizes the power in Christ, who is seated at God's right hand in the heavenly places "far above all rule and authority and power and dominion, and above every name that is named" (Eph 1:21), he does not emphasize the marginal status of the believers because they, too, are raised up with Christ and are seated "with him in

---

49. Horace, *Carmen Seculare*; Virgil, *Fourth Eclogue*; Suetonius, *Augustus*. Some have also considered these as direct challenges to the Roman imperial cult; cf. Allen Brent, "Luke-Acts and the Imperial Cult in Asia Minor," *JTS* 48 (1997) 411–38.

the heavenly places in Christ Jesus" (2:6). Paul does, however, emphasize his own vulnerability by noting that he is a "prisoner for Christ Jesus" (3:1; cf. 4:1), a phrase that points to his own imprisonment in Rome. It is striking, therefore, to find Paul providing us with his most extensive discussion on divine warfare in this prison epistle (6:10-17).[50] His "suffering" becomes the "glory" of the Gentiles (3:13) because such suffering points back to the cross, a symbol of humiliation that is able to destroy the stronghold of the cosmic powers (2:16). Paul's powerlessness, therefore, becomes the ultimate weapon against the power of this world.[51]

As is the case with other Jewish apocalypses, the Book of Revelation reveals a worldview that reflects the self-perception of a community that is marginalized by society at large.[52] This self-perception does not, however, prevent the author from providing a strong critique of Roman imperial power. In Revelation 4-5, one finds the affirmation of God and his Lamb as the Sovereign One through the use of an imperial courtroom scene. In these chapters, the expected Roman Emperor, who is supposed to be the one sitting on the throne, is replaced by the one who "created all things" (Rev 4:11).[53] The critique of Rome's claim to power continues in Revelation 12-14, where the dragon and the two beasts representing the evil forces behind the institution of the Roman imperial cult are not able to compete with the one "seated on the cloud," who is "like a Son of Man, with a golden crown on his head, and a sharp sickle in his hand" (Rev 14:14; cf. Dan 7:13).[54] Not to be missed is the critique of Roman

---

50. Note also that Paul concludes his discussion of divine warfare by asking for prayers for his mission as "an ambassador in chains" (Eph 6:20).

51. For a response to the false perception that this epistle promotes an ecclesiastical triumphalism, see Clinton E. Arnold, *Power and Magic: The Concept of Power in Ephesians*, 2nd ed. (Grand Rapids: Eerdmans, 1997), 139-42.

52. See Adela Yarbro Collins, *Crisis and Catharsis: The Power of the Apocalypse* (Philadelphia: Westminster, 1984), 84-107.

53. See David E. Aune, "The Influence of Roman Imperial Court Ceremonial on the Apocalypse of John," *BR* 28 (1983) 5-26. Aune, "The Form and Function of the Proclamations of the Seven Churches [Revelation 23]," *NTS* 36 (1990) 182-204, also suggests that the seven messages in Revelation 2-3 should likewise be considered imperial edicts, but these edicts were issued not by the Roman Emperor but by the one sitting on the heavenly throne.

54. This "one like a Son of Man" could refer to a heavenly agent, but in light of the use of Dan 7:13 in describing Christ in Rev 1:7, 13, this figure points to the victorious Christ; Gregory K. Beale, *The Book of Revelation*, NIGTC (Grand Rapids: Eerdmans, 1999), 770-71; and Grant R. Osborne, *Revelation*, BECNT (Grand Rapids: Baker Acaemic, 2002), 550.

imperialism as manifested in Rome's economic exploitation of her subjects (Rev 18:1–24).[55] Under the veil of a conquest account, this narrative provides the strongest critique of one that is recognized by the world to be the conqueror par excellence.

As in Paul's writings, John's critique originated from the position of perceived weakness and powerlessness. The power of the slaughtered lamb and the suffering of the saints in Revelation have already been noted,[56] and it is through this "army of the martyrs"[57] that the sovereignty of God's kingdom is established. The apparent contradiction within the symbol of this "army of martyrs" again provides a strong critique of the abuse of Rome's power. Such contradiction can also be found in the promise of "the crown of life" for those who are "faithful until death" (Rev 2:10). After all, it is both "the persecution" and "the kingdom" that John shares with his audience (1:9).

In these conquest narratives, one fails to find an exertion of power and an imposition of the ideology of a politically and/or economically dominant group upon the inferior group. What one finds instead is the prophetic call to justice and a critique of the unjustified claims of the dominant imperial power.[58] Once they attained positions of power, later generations of Christians often failed—and today continue to fail—to resist the temptation to exert unwelcome and unjustifiable control of others. To them, the prophetic critique offered by these New Testament conquest narratives are equally applicable.

Prophetic Self-Critique

A focus on the critique of the "other" may mask the significance of self-critique in these narratives. In the tradition of the Old Testament prophets, a critique of God's own people often precedes that of their en-

---

55. See in particular Richard Bauckham, "The Economic Critique of Rome in Revelation 18," in *Images of Empire,* ed. Loveday Alexander, JSOTSup 122 (Sheffield: JSOT Press, 1991), 47–90.

56. See the discussion in section above ("God and His Word as the Ultimate Warrior").

57. This phrase is borrowed from Richard Bauckham, *The Theology of the Book of Revelation,* New Testament Theology (Cambridge: Cambridge University Press, 1993), 76–80.

58. Some have also drawn attention to the parallelism between postcolonial literature and Old Testament prophetic traditions; see, for example, Laura E. Donaldson, "Postcolonialism and Biblical Reading: An Introduction," *Semeia* 75 (1996) 1–14.

emies. In these New Testament conquest narratives, the authors are no less concerned with the behavior of those who are supposed to subscribe to the ideology of the divine warrior. This critique prevents those who align themselves with the ultimate victor from automatically identifying themselves as the good who is fighting against the evil "other."

In describing the conquest of the Word, Luke is careful to make a distinction between the powerful Word and those who claim to adhere to this Word. Following the depiction of the early Christian community as having "simplicity of heart" (lit.; Acts 2:46) and being of "one heart and soul" (4:32), the episode of Ananias and Sapphira's deception (5:1–11) within this community served as a reminder to members of the early Christian community that membership in this group did not necessarily protect them from the wrath of God. That Luke does not see the church as the perfected ideal of God's people is reflected in the fact that in Acts the term "church" (ἡ ἐκκλησία) first appears only in the concluding note of this pericope, where the fear of God is emphasized: "And great fear seized the whole church and all who heard of these things" (5:11). The breaking down of the ideal harmony within the early Christian community provides a prophetic call to the church to be alert and to be faithful to the risen Lord whom its members worship.[59] The paradigmatic significance of this episode also provides a critical qualifying note on the depiction of the victorious Church, as those who follow the Word are not always able to be faithful to it.[60] The self-critique embedded in this conquest narrative further prevents one from regarding the adherents of the Word as inherently morally superior to those in the other camp.

Unlike the conquest narrative that one finds in Acts, the purpose of Ephesians is explicitly to modify the mindset and behavior of believers according to that which has been accomplished for them. Chosen to be "holy and blameless" (Eph 1:4), believers are "created in Christ Jesus for good works" (2:10). Paul, however, realizes that believers have yet to live out this reality. Therefore, he calls them "to lead a life worthy of the calling to which [they] have been called" (4:1). Although they have the honor of participating in this victory, they need to be reminded that they

59. Some have also compared the deception of Ananias and Sapphira to the deception of Adam and Eve who, at the beginning of time, destroyed the ideal harmony of the created order. See Marguerat, *The First Christian Historian*, 172–76.

60. See also the depiction of the dissension within the church (Acts 6:1–6; 15:1–2, 37–41). Luke is emphatic, however, that such dissension does not affect the progression of the Word.

"must no longer live as the Gentiles live, in the futility of their minds" (4:17). In the passage in which one finds the explicit call to "take up the whole armor of God" (6:13), Paul's urging of believers to "stand firm" (6:13) points to the fact that in describing the fight against the evil one, he is equally concerned with the lives of these believers. The discourse on divine warfare therefore becomes a parenetic one in which the focus on the destruction of God's enemies is shifted to the sanctification of the saints. In light of this reading, prophetic self-critique is not an excursus but the center of this epistle.

Jewish apocalypses often betray a stark dualistic framework in which the good is to fight against the evil, with the good prevailing. In the Book of Revelation, one also finds such dualism in the contrast between God and Satan, the Lamb and the Dragon, and the Bride and the Prostitute. Such theological dualism does not, however, extend unqualifiedly to a people group considered to be inherently good. Instead of simply identifying God's people as the good who are fighting against the evil ones, John begins his work by providing a stinging critique of the church. In the form of seven messages in Revelation 2–3, God, the ultimate judge, first delivers judgment to His own people before He fights against those who explicitly worship the evil one. Before unmasking the deceptive power of Satan lying behind those who worship the Dragon (Rev 12:1—13:18), John first points to the self-deception of those who claim to worship God. Among them are "those who claim to be apostles but are not" (2:2), "Jezebel, who calls herself a prophet and is teaching and beguiling my servants to practice fornication and to eat food sacrificed to idols" (2:20), those "who have a name of being alive, but . . . are dead" (3:1), those "who say that they are Jews but are not" (3:9), and those who say that "I am rich" but are "wretched, pitiable, poor, blind and naked" (3:17). Unless they repent, those who claim to be among God's people will also receive their share of God's judgment (2:5, 16, 21, 23; 3:3, 19). In these two chapters, therefore, it is clear that "[t]he great conflict between good and evil documented in Revelation . . . is more than a conflict *between* the seven Asian congregations and the Roman Empire. It is also a conflict *within* most of the congregations."[61] Through this conquest narrative, John is careful to describe the battle between

---

61. J. Ramsey Michaels, *Interpreting the Book of Revelation*, Guides to New Testament Exegesis 7 (Grand Rapids: Baker, 1992), 41.

God and Satan without automatically assuming that those who claim to be God's people are indeed fighting for God.

Without noticing the emphasis on self-critique in these conquest narratives, those who claim to be on the winning side could easily be "deluded . . . by the concept of [their] innocency."[62] The New Testament conquest narratives do not seek to affirm the power and status of those who receive such narratives; they seek, rather, to unveil the self-deception of those who assume that they are fighting for the good. On the other hand, in the postcolonial age it is equally tempting for the colonized to constantly assume the posture of a victim and thus shield themselves from the demands of the truth claims of the Gospel. To do so is likewise to be "deluded by the concept of our innocency."

BEYOND "THE COLONIZED" AND "THE COLONIZERS"

New Testament conquest narratives are unwavering in their affirmation that there is but one God and one Lord, and that all humanity will have to submit to this sovereign claim. These narratives also make it clear that God the Victor is not in the possession of one national or ethnic group, and that the theological confession of God as Victor serves as a critique to both the dominant power and those who see themselves as victims. It is in this sense that such conquest narratives can fulfill their prophetic function in calling all nations to repent and acknowledge the one and universal Lord of all.

In contemporary discussions of the idea of Holy War, one often finds a sharp distinction between the colonized and the colonizers. Our discussion of prophetic self-critique and the critique from the margin has revealed this distinction to be problematic. The contemporary historical reality of the twenty-first century further questions the continued usefulness of this distinction. Recent explosive political and economic developments in the so-called "developing countries" have prompted some to abandon the distinction between the first- and third-worlds, and the strength of economies and political systems in the non-Western world have further prompted many to question the validity of the East-West divide.[63] Moreover, the reality of globalization coupled with the rise

---

62. Catherine Keller, "Territory, Terror, and Torture: Dream-Reading the Apocalypse," *Feminist Theology* 14 (2005) 47–67.

63. See, for example, the discussion in Hans-Henrik Holm, "The End of the Third World?" *Journal of Peace Research* 27 (1990) 1–7.

of neo-colonialism has further highlighted the increasing complexity of interaction among nation states and traditional cultural entities.

More important, for our purpose, is the reality of global Christianity that forces one to acknowledge that Christianity is no longer to be considered a "Western" religion. Some have begun to see the shift of the center of Christianity to Africa, Asia, and Latin America, and the practice of faith in these regions will likely be "transplanted northward, either by migration, or by actual missions to the old imperial powers, to what were once the core nations of world Christianity."[64] While the once-colonized will probably not be perceived as the colonizers in the near future, they will have the same task of claiming the world for the risen Lord. In so doing, both the messengers and the recipients of the Gospel will be subjected to its demands. Recognizing that God is the only one to whom all must submit, both the messengers and the recipients will participate in one global fellowship of believers.

---

64. Philip Jenkins, *The Next Christendom: The Coming of Global Christianity* (New York: Oxford University Press, 2002), 107–8.

8

The Group and the Individual in Salvation

The Witness of Paul

Frank Thielman

WHEN THE NEW TESTAMENT speaks of salvation, does it refer primarily to the salvation of the individual or to the salvation of a people? This is an important question for at least two reasons.

First, evangelical Christianity, with its emphasis on the worldwide proclamation of the Gospel, has traditionally been strongest in North America.[1] The roots of evangelical Christianity in North America, however, lie firmly planted in the middle-class values of nineteenth-century American culture.[2] Did the missionaries who were a product of North American evangelicalism export the individualism of their culture to other places along with the Gospel, as if it were an integral part of the Gospel? Did they impose it on more collectivist cultures, where it did not easily fit, as if it were a critical element of the Gospel? If so, did they place an unnecessary stumbling block in the way of accepting the Gospel and thereby hinder the development of an authentically indigenous form of Christianity in the more collectivist cultures to which they traveled?

---

1. This now seems to be changing with the growth of evangelical Christianity in the so-called global South.

2. George M. Marsden, for example, tells us that the widely influential nineteenth-century evangelist Dwight Lyman Moody "rose to fame in the heyday of American individualism and his thought is pervaded by its assumptions." See Marsden, *Fundamentalism and American Culture: The Shaping of Twentieth-Century Evangelicalism 1870–1925* (New York: Oxford University Press, 1980), 37.

The cultural roots of the evangelical missionary movement make these reasonable and important questions.

Second, since the early 1960s, New Testament scholars, particularly those interested in the apostle Paul, have wondered whether Paul's writings have not been misread through the individualistic eyes of northern European, Protestant piety.[3] In the early 1960s, Krister Stendahl published a now famous essay entitled "The Apostle Paul and the Introspective Conscience of the West," in which he argued that the dominant understanding of Paul among Protestants since the Reformation is incorrect.[4] That understanding found at the center of Paul's theology an answer to the question, "How can the guilty individual find forgiveness for sin?" Protestants believe that the basic human problem is that every individual is a sinner, and that God has provided the solution to this problem by justifying, or acquitting, those guilty of sin through faith in Christ. Stendahl argued that this understanding of Paul was mistaken, an error that went back to Luther and, before him, to Augustine. Luther and Augustine emphasized that the Gospel was the solution to the plight of the individual in bondage to sin. According to Stendahl, the error in this approach is perhaps most clearly visible in the simple observation that Paul himself gives no evidence of having been plagued at any time in his life, whether before he was called to preach the Gospel or afterward, by an introspective conscience.

Once this culturally driven reading of Paul is stripped away, said Stendahl, Paul's teaching on justification by faith alone apart from works of the law can be seen for what it really is: a social doctrine that seeks to include Gentiles within the people of God on the basis of faith. In a book published in the 1970s, Stendahl put it this way: "Paul's thoughts about justification were triggered by the issues of divisions and identities in a pluralistic and torn world, not primarily by the inner tensions of individual souls and consciences. His searching eyes focused on the unity and the God-willed diversity of humankind, yes, of the whole creation."[5]

---

3. On this and on the "'social' interpretation of justification," see Francis Watson, *Paul, Judaism, and the Gentiles: Beyond the New Perspective* (Grand Rapids: Eerdmans, 2007), 4.

4. I cite the edition of this article reprinted in Stendahl, *Paul among Jews and Gentiles* (Philadelphia: Fortress, 1976), 78–96, but according to the note on p. 78, the article first appeared in Swedish in 1961 and in English in 1963.

5. Ibid., 40.

Other New Testament scholars reached similar conclusions around the same time. In 1968, Markus Barth published a less well-known essay entitled "The Social Character of Justification in Paul," in which he argued against what he called "the danger of a crass individualism" that the Protestant doctrine of justification by faith alone encouraged.[6] According to this theological scheme, each person, as an individual, found his or her own peace with God and seemed to forget about his or her fellow human beings.[7] Barth argued that if Paul is read correctly, then, to the contrary, "there is no personal justification by God without justification of fellow-men by God. And there is no faith in the justifying God without acceptance of the witness given by a neighbor. Briefly: where there is no love there is no faith and no justice."[8]

Like Stendahl, Barth understood Paul's teaching on justification by faith as primarily concerned with the inclusion of the Gentiles within the people of God. Paul's description of the incident in Antioch in Galatians 2:11–21 and his argument in the early chapters of Romans were concerned with two people groups, Jews and Gentiles, and the acceptance of both peoples by God. "The two themes, justification by faith and unity of Jew and Gentile in Christ," said Barth, "are for [Paul] obviously not only inseparable but in the last analysis identical."[9]

In his 1977 essay on the "social function" of justification, Nils Alstrup Dahl went beyond exegesis to an analysis of how the individualism of the pietistic and evangelical doctrine of justification had harmed the mission of the church: "It is hard to deny, precisely on the basis of the experience of the missionary churches, that a Christianity which limits the doctrine of justification to personal religious experience and salvation is insufficient. Young Asian, African and Indian Christians today ask for guidance to overcome the problems which their societies and their churches confront. Like many Westerners, they have trouble finding the answers in pietistic-evangelical religiosity."[10]

---

6. Markus Barth, "Jews and Gentiles: The Social Character of Justification in Paul," *JES* 5 (1968) 241–61; Watson, *Paul, Judaism, and Gentiles*, 5, calls Barth's piece "unjustly neglected."

7. Barth, "Jews and Gentiles," 243.

8. Ibid., 245.

9. Ibid., 258.

10. "The Doctrine of Justification: Its Social Function and Implications" in Nils Alstrup Dahl, *Studies in Paul* (Minneapolis: Augsburg, 1977), 95–120, here at 119.

The emphasis of Stendahl, Barth, and Dahl on the social character of justification by faith has received a large amount of careful exegetical support from the early 1980s to the present in the work of James D. G. Dunn and N. T. Wright, among others. In numerous essays, monographs, commentaries, and studies of Paul these two scholars have argued that, as Wright puts it, "the doctrine of justification was born into the world as the key doctrine underlying the *unity* of God's renewed people."[11] Although justification by faith involves the forgiveness of sins and does not threaten the Reformation's insight that salvation is entirely a matter of God's grace, it does not primarily refer to these concepts. Rather, it refers chiefly to God's declaration that those who have faith belong to his people.[12]

If these scholars are correct in emphasizing social concerns as primary in Paul's soteriology, then evangelical Christianity has probably overemphasized the individual and exported this imbalance to other cultures in its missionary ventures. Dunn's and Wright's exegetical work would dovetail with the observation that American evangelicalism was born in an individualistic environment: if Paul's understanding of justification by faith apart from works of the law was mainly about the inclusion of Gentiles into the people of God, then it becomes plausible that evangelical Christianity's emphasis on the individual is the product of its own cultural baggage rather than its commitment to biblical authority.

Although at first this may seem like a plausible scenario, I would like to argue that there is an indelibly individual element in the Gospel as Paul explains it, and that this individual element is as important as the social element in Paul's soteriology. Whereas it is entirely possible that American evangelicalism has overemphasized the individual side of Paul's soteriology and is in need of correction, the individual element is nevertheless both prominent and important in the apostle's understanding of the human plight and God's solution to it.

It will be useful, for brevity's sake, to make this argument from three texts: Galatians, Romans, and Ephesians. If the individual is important in the soteriology articulated in these letters—one from near the chronological beginning of Paul's extant correspondence, one from the middle, and one from near the end—then it seems likely that this is an enduring and important emphasis in his theology generally.

---

11. N. T. Wright, *Paul in Fresh Perspective* (Minneapolis: Fortress, 2005), 113.
12. Ibid., 121–22.

We begin, then, with Galatians. As emphasized in the more recent exegesis of this letter, Paul's opponents in Galatia were not concerned with matters of individual salvation, but with social and ethnic issues. They were trying to compel Paul's Gentile churches in Galatia to accept circumcision and thereby come under the social umbrella of Judaism. Paul tells us that their motives were to avoid persecution for the cross of Christ (Gal 6:12; cf. 5:11; 6:14, 17). Although it is unclear exactly how their strategy of promoting Jewish practice among Gentile Christians would prevent their persecution, it is reasonable to speculate that they were attempting to make Christianity more intelligible to the surrounding unbelieving society. Circumcision would provide ethnic and religious definition for Christians in a Roman context, where this sort of social definition was thought to be vitally important for the stability of the empire. Jews may have been widely misunderstood in the first-century Roman empire, but they were not regarded as a social threat at the time Galatians was written. Their ethnic group offered sacrifice to their god for the welfare of the emperor, and, from the Roman perspective, that was what mattered. Perhaps, then, Paul's opponents in Galatia hoped to convince the local magistrates to respond to Christianity in the same way that Gallio responded to charges leveled against Christians in Achaia—Christianity was an inner Jewish affair related to rather arcane theological issues, the resolution of which was hardly a concern for Roman governors (Acts 18:12-17).[13]

Whatever the precise historical explanation for their effort to bring Gentile Christians under the yoke of the Mosaic law, the desire of Paul's opponents to escape persecution shows that their ultimate concern was not the fate of individual Gentiles on the final day of judgment but group identity. Their tactic of "excluding" (ἐκκλεῖσαι) the Galatian Gentile Christians from their fellowship (Gal 4:17), like Peter's earlier withdrawal from table fellowship with Gentile Christians in Antioch (Gal 2:11-14), was designed to encourage them either to join their particular social group—the Jews—or to stop violating its boundaries.

It was Paul who turned the discussion toward the individual. Whereas his opponents were concerned with clearly defining social boundaries, Paul believed that their approach to his Gentile churches

---

13. Thanks to Bruce Winter for pointing out in private conversations the parallel to the Gallio encounter and for helping shape my thoughts about the references to persecution in Galatians.

had ramifications both for the relationship of believers to each other and for the relationship of each believer with God. On the social side, a large part of his argument focuses on the idea that the Gentile Galatians were already part of the people of God when they believed the Gospel of Christ crucified and when the Spirit became active in their midst: no further action was necessary, and to submit to the Mosaic law at this point would mean turning the clock back from the time of the fulfillment of God's promise to Abraham to the prior period when the Mosaic law was in force as the boundary marker of the Jewish people. To do this would be to deny the work of God in fulfilling his promise that he would bless all nations through Abraham (Gal 3:1–29).

Equally important to Paul, however, was something that apparently concerned his opponents little, if at all: the implication for the individual that adopting the Mosaic law would have on his or her standing before God. This implication is especially clear in three passages.

First, in Galatians 2:15–21, Paul reflects on the theology implied by the withdrawal of Peter, Barnabas, and "the rest of the Jews" from table fellowship with Gentile Christians in Antioch (2:11–14). The situation in Antioch was analogous to the situation in the churches of Galatia. Here too, Jewish Christians advocated circumcision for Gentile Christians as a way of enforcing group boundaries. Paul begins his reflection on this situation by speaking in group terms—"We ourselves are Jews by birth and not Gentile sinners" (2:15, NRSV)—but then immediately shifts his focus to the individual: "Yet we know that a person is justified not [οὐ δικαιοῦται ἄνθρωπος] by the works of the law but through faith in Jesus Christ. And we have come to believe in Christ Jesus, so that we might be justified by faith in Christ, and not by doing the works of the law, because no one will be justified by the works of the law" (2:16, NRSV).

Paul then begins to speak autobiographically of how he personally "died to the law," was "crucified with Christ," and now lives "by faith in the Son of God, who," he says, "loved me and gave himself for me" (2:19). Here the pathway to justification in Christ (2:17) is defined in terms of the faith of an individual in God's Son, and, more particularly, faith that the substitutionary, atoning death of God's Son solved the problem that failure to keep the law presented to the individual. Paul then concludes his argument with this statement: "I do not nullify the grace of God;

for if justification comes through the law, then Christ died for nothing" (2:21, NRSV).

In this context, the justification, law keeping, and divine grace revealed in the death of Christ are all concerns of the individual, as the use of the first person singular pronouns show. Paul's opponents both in Antioch and Galatia may have thought that they were simply enforcing social boundaries by pressuring Gentiles to live by the Mosaic law, but Paul draws their attention to the impact of their tactics on the justification of the individual. God holds sinners, whether Jewish or Gentile, responsible for their sins as individuals, and he acquits them of their sin as individuals on the basis of the atoning death of Christ. All of this is appropriated by the individual through his or her faith.

Second, in Galatians 3:10–14, Paul makes the case from the law itself that a person must carry out all the law's commands or stand under its curse (Deut 27:26) and that the law gives life to the one who "does" it (Lev 18:5). He also implies that no one can obey the law and that all stand under its curse when he says, "Christ redeemed us from the curse of the law by becoming a curse for us" (3:13, NRSV). If Christ redeemed "us" from the curse, then whoever is represented by this "us" must have needed redemption due to their disobedience. Paul probably has everyone in mind here, which would mean that no one could keep the law. As Paul puts it in Galatians 3:11, now substituting the concept of justification for the concept of redemption, and apparently viewing them as roughly equivalent, "no one is justified before God by the law" (NRSV). Life is only possible through trusting God that the death of Christ accomplishes one's redemption from the curse that the law pronounces on those who disobey it.

For our purposes, what is especially interesting is the oscillation between the plural and the singular in this passage. Paul begins by saying that "as many as are from the law are under a curse," but then, in his quotation of Deuteronomy 27:26, keeps the singular of the LXX text, "Cursed is everyone [singular] who [πᾶς ὅς] does not remain in all the things written in the scroll of the law in order to do them" (my translation). His comment on this quotation is also in the singular, "now, that no one [οὐδεὶς] is justified by the law is clear because the one who is righteous [ὁ δίκαιος] by faith shall live" (3:11; my translation), and he again preserves the singular in his quotation of Leviticus 18:5, "the one who does [ὁ ποιήσας] them shall live by them" (3:12). He then shifts back to the plural when he says that Christ redeemed "us" from the curse of the law (3:13), and he also draws conclusions for the unity of Jews and Gentiles as one people of God at the end of the paragraph. There he says that Christ became "a curse for us" so that the blessing of Abraham might come to the Gentiles in Christ Jesus (3:14).

The singular forms imply a plight of disobedience to the law for every individual, as well as rescue from that plight through the individual's faith in Christ's redemptive death. The plural forms suggest that the plight of the Gentiles as a group who stood outside the people of God has also been overcome by the death of Christ. Because he himself absorbed the curse that fell upon the Gentiles, they are now included in the family of Abraham in accordance with God's promise in Genesis 12:3. The collective implications of justification by faith are clearly present here, but they are intertwined with, and secondary to, the justification of disobedient individuals by faith.

Third, in Galatians 5:2–3, Paul tells the Galatians that if they let themselves "be circumcised, Christ will be of no benefit" to them (v. 2, NRSV). Paul then restates this principle for emphasis: "Once again I testify to every man who lets himself be circumcised that he is obliged to obey the entire law" (v. 3, NRSV). Although he used the plural in the first statement, Paul's reversion to the singular in his restatement shows that even in the first statement he was thinking of a group of *individuals*. Moreover, there is a clever play on words here between the failure of these individuals to "benefit" (ὠφελέω) from Christ's death if they accept circumcision and the "obligation" or, more literally, "debt" (ὀφειλέτης) that they will incur to keep the whole law if they accept circumcision.[14] These two options are presented as opposites: acceptance of circumcision, and, with it, acceptance of the yoke of the Mosaic law or benefit from Christ's death. The individual must choose between them.

Why are these two options regarded as mutually exclusive? At least from Paul's perspective, the reason probably lies in the theology articulated in Galatians 3:10–14. In Galatia, accepting circumcision was a sign of commitment to obey the law. One cannot obey the law, however, and so the commitment to do so can only lead to the law's curse on the disobedient. To experience redemption from the curse that falls on the disobedient, one must trust God that Christ's crucifixion atoned

---

14. Cf. James D. G. Dunn, *The Epistle to the Galatians*, BNTC (Peabody, MA: Hendrickson, 1993), 265.

for one's disobedience to the law. Accepting circumcision excludes one from the benefit of Christ's death, then, not because it identifies one with the wrong group but because it puts one in the impossible position of having to "do" all the law. It implies that Christ's death is not sufficient for redemption and that obedience to the law is also necessary. Although Paul does not explicitly frame it this way, he implies that those who accept circumcision have shifted their trust from Christ to the law.[15]

Here again, the atmosphere is thick with social issues: Paul's opponents in Galatia were trying to convince the Gentile Galatian Christians to identify with their social group. From their perspective, this was the goal of circumcision and adoption of the Mosaic law. What they regarded as a social issue, however, Paul understood in terms of personal soteriology. Every individual who accepted circumcision because he thought it was necessary for membership in God's people lost the redemptive benefit of Christ's death. Such a person implied that confidence in what God had done through Christ needed to be blended with confidence in what the convert to Judaism could do through becoming circumcised and following the rest of the Mosaic law. He hoped to "live," at least in part, by "doing" the law (cf. Lev 18:5).

Is it possible, however, that the emphasis on the individual in Paul's letter to the Galatians arises more from the rhetorical needs of the moment than from an abiding place in Paul's theology? If we move from Galatians to Romans, we can see that this is probably not the case. It is true that, like Galatians, Romans is often concerned with the question, "Who belongs to the people of God?" Paul asks in Romans 3:29, "Is God the God of the Jews only? Is he not also God of the Gentiles? Yes, of the Gentiles also!" (my trans.). It would be a major interpretive and theological mistake to play down this theme: it appears over and over again at critical points in the letter's argument.

It would also be a mistake, however, to try to explain the concern of the entire letter in terms of this theme. The perilous situation of the individual before God apart from faith that Christ's death has atoned

---

15. That the inner attitude of trust is at issue here is confirmed when Paul says only a few sentences later, "For in Christ Jesus neither circumcision nor uncircumcision counts for anything" (5:6, NRSV; cf. 6:15). On one level, it does not matter whether one is circumcised: circumcision only begins to matter when one puts his confidence in it (cf. Phil 3:3).

for his or her sin is also a prominent theme. Three passages show this clearly.

First, most of Romans chapter two, in which Paul describes the necessity of keeping the law in order to be justified before God, is framed in the singular. Other than the plurals in 2:7–16, this chapter is addressed to "the person who judges" (ὁ κρίνων, v. 1) and to "you (singular) who call yourself a Jew and rest in the law and boast in God" (v. 17). It speaks to a single individual who is "treasuring up" for himself "wrath in the day of wrath and the revelation of the righteous judgment of God, who will render to each person according to his works" (vv. 5–6). The problem is that the person to whom Paul speaks thinks that because he is a Jew and circumcised, God will give him special treatment on that day. Paul denies this, arguing forcefully that God is an impartial judge who will look on that day only at one's record of "good work" (v. 7). This is a test, Paul goes on to say in chapter three, that no one will pass, "for we have already charged that both Jews and Greeks—all of them—are under sin" (3:9).[16]

It is true that the Jew whom Paul addresses in this passage is a fictional dialogue partner and that Paul's concern here is primarily to undermine an attitude of ethnic privilege. Paul's fictional Jew thinks that God will privilege Jews over Gentiles on "the day of wrath, when God's righteous judgment will be revealed" (2:5, NRSV). Paul's argument presupposes, however, that every individual will one day account for himself or herself before God. This presupposition is confirmed by the two other places in Paul's letters where he mentions the eschatological judgment of the individual. "All of us must appear before the judgment seat of Christ," he says in 2 Corinthians 5:10, "so that each [ἕκαστος] may receive recompense for what has been done in the body, whether good or evil." Similarly, in Romans 14:12, Paul writes, "So then, each [ἕκαστος] of us will be accountable to God" (both NRSV). Paul's point about ethnic groups in Romans 2 is based upon his theological conviction that every human being shares something in common: each person is destined to appear before God on the day of wrath. Just as in Galatians, then, Paul here speaks of the individual's day of reckoning as part of his social concern to include Gentiles within the people of God on the basis of faith: circumcision, and the social status it represents, will be irrelevant on that day.

---

16. The translations in this paragraph are my own.

Second, the importance of the individual in Paul's soteriology also comes to the fore in Romans 4:1–8. Paul has just finished making a socially oriented argument that was at the heart of his concern in Romans 2, as we have just seen. By the time we reach the end of Romans 3, Paul has asserted more emphatically that justification, or acquittal in God's eschatological court, is not a matter of social affiliation but of accepting by faith God's gracious gift of justification through the death of Christ. The reason that social affiliation will not count before God on the day of judgment is that both Jews and Gentiles will be judged on the same basis, and that basis will be the law of God, which even the Jews have not kept (3:19–20). God has graciously provided a way out of this desperate situation by the atoning death of Christ, and everyone, whether Gentile or Jew, has access to its benefits through faith (3:21–26). Boasting, then, is excluded (3:27–31).

Although much of the boasting Paul has in mind is boasting in one's ethnic identity, he does not stop there. As we saw above in our study of Galatians, Paul implies that the movement of a Gentile Christian into Judaism through accepting circumcision entailed placing confidence in the law rather than in Christ. This understanding of the situation also seems to lie behind Romans 4:1–8. Here too, the primary concern is circumcision and the implied question, just as in Galatians, is whether circumcision is necessary in order to receive the blessing of forgiveness and be declared righteous by God (4:9–12). Yet Paul also seems to view circumcision as one of the "works" in which some might assume that Abraham could boast (Rom 4:2). This attitude of boasting in works, Paul argues, is the opposite of the attitude that Abraham actually had before God, which was an attitude of trust. This attitude of trust, and not of boasting in circumcision or any other "works," is what God counted to Abraham as righteousness (4:3). The impiety of Abraham places him on the same footing with everyone else. As Paul says, God could only reckon him righteous on the basis of faith, not on the basis of works, including circumcision (Rom 4:3, 5, 9–12; cf. 4:18–22).

Here Abraham stands before God as an individual, just as a day laborer stands before the pay master. Unlike the day laborer, however, he has not done an honest day's work (4:4–5). Abraham has no good works sufficient for his acquittal in God's court, but God justifies him anyway through the faith that he, as an individual, has placed in God.

Third, the first person singular pronouns in Romans 7:7–25, whatever else they may mean, at least refer to the plight of the fleshly and therefore weak individual before the massively powerful figure of Sin. This seems clear from both parts of this much debated passage. In the first part (7:7–13), for example, Paul describes the inability of the "I" to keep the tenth commandment. That commandment says to the "I," "You shall not have illicit cravings," (Exod 20:17; Deut 5:21, LXX), but instead of prompting the "I" not to covet, he covets that much more (v. 8). The commandment, which would bring life if obeyed, becomes instead the source of death since it cannot be obeyed (v. 10). If the "I" here at least includes a reference to the state of every individual human being, as seems likely, then the message is reasonably clear. Every individual faces an insuperable problem: he or she has received God's commandments which, if kept, lead to life; however, no one is able to keep these commandments, since they only prompt the individual to sin that much more.

This understanding of the human individual also emerges in the second part of the passage (7:14–25). In Romans 7:22, for example, Paul describes the struggle of the "I" to do what is right as taking place "in the inner human being" (ὁ ἔσω ἄνθρωπον). Here a war is underway between the law of sin that is present in the individual's members and the law of the mind that wills what is good (v. 23; cf. v. 25b). Sin proves to be too powerful, however, and the "I" can only cry out in defeat and anguish, "I am a wretched human being! Who will rescue me from this body of death?" (v. 24).

A large part of the human plight to which the Gospel responds in Romans, therefore, is a plight experienced at the level of the individual human being. This plight is the desperate condition of the individual who knows that keeping the law of God is the pre-condition for life, but who also knows that he or she is incapable of such obedience.

Where did Paul get this idea? He believed that it came from the Scriptures.[17] If we move sequentially through the three passages in

---

17. It is also true, as Gary W. Burnett has argued, that an interest in the individual was current in Paul's first-century Greco-Roman and Hellenistic Jewish environment, despite its predominantly collectivist orientation. See Burnett, *Paul and the Salvation of the Individual*, Biblical Interpretation Series 57 (Leiden: Brill, 2001), 23–87. Cf. the comments of Troels Engberg-Pedersen, "Ephesians 5, 12–13: ἐλέγχειν and Conversion in the New Testament," *ZNW* 80 (1989) 89–110, here at 110: "I believe that there is no single concept that better sums up the shared Greek and Jewish, Hellenistic 'mentality' (as opposed to the worldviews of Old Testament Judaism and of classical Hellenism)

Romans we have just reviewed, we will discover that the source in each for Paul's soteriological concern for the individual is Scripture. Paul backs up his argument in Romans 2 that God will judge both Jew and Greek impartially with the claim that God is a judge "who will repay each person according to his deeds" (ὃς ἀποδώσει ἑκάστῳ κατὰ τὰ ἔργα αὐτοῦ, 2:6, my translation). Although Paul does not introduce this statement with a quotation formula, it nevertheless matches almost exactly a description of God that occurs in Proverbs 24:12: he is the God "who renders to each person according to his works" (ὃς ἀποδίδωσιν ἑκάστῳ κατὰ τὰ ἔργα αὐτοῦ).[18]

If we move to Romans 4:1–8, Scripture is again of critical importance to Paul's argument, and here Paul is explicit. Paul begins his proof that Abraham was not justified by works and had no right to boast before God on the basis of works with the rhetorical question, "For what does the Scripture say?" He then quotes Genesis 15:6: "And Abraham believed God, and it was counted to him as righteousness" (4:3).

Similarly, the description of the struggle of the "I" with the command of God in Romans 7:7–25, begins, as we have seen, with a quotation of the Decalogue's tenth commandment (Exod 20:17; Deut 5:21, LXX). The wretchedness of the individual is a struggle induced by the encounter of the individual with a requirement laid down in Scripture.

Has Paul imposed his individual understanding of the human plight on biblical texts that are actually concerned with people groups? It would be extraordinarily difficult to argue that he has done so. All of these texts are emphatically in the singular. In Proverbs 24:10–12, a father instructs his son not to think that he can escape his duty to save endangered people from death in the "day of adversity" by arguing that he did not know about the situation: "If you [singular] say, 'We knew nothing about this,' does not even he who weighs motives discern [the truth]? As for him who protects your [singular] life, does he not know, and will he not repay a person [singular] according to his conduct?" (24:12).[19]

---

than the experience and consciousness of the divided self. This is the mentality out of which Christianity arose."

18. Paul's phrase is also similar to Psalm 62:11 and Sirach 16:12 and 14, but the presence of the relative pronoun, which is missing from these texts, and of the verb ἀποδίδωμι, which is missing from the Sirach texts, make it probable that Paul is thinking of the phrase as it occurs in Proverbs.

19. The translation belongs to Bruce Waltke, *The Book of Proverbs*, vol. 2, NICOT (Grand Rapids, Eerdmans, 2005), 270.

Here the concern is for a person who might try to excuse himself for having failed to rescue others with the claim that he did not know that the people he could have saved were in any danger. His excuse is formulated in the plural, but this is part of the lie that he tells in his defense. He is cloaking himself in a larger group when, in fact, he alone is responsible for his own conduct.[20] This subterfuge will not fool the Lord, however, because the Lord examines hearts, knows what is there, and will, as the LXX puts it, "repay to each person according to his works."

There is certainly a concern here for the community, which has been destroyed through irresponsible behavior. But this misbehavior was the conduct of a single person who is pictured standing in the Lord's courtroom, unable to make a plausible case for his innocence because the Lord knows his inner thoughts. The focus, then, is on an individual with an inner life that prompts outward behavior, and both the inner, individual element and the outer, communal element of his existence figure in the Lord's judgment of him.

This is basically the same scenario that Paul has in mind in Romans 2. There, ill-founded inner attitudes of moral superiority (2:1), impenitence (2:5), and "selfish ambition" (ἐριθεία, 2:8) are spoken of as being uncloaked on the day of God's wrath and counted among the works by which even the Jew will be judged (2:6–11, 16).[21] No one will be able to hide behind his or her group identity (2:9–10, 25–29).

A similar premise is seen in Paul's use of Genesis 15:6 in Romans 4:1–8. As previously mentioned, ethnic concerns permeate this section of Romans, just as they do the Genesis narrative. The promises that Abram (or, as he becomes in 17:5, "Abraham") believes are that he will have a son, that he will become a great nation, and that "all the families of the earth shall be blessed" in him (Gen 12:3, NRSV; cf. Rom 4:17, citing Gen 17:5). But there is also an emphasis in the Genesis narrative at this point on Abram's own trusting relationship with God. Abram left Haran for Canaan because the Lord told him to do so. Four times in chapters twelve and thirteen, the narrative says that Abram built an altar to the Lord, and twice the text says that he called upon the name of the Lord. The Lord appears to Abram (12:7) and speaks with him (12:1, 7; 13:14),

---

20. Ibid., 277.

21. On ἐριθεία as "selfish ambition," see Frederick William Danker, ed., *A Greek-English Lexicon of the New Testament and Other Early Christian Literature*, 3rd ed. (Chicago: University of Chicago Press, 2000), 392.

so we are not surprised to learn at the beginning of chapter fifteen that "the word of the Lord came to Abram in a vision" (15:1). As a result of the conversation that Abram has with the Lord in this vision, Abram believes God's promise against the logical probabilities to the contrary, and God counts this trust in his promise as righteousness (15:6).

Whatever the precise definition of "righteousness" may be here, it is something that is counted to Abram in the midst of a personal encounter between him as an individual, with his various hopes and fears (15:1), and the God whom he worships. This personal and relational aspect of the Abraham story in Genesis probably accounts for the ancient designation of Abraham as "the friend of God" (2 Chr 20:7; Isa 41:8; Jas 2:23).[22] If, as I have argued previously, the soteriology that Paul explains on the authority of Genesis 15:6 is primarily about the relationship of the individual to God, then it would be difficult to claim that this element is unfaithful to the emphases of the biblical narrative to which Paul appeals.

The same is true of Rom 7:7-25, where the description of the wretchedness of the "I" begins with a quotation of the law of Moses: "You shall not have illicit cravings." Both in Hebrew and in the Greek translation that Paul uses, the "you" here is singular, just as it is throughout the Decalogue. Although the Decalogue is for all the people of Israel, it confronts them both as people and as individuals.[23] There is thus an inner aspect to the commandment, "You shall not have illicit cravings."[24] This law prohibits the sinful inner deliberations of an individual person's thoughts. Given this way of framing the commandment, it would be difficult to maintain that Paul has violated the sense of the commandment

---

22. Perhaps this phrase φίλος θεού supplies the answer to N. T. Wright's puzzlement about "how Paul would express, in Greek, our notion of 'relationship with God'" (Wright, *What Saint Paul Really Said* [Grand Rapids: Eerdmans, 1997], 120).

23. Nahum M. Sarna, *Exodus*, JPS Torah Commentary (Philadelphia: Jewish Publication Society, 1991), 109: "On the one hand it is 'all the people' as a corporate entity, a psychic unity, that enters into the covenantal relationship with God. On the other hand, each member of the community is addressed individually, as is shown by the consistent use of the second-person singular." Cf. Jeffrey H. Tigay, *Deuteronomy*, JPS Torah Commentary (Philadelphia: Jewish Publication Society, 1996), 62: "The fact that the people are addressed in the singular emphasizes the responsibility of each individual, while their collective responsibility is indicated by the fact that the commandments were proclaimed in a public assembly to the entire people."

24. Douglas Moo, *The Epistle to the Romans*, NICNT (Grand Rapids: Eerdmans, 1996), 435-37.

itself by moving from it to a discussion of the frustration that the individual it confronts feels in attempting to obey it. It is, to an important degree, this inner plight of the individual that the Gospel solves. "For," Paul says, "the law of the Spirit of life in Christ Jesus has freed you [singular] from the law of sin and death" (8:2, my translation).

Is it possible, however, that Paul's focus on the individual is contingent on his polemical dialogue with Judaism and Judaizing Christianity and that the concern disappears when the circumstances change? In answer to this question, it is helpful to consider a letter that stands outside this dialogue and comes from a different phase of Paul's ministry. Ephesians is well suited for this purpose.[25] If Galatians comes from the chronological beginning of the Pauline corpus and Romans from a period closer to its middle, Ephesians comes from a time near the end. Paul probably dictated this letter to a secretary during the Roman imprisonment described in Acts 28:16–31.

Moreover, the letter is perhaps the least contingent text in the Pauline corpus. It is addressed to Gentiles who needed to be reminded of their inclusion with Israelite believers in the newly created people of God (2:11; cf. 3:1; 4:17), but there is no dialogue in the letter either with Jewish Christians or with unbelieving Jews. It contains only brief, general references to false teaching (4:14; 5:6; cf. 4:25) and to the possible discouragement of Paul's readers (3:13). Because of these characteristics, Ephesians offers a good test case for the enduring importance of the individual in Paul's soteriology: if we find an emphasis on the individual here, that emphasis is likely to be a non-negotiable in Paul's theology.

As it turns out, Ephesians is primarily about corporate Christian existence. When Paul speaks of faith and salvation in this letter, he never describes those who have faith or are saved in the singular: they are always referred to as a group. This is consistent with the letter's intense interest in the church as a cohesive, smoothly working society whose mission is to proclaim to the invisible, inimical powers of the universe the wisdom of God (3:10). God's wisdom is demonstrated in something Paul calls "the mystery" (3:9), and this mystery is defined as the full equality of Gentile believers with Jewish believers in the people of God (3:6).

---

25. On the Pauline authorship and setting of Ephesians, see, e.g., Peter T. O'Brien, *The Letter to the Ephesians*, Pillar New Testament Commentary (Grand Rapids: Eerdmans, 1999), 4–47, 57–58; Harold W. Hoehner, *Ephesians: An Exegetical Commentary* (Grand Rapids: Baker Academic, 2002), 2–61, 92–97.

Paul develops two metaphors for the unity that should exist in the church: it is both a "temple" and a "body." In his description of believers as a temple, Paul's focus is on unity among believers across ethnic lines. The death of Christ has torn down the Mosaic law, which functioned as a "dividing wall of hostility" between Jews and Gentiles (2:14–15). Jews and Gentiles who are "in Christ" are now part of the same society (they are συμπολῖται) and the same household (οἰκεῖοι). This household dwells in a building, the stones of which are carefully tooled to fit tightly together (οἰκοδομὴ συναρμολογουμένη), and this building "is growing" (αὔξει) into a temple in the Lord (2:19–21).

This organic imagery of growth is probably related to the metaphor of a growing body that Paul uses in Ephesians 4:7–16 (cf. αὔξησιν, v. 16) to refer to believers. Here Paul envisions the ascended and victorious Christ giving gifts to his people. The gifts turn out to be individuals ("each one," 4:7) who use their abilities to equip other believers to do the work of ministry "for the edification of the body of Christ." This body is in the process of growing to "mature manhood;" when it reaches that goal, it will have attained "the measure of the stature of the fullness of Christ" (4:13). Like the temple, it is tightly joined together (συμβιβαζομένη). It is also united (συμβιβαζόμενον) by each assisting connection, which does its assigned job to bring about the body's growth (4:16; cf. 4:7).

Even two of the most prominent individuals in the letter, Christ and Paul, are depicted as having more than an individual existence. As the metaphor of the growing body shows, the group of believers is Christ's body (4:12–13), and Christ is the head of his body (4:15). Paul suffers on behalf of the Ephesian Christians and his suffering is their glory (3:13).

This, then, is not the biblical text in which we would expect Paul to develop an individual soteriology. His focus seems to be on the body of believers as a united group, working and living together harmoniously, each with his or her assigned place, for the mission of the entire group.

Nevertheless, here too Paul reveals the importance of the notion that the human plight is, fundamentally, the plight of individuals before the wrath of God, and that God in his grace has provided salvation for these individuals. This becomes clear in 2:1–10 where Paul describes the human plight in terms that are especially appropriate to the individual.[26] Here, both the human plight and God's gracious response to it are framed in terms that are more applicable to individuals than to societies.

---

26. Cf. Hoehner, *Ephesians*, 205.

The transgressions, sins, and servility to the world, the devil, and the flesh in verses 1 and 2 are summarized in verse 3 in the language of individual existence. We all lived among the sons of disobedience at one time, Paul explains, and this was an existence "in the cravings of our flesh, doing the desires of the flesh and of the thoughts." While it is possible to think of whole people groups as having cravings, fleshly desires, and fleshly thoughts, this language is most naturally interpreted as a reference to the inner life of the individual. This is clear from the affinity of this language with the language that Paul uses in Rom 7:7–25 to describe the plight of the individual "I." There too, the plight was framed in terms of craving, the flesh, the will, and the mind.[27]

God's gracious response to sin, rebellion, and death is also framed in 2:4–10 in terms that show that the individual person is being addressed. It is true that the statement "you are saved by grace" (2:6, 8a) is formulated in the second-person plural, but the all important purpose statement for this mode of salvation is formulated in the singular: "lest anyone (τις) should boast" (2:9b). If the result of the gracious nature of salvation is that no individual may boast before God, then salvation itself must have an individual element. This means that "not from you" and "not from works" in 2:8–9 refer to the existence and efforts of the individual.

Galatians, Romans, and Ephesians show, then, that the individual is critically important in the soteriology of Paul. People will stand before God on the final day not as members of various ethnic groups but as individuals, and apart from a personal faith in God's power to save them through the Messiah Jesus, they will stand condemned on that day. This is not a fleeting element in Paul's theology, but persists through his letters as its visibility in texts from different times and different settings shows. It is entirely possible, indeed probable, that Western individualism has led Western evangelicals to lay too much stress on this element of the Gospel in their various missionary movements. But in our enthusiasm to correct mistakes of the past, it is important not to go to the opposite extreme of denying or neglecting the Bible's own concern with the salvation of the individual.

---

27. Cf. the use of ἐπιθυμία, σάρξ, θέλημα, and διάνοια in Eph 2:3 with the use of ἐπιθυμία, ἐπιθυμέω, σάρκινος, θέλω, σάρξ, and νόος in Rom 7:7–8, 14, 15–16, 18, 19–21, 23, 25.

9

Boundaries in "In-Christ Identity"
Paul's View on Table Fellowship and Its Implications for Ethnic Identities

MAUREEN W. YEUNG

INTRODUCTION

FRANK THIELMAN'S CHAPTER, "THE Group and the Individual in Salvation: The Witness of Paul," cautions us not to belittle the individual dimension in salvation at the expense of the collective one, a tendency which is in vogue in Pauline scholarship today. Indeed, the individual and the collective aspects in salvation are closely related. This is clearly seen in the issue of identity. The identity of a person is always defined in relation to others.[1] When a person accepts Jesus Christ as Lord, he or she immediately gains a new identity: he or she is now a Christian, or a person in Christ, in contrast to someone who has not accepted Christ as Lord. He or she is born into a family with God as Father and fellow Christians as brothers and sisters, a relational reality not enjoyed by non-Christians.

---

1. One of the definitions of "identity" listed in Della Summers, ed., *Longman Dictionary of Contemporary English*, 4th ed. (Harlow, Edinburgh Gate: Pearson Education, 2005), 805 is, "the qualities and attitudes that a person or group of people have, that make them different from other people." Another definition, listed in Philip Babcock Gove, ed. *Webster's Third New International Dictionary of the English Language* (Springfield, MA: Merriam-Webster, 1993), 1123, is, "sameness of essential or generic character in different examples or instances."

The hard question is how this new "in Christ" identity relates to a person's ethnic identity. In the context here, the question is how a Chinese Christian should relate his or her Christian identity to his or her Chinese identity. Questions commonly arise such as, "Can a Chinese person who converts to Christianity still be a 'full' Chinese?" "Is he or she a 'Chinese Christian' or a 'Christian Chinese'?" The distinction between "Chinese Christian" and "Christian Chinese," however subtle, is significant. It is similar to the difference between "Chinese American" and "American Chinese." Many American-born Chinese teenagers regard themselves as "Chinese American" rather than "American Chinese." For them, their American identity takes priority over their Chinese identity. What about Chinese people who have become Christians? Are they first and foremost Christians, and only secondarily Chinese? Or are they first and foremost Chinese, and only secondarily Christian?

The complexity of such questions regarding identity is underscored with the issue of ancestral worship. Is it acceptable for a Chinese Christian to continue to practice ancestral worship? Given that honoring one's parents is part and parcel of traditional Chinese culture, and that ancestral worship is a common outward expression of reverence for ancestors, should or can a Chinese Christian practice it? In the history of Western missionary activities in China, the rulings of Western missionaries banned ancestral worship. Was this a correct move? Were the missionaries imposing their Western culture on Chinese Christians? Were they robbing the Chinese Christians of their Chinese identity?

Lo Lung-kwong, a Hong Kong Chinese scholar, recently addressed this issue by studying the identity crisis reflected in Romans 14:1—15:13.[2] After careful analysis of the difficulties encountered in table fellowship between Jews and Gentiles in Rome, he concluded that Jewish Christians and Chinese Christians face a similar identity crisis. Just as Paul says it is wrong for the "strong" Christians in Rome (Gentile Christians) to force the "weak" Christians (Jewish Christians) to give up their Jewish identity (expressed in refraining from eating meat), the Western missionaries (in a strong position) were wrong in forcing the Chinese Christians (in a

---

2. Lo Lung-kwong, "Identity Crisis Reflected in Romans 14:1—15:13 and the Implications for the Chinese Christians' Controversy on Ancestral Worship," *Ching Feng* 3 (2002) 23–59.

weak position) to give up their Chinese identity (expressed in ancestral worship).³

To what extent is Lo's conclusion justified? Does a single passage provide sufficient evidence to support such a conclusion? Is there a viable analogy between the identity crisis of Jewish Christians and Chinese Christians? Two hundred years after the arrival of Robert Morrison in China, it is high time that we assess the legitimacy of the Western missionaries' approach by delving into the biblical text.

A good starting point is to explore the relationship between "in-Christ identity" and ethnic identity by studying Paul's view on table fellowship. As the gospel spread from Jews to Gentiles, conflicts often arose over matters of eating. Such disputes were evident in Jewish and Gentile Christians' clashes over "clean" and "unclean" foods, the Lord's Supper, and ethnic identities. Three passages in Paul's letters are related to table fellowship: Galatians 2, 1 Corinthians 8–10,⁴ and Romans 14–15. The issues raised in these texts are each different and thus provide us with a variety of circumstances, rather than just one case as in Lo's study, to explore the relationship between Christian identity and ethnic identity.

Our methodology is first to see if there is discussion of "in-Christ identity" in each of these passages, which will involve specifically looking for actual "in Christ" terminology. It is scholarly consensus that "in Christ" terminology is a distinctive feature of Pauline theology.⁵ It expresses well what Paul thinks is the essential identity of a Christian. This identity takes priority over ethnic identity, so that Paul says he became as a Jew to Jews and as a Gentile to Gentiles (1 Cor 9:20–21). How does this actually work out in daily living? Are there limits to this "in-Christ identity" when it comes into conflict with ethnic identity?

After locating the "in Christ" terminology, we shall place the expression "in-Christ identity" in the broader context of the passage and/or book's Christology. Particular attention will be given to how the

---

3. Ibid., 58–59.

4. Although the issue in Corinthians is not table fellowship between Jews and Gentiles, it concerns table fellowship with demons.

5. A. J. M. Wedderburn offers a helpful discussion of ἐν Χριστῷ terminology in "Some Observations on Paul's Use of the Phrases 'in Christ' and 'with Christ,'" *JSNT* 25 (1985) 83–97. He points out the Jewish origin of ἐν Χριστῷ, developed from the "in Abraham" terminology. Paul expands this link to encompass "in Adam." This is followed by Lars Klehn, "Die Verwendung von ἐν Χριστῷ bei Paulus. Erwägungen zu den Wandlungen in der paulinischen Theologie," *BN* 74 (1994) 66–79.

Christology affects Paul's view on table fellowship. We shall then be in a position to ascertain the relationship between "in-Christ identity" and ethnic identity as revealed in these case studies on table fellowship.

I want to argue that there are boundaries established around Paul's "in-Christ identity." Such limits are set by Christology and soteriology. A Christian acquires his or her identity on the basis of who Christ is and what he has done. The significance of Christ's attributes and works determines how a Christian should act in different cultural settings. The Christological and soteriological contributions of the three passages are "freedom in Christ" (Galatians), "Christ as the same Lord" (Romans), and "Christ as one Lord" (1 Corinthians).[6] These emphases draw the boundaries around "in-Christ identity" and shape the contours of ethnic expressions. The implications for ethnic identities are that ethnic expressions should be respected with a view to promoting harmony and unity among Christians, but must be abandoned if they infringe upon Christians' freedom from the Law, or if they are idolatrous or immoral.

GALATIANS 2: FREEDOM IN CHRIST

Christology and Soteriology

Christ died to set us free from the Law so that we may be justified by faith apart from works of the Law.

Boundaries in "In-Christ Identity"

The Law, in its different ethnic expressions, may be observed so long as it is not regarded as a condition for salvation. Ethnic differences should also never be hindrances to equality and unity in Christ.

The book of Galatians' most significant theological contribution to the definition of "in-Christ identity" is its focus on the Christian's complete identification with Christ on the cross, which frees the Christian from the Law. Any infringement upon such freedom amounts to tearing down this "in-Christ identity." Jewish ethnic identity has no part to play in attaining this freedom, and Jewish ethnic expressions such as circumcision and food laws should therefore not be imposed on Gentile Christians.

---

6. The chronological order of the three books focused on in this chapter is Galatians, 1 Corinthians, and Romans. For smooth transitions of thought, I shall follow a different order.

Galatians deals singularly with the issue of justification by faith apart from works. The Galatians were under pressure to "complete" their conversion by circumcision, and Paul insists that succumbing to such pressure in order to be saved is contrary to the gospel message. Galatians 2:1–10 records Paul's meeting with the church pillars, during which he successfully resisted the pressure to circumcise the Gentile Titus, and in which there was mutual understanding as to Peter's and Paul's rightful ministries to Jews and Gentiles, respectively.

This is followed by the account in Galatians 2:11–14 (or possibly 2:11–21 if 2:15–21 was also spoken during the confrontation) of Peter's arrival in Antioch and Paul's confrontation with him. Peter acts insincerely by withdrawing from eating with the Gentiles when certain people came from James. Paul makes it clear to Peter that his withdrawal is tantamount to making Christ an agent of sin if he regards table fellowship between Jewish and Gentile Christians as sinful. In 2:15–21, Paul goes on to stress the complete identification of a Christian, by faith, with the crucified and risen Christ and his or her subsequent release from the Law.

In this chapter, two occurrences of "in Christ" terminology are present: ἐν Χριστῷ Ἰησοῦ in 2:4 and ἐν Χριστῷ in 2:17. These two phrases occupy strategic positions and convey important concepts. The ἐν Χριστῷ Ἰησοῦ in 2:4 occurs in the account of the Jerusalem meeting. It speaks of the "freedom" that a Christian gains in Christ, which refers obviously to freedom from the Law and the freedom not to observe Jewish practices. Such freedom is basic to "in-Christ identity" and explains why Paul resisted the pressure to circumcise Titus. The ἐν Χριστῷ in 2:17 is a postscript to the Antioch incident and speaks of the complete justification that both Jews and so-called "Gentile sinners" obtain in Christ. As Christ has already justified both Jews and Gentiles who put their faith in him, no Christian should consider himself or herself, or other Christians, to be sinners if the latter do not observe the Law.

The Christology and soteriology of Galatians 2 are profound. Christ is none other than the Son of God, who died to save sinners (2:20). As observed by Gordon Fee, Christ is prominently referred to four times as the "Son" in this book ("the Son of God" in 2:20 and "his Son" in 1:16; 4:4, and 4:6).[7] Jesus Christ is not merely the son of God in the sense of

---

7. Gordon Fee, *Pauline Christology: An Exegetical-Theological Study* (Peabody, MA: Hendrickson, 2007), 208.

a Davidic king (cf. 2 Sam 7:12–14), but is also the divine Son of God whom God sent to be born as a human being under the Law (4:4). This Son of God died on the cross to save sinners from the bondage of the Law. When a person puts his or her faith in Christ, he or she is fully identified with this Son of God, who died to the Law for sinners. The "in-Christ identity" means a Christian is so fully identified with Christ that he or she lives in complete union with him: with Christ living in the Christian and the Christian living in Christ, that is, two in one. As Christ has died to the Law, so a Christian is free from the Law (2:19–21). Freedom from the Law is therefore one of the most important aspects of "in-Christ identity." Whenever this freedom is infringed upon, a Christian's "in-Christ identity" is endangered. This explains why Paul so vehemently confronted Peter.

How does this "in-Christ identity" shape Paul's view on table fellowship between Jews and Gentiles? What is at stake in Antioch? It is difficult to reconstruct the scenario in Antioch with historical precision, as proper placement of the Antioch account in the story of Acts is debated. Most scholars identify Gal 2:1–10 with the Jerusalem Council in Acts 15. In this case, it is difficult to understand why Peter so quickly moved away from his position in the Council and also why James appeared to renege so soon on the Apostolic Decree. To resolve this perplexity, Esler suggests that Paul had obtained only right-hand blessing and not an oath from the church pillars; therefore, Peter and James were able to retract their decisions in the Jerusalem Council without appearing fickle.[8] Another scholar tries to reconcile this matter by saying that James' Apostolic Decree was actually a means to *separate* the Gentiles from the Jews. On the other hand, some scholars, including Richard Bauckham recently,[9] distinguish the Jerusalem meeting between Paul and Barnabas and the pillars (Gal 2:1–10) from the Jerusalem Council recorded in Acts 15. In this view, Galatians was written immediately after the incident in Antioch (Gal 2:11–14 = Acts 15:1–2a) but before Paul went before the Jerusalem Council (Acts 15:2a–4). This position has much to commend it, but space does not permit a full assessment of the various views.

---

8. Philip F. Esler, "Making and Breaking an Agreement Mediterranean Style: A New Reading of Galatians 2:1–14," *BibInt* 3 (1995) 285–314.

9. Richard Bauckham, "James, Peter and the Gentiles," in *The Missions of James, Peter and Paul: Tensions in Early Christianity*, ed. Bruce Chilton and Craig Evans, NovTSup 115 (Leiden: Brill, 2005), 136.

No matter how we attempt to harmonize the Pauline and Lukan accounts, it is clear that Peter somehow withdrew from eating with Gentiles and acted against his own convictions. From Acts 10:28, it is clear that Peter did not previously "associate with" (κολλᾶσθαι) or "visit" (προσ-έρχεσθαι) Gentiles for fear of being contaminated by them, as they were regarded as "common" (κοινὸν) and "unclean" (ἀκάθαρτον). However, the vision Peter saw on the roof prompted him to visit Cornelius. There, in a Gentile home, he witnessed the gift of the Holy Spirit upon the Gentiles (10:45–46). Peter stayed in Cornelius' house for several days, perhaps to have more time for fellowship (10:48). Obviously, he ate with Cornelius and his household during those days.

Cornelius, though a God-fearer, was nevertheless uncircumcised (11:3). For Peter to eat with an uncircumcised Gentile was unprecedented. It was also unacceptable to the Jews. This was exactly the complaint that the Jews launched against him (11:3). Why did Peter step out of his comfort zone to eat with uncircumcised Gentiles at Cornelius' home? It must be that Peter's vision (which declared "common and unclean" foods clean) and the gift of the Holy Spirit (which descended on the so-called "common and unclean" Gentiles) combined to teach him that God had cleansed the Gentiles' hearts by faith just as he had done for the Jews (15:8–9). Peter's repeated use of "just as we are" language (10:47; 11:15, 17; 15:8)[10] showed that he was thoroughly convinced that "there is no distinction between Jews and Gentiles" (15:9) and that both are saved through the grace of the Lord Jesus (15:11). His insight culminated in his offer to baptize Cornelius and his household in the name of Jesus Christ (10:47–48), thereby declaring the equality of Jews and Gentiles in Christ.

It is unclear if the Lord's Supper was celebrated at Cornelius' home. It would not be a surprise if Peter, who baptized Cornelius and his household, shared the Lord's Supper during table fellowship with Cornelius. The celebration of the Lord's Supper in the midst of a love feast was common practice among early Christians. If Peter did in fact share the Lord's Supper with uncircumcised Gentile converts, he was not only acknowledging the equality of Jewish and Gentile Christians, but also living out the unity of the two ethnic groups.

---

10. "Just as we have" (ὡς καὶ ἡμεῖς, 10:47), "just as it has upon us" (ὥσπερ καὶ ἐφ' ἡμᾶς, 11:15), "as to us" (ὡς καὶ ἡμῖν, 11:17), and "just as to us" (καθὼς καὶ ἡμῖν, 15:8).

This probably became Peter's standard practice after he converted Cornelius. Hence, he was also eating with the Gentiles in Antioch before certain men from James came (Gal 2:12). His sudden withdrawal from eating with the Gentiles was perplexing. What was he afraid of? We do not have the full picture before us. The evidence from the text is that he feared "the circumcision party" (2:12) and thus fell in line with its dictate that Gentiles should live like Jews (ἰουδαΐζειν, 2:14).

The word ἰουδαΐζειν has been much discussed. It means "to follow Jewish practices." Bauckham fairly grants that this word need not mean circumcision, but, on the other hand, it need not exclude it.[11] The context of the letter favors the reference to full observance of the Law and Jewish practices, including circumcision. Paul is saddened that the Galatians observe "days, and months, and seasons, and years" (4:10), which probably refer to the Jewish Sabbaths and feasts given Paul's later assertion that the Galatians desire "to be under law" (4:21).[12] Moreover, not only does Paul repeatedly speak against circumcision (2:3–5; 5:3, 6, 11–12, 13, 15), but he also explicitly tells the Galatians to resist the pressure to be circumcised (5:2; 6:12).

What pressure, then, was Peter under when the men from James arrived? If the men genuinely represented James, can we determine what James demanded without having to necessarily conclude that he reneged on his previous decision to give Paul and Barnabas the right to preach to the Gentiles?

An important clue to understanding James' request is contained in Paul's words to the Galatians: "having begun with the Spirit, are you now ending with the flesh?" (3:3) I suggest that the men from James accepted the Galatian converts' "beginning," but then exerted pressure on them to "end with the flesh." James probably approved of the preaching of the gospel to the Gentiles and also of the Galatians' baptism. Such practices were acceptable as long as winning converts did not require the Jews to have much social contact with the Gentiles. That was why previously James could extend the right hand of fellowship to Paul and Barnabas. However, for Jewish and Gentile Christians to eat together and to share the Lord's Supper was quite another matter. Questions naturally arose in Jewish minds: Is the food prepared by the Gentiles "clean" food accord-

---

11. Bauckham, "James, Peter and the Gentiles," 126.
12. So is I. Howard Marshall's view; see *New Testament Theology* (Downers Grove, IL: InterVarsity, 2004), 210.

ing to the Law? Will the Jews become defiled as a result of eating with the Gentiles? A safe precaution was to require the Gentile converts to be circumcised and to fully conform to Jewish practices before Jews could establish such close contact with Gentiles. In all likelihood, the men from James demanded circumcision and full observance of the Law as a sign of "complete conversion." It was probably at this juncture that Peter succumbed to the pressure of the circumcision party. Peter chose to avoid an open conflict with the representatives from James by withdrawing from eating with the Gentiles. After all, James did not deny the "beginning" of the Galatians and apparently still upheld justification by faith as a condition for salvation. The demand from James' representatives thus did not appear that anti-gospel after all. This would explain why the rest of the Jews and even Barnabas withdrew from table fellowship with the Gentiles. If James had rejected justification by faith altogether, it is inconceivable that Peter and Barnabas would have given in to his representatives.

While Peter did not seem to be aware of the implications of his action, Paul denounced his withdrawal as contrary to "the truth of the gospel" (2:14). What is the implication of Peter's action? To Paul, Peter's withdrawal ran counter to the freedom a Christian has in Christ. Once a person is in Christ, he or she is free from the Law. Peter's withdrawal from eating with the Gentiles reflected his belief that Gentiles were not completely "clean" solely as the result of having put their faith in Christ. Rather, Gentile converts had to observe fully the Jewish Law, including circumcision, before he or she could attain equal footing with Jewish Christians and be permitted to share food and the Lord's Supper with their Jewish brothers and sisters without polluting them. In other words, Gentiles were required to live like Jews before they could be completely saved. Paul thought this was ridiculous. Peter, himself a Jew, preached justification by faith and was thereby released from the Law. He had, in fact, been living "like a Gentile" without the Law. How could he then require the Gentiles to live as he did in his own pre-conversion Jewish days in order to be saved (2:14)?

Peter also committed no sin by eating with Cornelius and other Gentile converts. His withdrawal from eating with the Gentiles implied, however, that it was a sin to eat with Gentiles. Does that mean that Christ promotes sin? The answer to Paul's rhetorical question is clearly negative. Christ has justified both Jews and Gentiles apart from works and made table fellowship between the two ethnic groups not only possible, but mandatory. Bauckham is probably correct when he says "the difference between Peter and Paul might be . . . [that] for Peter 'the truth of the Gospel' . . . meant that fellowship between Jewish Christians and uncircumcised Gentile Christians was permissible, whereas for Paul it meant that it was mandatory."[13] There should be no further condition for Gentile converts to be able to share the Lord's Supper with Jewish Christians. The Gentiles are not required to keep the Law. In other words, the difference between Peter and Paul is that the former accepts justification by faith but the latter insists on justification by faith *apart from works*.

The Law is actually time-bound. It was the παιδαγωγός, which guarded people until Christ came (Gal 3:24). The Law has its various expressions and distinctions. It has *ethnic* expressions such as Jewish food laws, circumcision, and feasts. Distinctions are made between Jews and Gentiles. The Law has *social* distinctions. For instance, the master who gave his slave a wife had the right to keep the woman and any children she bore if the slave chose to leave him after six years of slavery (Exod 21:4). The Law also has *gender* distinctions. For instance, the time of purification after giving birth to a girl is double the length of that after giving birth to a boy (Lev 12:1–5). These distinctions are part and parcel of the Law. However, they have no place in "in-Christ identity" because a Christian has fully identified with Christ, who set his people free from the Law. Paul declares boldly, "there is neither Jew nor Greek, there is neither slave nor free, there is nether male nor female; for you are all one in Christ Jesus" (Gal 3:28). None of the distinctions among members of the human race, whether rooted in ethnicity, social status, gender, age, intelligence, physical capacities, etc., should be allowed to infringe upon the "in-Christ identity," which is obtained on only one condition: justification by faith apart from works.

Paul thus ties "in-Christ identity" to the acceptance of Christ's redemptive work—and nothing else. With regard to ethnicity, while Paul does not oppose Jews receiving circumcision so long as they do not depend on it for salvation,[14] he is adamantly against circumcising Gentiles in order to make them "clean." Ethnic expressions are accept-

---

13. Bauckham, "James, Peter and the Gentiles," 127.

14. For the sake of his ministry among Jews, Paul even circumcised Timothy so as to remove a possible stumbling block to the reception of the gospel (Acts 16:1–3).

able to retain so long as they are not regarded as conditions for salvation, because Christ has already set the Christian free from the Law. Ethnic expressions should in no way undermine or hinder equality and unity in Christ, however.¹⁵ In the words of Bengt Holmberg, "Jewish identity must cede to the common Christian identity."¹⁶

ROMANS 14:1—15:13: CHRIST AS THE SAME LORD

Christology and Soteriology

Jesus Christ is the same Lord of all, accepting both Jews and Gentiles so as to give unified glory to God. He unites his people under his lordship with unity in diversity: unity based on the same terms of salvation; diversity exemplified in cultural expressions of love for the Lord.

Boundaries in "In-Christ Identity"

Respect for cultural differences should be paid to different ethnic groups so as to promote unified worship of the Lord.

Paul's view on table fellowship in Romans 14–15 appears to contradict his view in Galatians. Whereas in Galatians Paul is against observance of Jewish Law such as circumcision, food laws, and feasts, in Romans 14–15 he accepts those who observe feast days and probably food laws. In fact, although identifying himself with the "strong" (Rom 15:1), he admonishes the "strong" to accommodate the needs of the "weak," which the majority of scholars take to refer to Jewish Christians who refrain from eating meat for fear of violating the food laws. Does Paul uphold the Law in Romans 14–15? If so, he contradicts himself not only in Galatians, but also in the first half of Romans.

Paul's thought is actually consistently controlled by Christology and soteriology. As pointed out by Gordon Fee, Pauline Christology is characterized by κύριος Christology. In Romans, the prominent Christological

---

15. While I understand "works of the Law" (Gal 2:16 et al.) to mean "works required by the Law" and to include Jewish identity markers such as circumcision, food laws, and festivals, I do not equate the term with these markers as James Dunn does. For my critique of Dunn's view, see Maureen W. Yeung, *Faith in Jesus and Paul*, WUNT 2/147 (Tübingen: Mohr/Siebeck, 2002), 227–47.

16. Bengt Holmberg, "Jewish versus Christian Identity in the Early Church?" *RB* 105 (1998) 397–425.

emphasis is Jesus Christ as Lord. It is worth noting that up through chapter 9, the word κύριος occurs only in the threefold combination "Lord Jesus Christ"; after that, it appears on its own frequently.[17]

According to Fee, Paul's κύριος Christology in Romans first appears in 8:34 by alluding to Psalm 110:1, although the actual use of κύριος as a Christological title does not occur until 10:9. The confession of Jesus as Lord in 10:9 has at least double significance. First, the application of Joel 2:32 (3:5 LXX) to Christ is tantamount to recognizing Jesus Christ as the Lord Yahweh. Second, God exalted Christ to be the "Lord over all" so that Christ can now assume rightful lordship over the lives of both Jewish and Gentile Christians. Indeed, there is profuse use of κύριος on its own after chapter 10, as Paul's teaching moves to the more practical level. In 14:1–12 alone, Christ is referred to as ὁ κύριος no less than eight times.[18]

In addition to emphasizing Jesus Christ as Lord, Romans stresses that this Lord is "the same Lord of all" (Rom 10:12) who accepts Jews and Gentiles on the same basis: justification by faith apart from works. There is therefore "no distinction" between Jews and Gentiles. The use of the word "distinction" is suggestive. Whereas in the Law the Israelites are told to "make a distinction" (διαστεῖλαι) between the "clean" and the "unclean" (Lev 10:10 LXX), Paul now declares that "there is no distinction" (οὐ ἐστιν διαστολή) between the Jews and the Gentiles (Rom 10:12).

In the passage of concern here (Rom 14:1—15:13), the Christological focus is therefore the same lordship of Christ in the lives of both Jewish and Gentile Christians. The ultimate purpose is to create one unified people out of Jews and Gentiles under the lordship of Christ to the glory of God (15:5–6, 8–9). The "in-Christ" terminology occurs once in 14:14. Nearly every word of this verse is theologically charged: "I know and am persuaded in the Lord Jesus (ἐν κυρίῳ Ἰησοῦ) that nothing is unclean (κοινόν) in itself; but it is unclean for anyone who thinks (τῷ λογιζομένῳ) it unclean (κοινόν)." Paul is totally convinced of the theological truth that follows. There are two parts of this "in-Christ" statement. The first part has to do with the objective reality, the second part the subjective reality.[19]

---

17. Fee, *Pauline Christology*, 254.

18. Ibid., 258–59.

19. In the structure proposed by Robert Jewett, 14:14 is "the Pauline ethical principle," with 14:14a as the "surety formula and formulaic thesis: 'nothing is unclean in it-

First, in Christ, nothing is unclean in itself. There is a revolution in values with the coming of the new epoch. Under the Law, some foods were clean and some were not. However, in Christ, there is no more distinction. This is actually another way of saying "Christ is the end of the Law" (Rom 10:4). What appears to be a statement about food is actually a statement about people in Christ. In Christ, no one is unclean. The person in Christ is a person holy and pure, fully acceptable to God. What he or she eats does not affect his or her saintly status.

The connection between food and people can be seen in the use of the word κοινόν, which literally means "common/profane," but is usually translated as "unclean" in this context in most English versions. This word is used together with ἀκάθαρτον ("unclean/impure") in the Cornelius story (Acts 10:14; cf. 11:8; 10:28). It is interesting that in this story, both the animals and Gentiles were regarded as "common and unclean" by Peter. However, the voice from heaven declared that what God "has cleansed" (ἐκαθάρισεν), Peter must not call "common" (κοίνου) (Acts 10:15; cf. 11:9). Finally, Peter admitted that God had shown him that he should not call any person "common or unclean" (κοινὸν ἢ ἀκάθαρτον) (10:28). Judging from the heavenly voice, κοινόν and ἀκάθαρτον are synonyms in this context. However, a distinction can still be maintained, as Peter repeatedly used these two words and did not collapse them. Κοινός means "common/profane" in the sense that a person or a thing is not separated from the ordinary sector for special use by the Lord. Ἀκάθαρτος means "unclean/impure" in the sense that something has moral impurity in itself. The word κοινός thus has a wider reference than the word ἀκάθαρτος in that an unclean person or thing is surely common, but a clean person or thing by itself may still be common and not yet sanctified. When God has cleansed a person, he or she is no longer "common" in the sense that he or she is not only cleansed from moral impurity but is also acceptable and holy before God. When used together, the two words connote the sense that Peter finally realized that Gentiles are not regarded as either morally impure or profane in God's sight.

With this as background, it is significant that Paul used the word κοινόν in Romans 14:14.[20] Paul uses strong words to introduce his con-

---

self" and 14:14a as the "exception based on the principle of ethical autonomy" in Jewett, *Romans: A Commentary*, Hermeneia (Minneapolis: Fortress, 2007), 856.

20. Contrast Paul's use of "unclean" (καθαρά) in 14:20, where he seems to be referring strictly to food.

viction: "I know and am persuaded," indicating that what follows is a result of deep theological reflection and missionary experience. Whether a person is accepted by God does not depend on the kind of food he or she eats, but on whether his or her sins have been cleansed by Jesus Christ. When a person is in Christ, he or she is fully accepted by God and no longer "common." Therefore nothing is "common" in itself in Christ. Paul uses the word "common" to indicate that a person in Christ is not only not "unclean" (ἀκάθαρτος), but also not "common" (κοινός). He is holy to the Lord (cf. the priestly and "holy" language in Romans 12:1).

This conviction corresponds to Paul's insistence in Galatians 2. Gentile believers are already cleansed, and it is mandatory that Peter fellowship with them. To withdraw from having table fellowship with Gentile believers who had not conformed to full-scale Jewish practice as if they were still sinners violates the truth of the Gospel. This "in-Christ identity" does not require a Gentile Christian to first take on Jewish identity. In fact, ethnic identity has nothing to do with "in-Christ identity." Both Jews and Gentiles are saved on the basis of faith regardless of their ethnic identities. Jewish Christians have to learn that Jewish practices including circumcision, food laws, and Sabbaths are not means of obtaining "in-Christ identity."

The first part of "in-Christ identity" as expressed in Romans 14:14a is therefore the essence of the objective aspect of faith. The objective aspect of faith is the work of God and Jesus Christ. For the person who puts his or her faith in Jesus Christ, God does not "reckon" (λογίζομαι) his or her sin (Rom 4:8) but "reckons" (λογίζομαι) him or her as righteous (Rom 4:23–25). As a result of God's "reckoning" (λογίζομαι), the believer should likewise "reckon" (λογίζομαι) the objective benefits of the death and resurrection of Christ to himself or herself (Rom 6:11). The objective benefits that Christ brings to his people are the same for every person, whether Jew or Gentile. This is what Paul insisted upon at Antioch.

However, a subjective aspect of faith is also introduced in Rom 14:14b. Those who have already put their faith in the objective redemptive work of Christ demonstrate different measures of faith (cf. Rom 12:3). Each believer grows in the knowledge of God at a different pace, being influenced by his or her background, including ethnic and cultural background. The same Lord Jesus Christ, however, as the gracious Lord, "welcomes" (Rom 15:7) each believer's subjective faith. He allows diversity as each believer seeks to please him according to his or her conscience. For the believer who "reckons" (λογίζομαι) a certain food as unclean and who does not want to dishonor God by eating it, the food becomes unclean (Rom 14:14b). The Lord Jesus accepts his or her conviction (although it does not correspond to objective reality), as this person's desire to please God is more important than the knowledge he or she possesses. If this person eats against his or her own faith, it is sin (Rom 14:23).

Paul urges the Roman believers to take into account this subjective aspect of faith in relating to each other. The conflict between the "strong" and the "weak" probably arose when the Lord's Supper was celebrated during table fellowship.[21] As most scholars today accept, the Roman church was probably not a mega-church, but consisted of many house churches. When meals were shared in a Jewish home, *kosher* food was served. For Jewish Christians who had difficulty buying *kosher* meat, they might avoid meat altogether by serving vegetables. Gentile Christians might fall into the temptation of despising their Jewish brothers' and sisters' "weak" conscience. Still larger problems arose when meals were served in Gentile homes. Gentile Christians, having a "strong" conscience, had no problem eating meat bought from the market. Jewish Christians would then find it hard to participate in such meals. Table fellowship therefore broke down because of the different eating habits of the two groups. Paul therefore appeals to the Gentile Christians, that is, the "strong," to bear the burden of the "weak." They should sacrifice their right to eat meat for the sake of the Jewish Christians, whose conscience was weaker. Only in this way could table fellowship be maintained and unity among Christians safeguarded. The higher purpose is to promote unity among Christians so as to offer unified praise to God.

It should be noted, though, that this subjective aspect of faith is itself rooted in the objective aspect of faith. The two components of Rom 14:14 are true only "in the Lord Jesus." One has to be "in the Lord Jesus" first before this subjective aspect of faith works. In fact, Paul wrote more than eleven chapters on the objective aspect of faith before he came to 12:3, where he introduces the "different measures of faith." In other words, the objective aspect of faith is a common denominator of all Christians. Diversity can only flourish when there is basic unity in Christ.

---

21. For a reconstruction of this scenario, see Lung-kwong, "Identity Crisis Reflected in Romans 14:1—15:13," 23–59.

In sum, in the same Lord Jesus Christ there is both unity and diversity. There is unity because the same Lord justifies people according to the same terms (justification by faith apart from works). There is also diversity because the same Lord accepts different ways of honoring him. The boundaries of "in-Christ identity" are such that ethnic and cultural expressions should be allowed to co-exist with a view to promoting harmony among Christians so as to glorify the same Lord of all.

1 CORINTHIANS 8–10: CHRIST AS ONE LORD

Christology and Soteriology

Jesus Christ as one Lord means He is a jealous God. A Christian who does not flee from idolatry (or demon worship) and immorality may end up losing his or her salvation.

Boundaries in "In-Christ Identity"

Respect for cultural differences should be paid to different ethnic groups as long as the cultural expressions are neither idolatrous nor immoral.

Like Romans, 1 Corinthians also emphasizes κύριος Christology. Whereas in Romans 14–15 the emphasis is on the *same* Lord, in 1 Corinthians 8–10 it is on the *one* Lord. A subjective aspect of faith is discussed as in Romans 14–15, and Christians are also described as being either "strong" or "weak." However, the issues are not identical and the terms "strong" and "weak" carry different connotations.

The main issue in these three chapters is the right to eat festive meals in pagan temples. The Corinthians argue for their right to do so, offering the rationale that there is only one God and all idols are nothing. Therefore, eating in pagan temples does not amount to idolatry. Paul objects to this position for two main reasons. First, for those Christians who had been used to worshipping pagan gods before conversion and who have a "weak" conscience, idols are a "subjective reality."[22] For these "weak" Christians to attend festive meals in pagan temples following the example of the "strong" Christians is an act of idolatry. Therefore, the "strong" Christians should not be a stumbling block to their "weak" brothers and sisters by eating in pagan temples (8:7–13). Second, al-

---

22. A term used by Gordon Fee. See his *Pauline Christology*, 89.

though idols are nothing, there are actually demons behind idol worship. Therefore, on no occasion should Christians, whether of strong or weak conscience, take part in such meals, as they amount to fellowship with demons (10:1–22).

Sandwiched between these two reasons is Paul's personal example of discipline (1 Cor 9). It is in this chapter that ἐν κυρίῳ occurs twice (9:1, 2), both in relation to Paul's apostleship. Paul sees his apostleship as commissioned and completed by Christ. His own rigorous discipline sets an example "in Christ" to the Corinthians in two respects, corresponding to the two reasons why Corinthians should not attend pagan temple feasts.

First, Paul forfeits his legitimate rights and identifies with others' ethnic expressions in order to save more people. This sets an example of not seeking one's own interests, but the interests of others. To the "weak" Paul is "weak" (9:22), as evidenced by his willingness to give up eating meat for their sake (8:13). This implies that the Corinthians should in no way be a stumbling block to their "weak" brothers and sisters by attending festive meals in pagan temples.

Second, Paul disciplines himself so that he will not lose his salvation. Although some scholars regard the "disqualification" (9:27) as referring to the failure to obtain reward, the subsequent context is in favor of understanding it as the loss of salvation. Paul's rigorousness is an example of disciplining one's natural desires, including the desire to eat meat in pagan temples. Such discipline is not asceticism, but a serious attempt to flee from idolatry and immorality so as not to endanger one's salvation.

Paul's personal testimony is flanked by two important Christological passages that explain his lifestyle. In 1 Corinthians 8, the first few verses are important declarations emphasizing Jesus Christ as one Lord. As Gordon Fee observes, Paul separated the *Shema* into two parts in 8:6:

> Deut 6:4—Hear, Israel, the Lord our God the Lord is one.

> 1 Cor 8:6—There is one God the Father, from whom are all things and for whom we exist; and one Lord, Jesus Christ, through whom are all things and through whom we exist.[23]

Paul here equates "God" with "the Father" and "Lord" with "Jesus Christ." In such a way, Paul shows that Jesus Christ is none other than the

---

23. Ibid.

creator God of the Old Testament. As such, there is only one God and one Lord—all other gods and lords are false gods. While idols are nonexistent, idolatrous people cling to such false gods. There is only one lord God, Yahweh, but the idolatrous Israelites chose to worship false gods like Baal. New Christians who are used to worshipping idols and whose conscience is weak may be tempted to continue doing so. Therefore, Paul asks the "strong" in faith to be considerate to the "weak." Christians with "knowledge" who eat at idols' temples may be a stumbling block to their weaker brothers and sisters who are used to worshipping idols. When the latter follow suit and eat at idols' temples, they worship God against their conscience and thus sin against him. Paul can become as a Jew to a Jew and as a Gentile to a Gentile in the sense that he respects and takes care not to act in ways that are counter to another person's conscience, which is influenced and molded by ethnicity and culture.

In chapter 10, the first few verses are important Christological statements identifying Christ as the Rock in the Israelites' exodus. The first generation of Israelites, though released from Egyptian bondage, failed to reach the Promised Land because of their idolatry and immorality. Paul is saying that if he and other Christians do not flee from idolatry and immorality, they may be "disqualified" as well.

Paul's direct identification of the Rock as Christ is striking: "the Rock was Christ" (1 Cor 10:4). By using the past tense ἦν and placing the predicate noun after the verb, thus emphasizing the last word "Christ," Paul declares the preexistence of Christ before his incarnation. He says, in effect, that the Israelites sinned against Christ in the wilderness by committing idolatry and immorality, and the Corinthians are now also in danger of doing so.

Paul describes the history of the Israelites as a *type* (10:6 "type," τύποι; 10:11 "typical," τυπικῶς). The salvation history of the Israelites is a prefiguration of that of the Christians, and the nature of both is the same. Just as the Israelites sinned against Christ by committing idolatry and immorality, the Corinthians are in danger of sinning against Christ by committing idolatry by eating festive meals in pagan temples. The correspondence between the two groups is brought forth by several striking parallels:[24]

---

24. For a good discussion on the use of the Old Testament in this passage, see James W. Aageson, "Written Also for Our Sake: Paul's Use of Scripture in the Four Major Epistles, with a Study of 1 Corinthians 10," in *Hearing the Old Testament in the New*

Pentateuch	Exodus	Corinthians	New Exodus (Salvation in Christ)
Exod 14	Crossing the Red Sea	10:1–2	Baptism
Exod 16	Spiritual food (manna)	10:3	Spiritual food
Exod 17:1–7; Num 20:1–13	Spiritual drink	10:4	Spiritual drink
	Rock		Spiritual rock (Christ)
Num 11:4	Craving for food	10:6	Craving for evil things
Exod 32:6	Idolatry, immorality	10:7	Idolatry, immorality
Num 25	Immorality	10:8	Immorality
Exod 24:11	Eating after covenant	10:16–17	Lord's Supper
Deut 32:17	Sacrifice to demons	10:19–20	Sacrifice to demons
Num 21:6; 25:9	Judgment by God	9:27; 10:22	Possible judgment (on Paul and Corinthians)

Paul cites the exodus experience in order to bring home the severity of giving into temptation, which will lead to "disqualification" from salvation 9:27). Given that demons are real, feasting in pagan temples has spiritual significance. Such feasts are a kind of fellowship with spiritual beings, just as the Lord's Supper is fellowship with the Lord Jesus. As Jesus is one Lord, sharing the Lord's Supper means a Christian is having fellowship with the one Lord. To eat a festive meal in a pagan temple, however, is actually to fellowship with the demons behind the idols in temples. This is idolatry. Paul's admonition culminates in the rhetorical questions: "Shall we provoke the Lord to jealousy? Are we stronger than he?" This echoes Deuteronomy 32, in which God is repeatedly called the Rock (32:4, 18, 30) and the Israelites are censured for provoking God's jealousy by worshipping demons and non-gods (32:17, 21). Just as the judgment of the jealous and strong God on the Israelites is certain (Deut 32:36–43), the Corinthians are in grave danger of losing their salvation if they commit the same sin as the Israelites.

Testament, ed. Stanley E. Porter, McMaster New Testament Studies (Grand Rapids: Eerdmans, 2006), 152–81.

That Jesus Christ is the *one* Lord implies that he cannot and will not put up with idolatry and immorality. "Strong" Corinthians who think there are no idols and thereby have no qualms feasting in pagan temples just as they did prior to conversion are in grave danger. They trespass upon the boundaries of "in-Christ identity": ethnic and cultural identities that one has before conversion should be abandoned if they are of idolatrous or immoral nature.

CONCLUSIONS

The above discussion shows that Paul's view on table fellowship is consistent. His Christology and soteriology contribute to the definition and mark the boundaries of "in-Christ identity" in relation to ethnic identities. The Christological truths emphasized by Paul are "freedom from the Law in Christ" (Galatians), "Christ, as the same Lord of all, acceptance of different ethnicities" (Romans), and "Christ as one jealous Lord" (1 Corinthians). These truths determine how "in-Christ identity" should relate to ethnic identities. We may group the principles under three main points:

1. "In-Christ identity" can be attained only through justification by faith apart from works. This identity takes priority over ethnic identity; therefore, ethnic expressions should never infringe upon this freedom from works.

2. Positively, ethnic expressions should be respected with a view to promoting unity among Christians.

3. Negatively, ethnic expressions should be abandoned if they are idolatrous or immoral in order to prevent the loss of salvation.

Paul's view corresponds to the Apostolic Decree described in Acts 15, in which Gentiles are not required to be circumcised in order to be saved, but must refrain from the eating of strangled meat and blood (measures taken to avoid offending the conscience of the Jewish Christians and thus to promote unity, point 2), idolatry, and immorality (measures both taken to avoid provoking the anger of the jealous God, point 1).

The findings of the above study provide us with a more comprehensive picture than the one discussed by Lo Lung-kwong. We are therefore in a better position to ascertain the implications for Chinese Christian identity. With regard to ancestral worship, such practice should never be seen as good works meriting salvation (point 1). The cultural elements that are not idolatrous should be respected (point 2). For instance, the traditional mourning dress of Chinese (white linen, symbolizing grief) need not be discarded if a Chinese Christian chooses to wear it (currently most Christians wear black). On the other hand, cultural expressions in ancestral worship that are idolatrous in nature should be abandoned (point 3). For instance, the custom of crossing the fire basin in order to receive good luck should be banned.

10

"Who Am I?"

Theology and Identity for Children of the Dragon

Robert J. Priest

My family and I enjoy movies made by the Hong Kong actor and movie producer Jackie Chan. In one movie, Jackie loses his memory and cries out, "Who am I?" For the rest of the movie, he goes by the name "Who am I?"

"Who am I?" is an important question, historically answered by different people in different ways. Who am I? *I am the son of my father, and I bear his surname, Priest. I am the grandson of my mother's father Robert, and my father's father, Joseph. My name is Robert Joseph Priest. I am American, not British; notice my accent. I am a professor; my students call me "Doctor." I am a father; my children call me "Dad." I am a husband; my wife calls me "honey." I am an anthropologist; I write about culture. I am a Christian; I read my Bible, pray, and go to church. I am an evangelical; I subscribe to* Christianity Today *and believe the gospel should be shared. I am a human being—made in the image of God, sinfully flawed, and saved by grace.*

Who am I? How is this question answered in Hong Kong?[1] Some might reply:

---

1. I want to thank Min-Fu Hsu, Paulus Pan, Mark Dominey, Pei Fang Cook, Richard Cook, David Pao, How Chuang Chua, Jonathan Seitz, Nathan Showalter, Carl Brown, Clive Chen, Kevin Yao, and Tenny Li Farnen for providing suggestions, research leads, and correctives to an earlier draft of this chapter. Any errors in the current piece are purely my own.

I am a Hong Konger, a citizen of Asia's world city. As Hong Kongers, our collective identity, our Brand Hong Kong,[2] is portrayed by a catchy image of a dragon—a modern symbol linking us back to an ancient and prized cultural heritage. I am the son of my father, a descendant of my ancestors. I am Han Chinese, born in the year of the dragon. I am modern. I am a Christian.

Our various identities are sometimes difficult to integrate. When I meet strangers and tell them I am an anthropologist who is also a Christian and that I teach seminarians preparing to be missionaries, they are often puzzled and even disturbed. In their minds, one can be an anthropologist and not a Christian or missionary, or one can be a Christian and missionary but not an anthropologist. One cannot and should not attempt to be both. Just as I face interesting challenges in integrating my identities and corresponding commitments, so around the world Christians face diverse challenges related to identity.

When Chinese become Christian, this sometimes raises profound questions about their valued identification with Chinese ancestry, heritage, and culture. Who am I? Does becoming a Christian mean a Chinese person is no longer Chinese? Must such a Christian cease to identify with and honor one's parents and ancestors? And how should Han Chinese, who may proudly claim descent from the dragon, and who may even refer to their own Chinese culture as "dragon culture," respond to the book of Revelation in the Christian Bible that also speaks of the dragon, but which identifies the dragon with Satan, the source of evil? For more than one hundred years, Chinese Christians have heard other Chinese voice the criticism, "One more Christian, one less Chinese." That is, in the minds of many, one must choose between being Christian and being Chinese. One cannot be both. Chinese Christians are not, of course, the only Christians to face profound identity challenges. But such challenges are historically and culturally situated, with Koreans or Japanese or Africans or Europeans experiencing identity issues in their own context in distinctive ways.

To take but one example, as studied by Robert Hefner,[3] nineteenth-century Dutch missionaries in Java framed Christian identity as requir-

---

2. "Hong Kong: Asia's World City," Website. Online: http://www.brandhk.gov.hk/.

3. "Of Faith and Commitment: Christian Conversion in Muslim Java," in *Conversion to Christianity: Historical and Anthropological Perspectives on a Great Transformation*, ed. Robert W. Hefner (Berkeley: University of California Press, 1993), 99–127.

ing that men cut their hair short to signify conversion, adopt European dress, learn to sing using European musical genres, repudiate Javanese shadow plays, and forsake pagan names such as *Ajisaka* for Christian names like Hendrik. Few became Christian. Then one Javanese started a new church requiring that Christian Javanese retain markers of Javanese identity; that men not cut their hair; that birth names be retained; that worship make use of already familiar musical patterns; that shadow plays be regarded as an appropriate way to set forth the biblical message; and that indigenous religious vocabulary be used to communicate biblical truth, with no need for Dutch loan words. This church quickly grew, until Dutch colonialists, threatened by its repudiation of identification with the Dutch, acted decisively against the church by taking property from its leadership. They squelched the movement, simultaneously creating a situation where conversion to Christianity in subsequent decades required embracing a new identity aligned with that of the Dutch colonialists. To be Christian was to be pro-colonialist.

While in some ways extreme, this scenario illustrates a not uncommon pattern in the history of missions. For centuries, European missionaries insisted that converts in certain places such as India, Bangladesh, Africa, or Java renounce the name their parents gave them and take a Christian name instead. Conversion, they insisted, required a change of identity marked by the adoption of a new name. And while Protestants sometimes argued that Christian names must be biblical names, the missionaries themselves often had names like Charles, Helen, or William; these names thus became part of the name set defined as Christian. As recently as the 1950s, European Catholics raised money for missions in Africa under the slogan of "saving black babies." Each person donating a designated amount was allowed to offer a name, such as the name of a deceased grandparent, that the European missionary who received the money was obligated to bestow on a new convert at baptism. African Christians were expected to adopt new identities assigned by Europeans, identities that were supposedly Christian but also simultaneously European. An African Christian wishing to name his son after an African grandfather would be required to renounce this identity link as pagan and to instead accept the name submitted by a European donor. Let me be clear that I am not talking here about African Christian parents' spontaneous and voluntary decision to name their child after a biblical hero or admired missionary. I am talking, rather, about a mode of impositional naming involving issues of power in the context of inappropriate understandings of identity.

When names flowed from Europeans to Africans and when traditional names linking one to his or her own African heritage and ancestry were disavowed as pagan, Christian identity and European identity became confused. Christian identity was defined against the ethnic identity of receiving communities. One was asked to choose between being Christian and being African, between being Christian and being Javanese.

The name change requirement sent the signal that a new Christian's given name was associated with something bad, something inherently unchristian. And indeed, if even an innocent African name such as Nzuzi was considered evil and required abandonment, other elements of African culture and identity, such as the drum, music, and dance, were even more disparaged. That is, the rejection of one identity element (a person's name) signaled a whole manner of assessing aspects of indigenous identity—a mode best described by Niebuhr under the type of "Christ against culture."

Naming is often tied to power and dominion. Adam's naming of the animals was linked to the exercise of dominion. When Babylonian officials gave Daniel and his three friends new names associated with Babylonian deities, this reframing of identity was also an exercise of dominion, of assimilating them into the Babylonian colonial hegemony. In a famous European book from the eighteenth century, after Robinson Crusoe saved the life of a Pacific Islander, he did not ask "What is your name?" Rather, Crusoe said, "I made him know that his name should be Friday." Mythically, Crusoe and many Western colonialists acted as if they were a second Adam, facing an unnamed world that needed naming. Instead of asking, "What is your name?" or "What is the name of this place?" they declared, "I so name you (or this place)." Because the power to name is the power to exercise dominion, Crusoe said, "I taught him to say 'Master,' and then let him know that was to be my name." The story, of course, is fiction. But in a story many European Christians have considered a classic, in which Crusoe shares the Gospel with Friday and Friday voluntarily places his neck under the foot of Crusoe, it is clear that fantasies of missionary evangelization sometimes merge with fantasies of power and cultural and racial superiority. Crusoe constructs for himself and his convert new identities that help to ratify colonial hierarchies of power.

Such issues of power and identity often get skipped in our histories of the church. One thinks of the Genevan fathers who brought their sons to John Calvin's French ministers, wanting to name their sons after themselves, with names such as "Claude." The French ministers insisted that names like Claude were Roman Catholic and unbiblical, and they unilaterally insisted on assigning other names, such as Abraham, at baptism. This was experienced as the usurpation of a parent's right to name his child. Indeed, so resentful, and on occasion violent, did Genevans become at this French usurpation of parental naming prerogatives that John Calvin wondered if an armed guard would not need to be posted at every baptism—protecting the ministers who insisted on assigning names of their own choosing against the wishes of parents.[4] When mission schools admitted only students with "Christian names,"[5] this too constituted hegemony.

When asked to justify the requirement of a name change at conversion, nineteenth-century missionaries pointed to the switch from Saul to Paul in the New Testament. But while missionaries sometimes claimed that this name change marked Saul's conversion, the narrative of Acts continues to refer to "Saul" for years after his conversion and only switches from Saul to Paul in the middle of Paul's first missionary journey. At this point in the Acts narrative—when a Gentile government official named Sergius Paulus calls them in, listens to their message, and believes the Gospel despite having no prior relationship to Jewish religious institutions—several transitions occur. Until this point, systematic evangelism occurred only in the context of Jewish synagogues, with Gentiles evangelized only as an adjunct to ministry with Jews and in the context of the Jewish synagogue. After this conversion, Paul and Barnabas began a pattern of moving from the synagogue out into the community at large in an announced "turning to the Gentiles" (Acts 13:46). This new pattern of independent witness to Gentiles, a pattern forged in the second half of Paul's first missionary journey, involved the opening of "a door of faith to the Gentiles" (Acts 14:27). Judaizers soon learned of this new pattern of Gentile evangelism (perhaps through the return of John Mark, who may have been unhappy with this change of paradigm, to Jerusalem at this

---

4. W. G. Naphy, "Baptisms, Church Riots and Social Unrest in Calvin's Geneva," *Sixteenth Century Journal* 26 (1995) 87–97.

5. Taiye Aluko, "Naming Ceremony in African Independent Churches: A Cultural Revolution," *The Indian Journal of Theology* 35 (1993) 28.

point in the journey), and they followed Paul and Barnabas, attempting to insist that Gentile converts embrace markers of Jewish identity. But the book of Galatians, as well as the Jerusalem Council in Acts 15, each affirm that Gentiles could become followers of Jesus without adopting a Jewish identity.

It as at the point where Sergius Paulus believes, that the text of Acts signals a transition. Until this point, the two names "Barnabas and Saul" are used; after this point, the references are to "Paul and Barnabas." This linguistic shift consists of two elements. First, there is a shift in the order of names, with Barnabas's name, which formerly appeared first, now being listed second. This suggests that Paul is now taking the lead role in this new approach to Gentile missions. Second, the text also transitions from "Saul" to "Paul." "Barnabas and Saul" now becomes "Paul and Barnabas." "Saul" was, of course, a distinctively Jewish name. Indeed, for Saul, who later indicates that he had been "extremely zealous for his ancestral tradition" (Gal 1:14), who took pride in his ethnic identity (cf. Phil 3:7), and who was a Benjaminite named after the first great Benjaminite king in the Old Testament, it would have been natural to cling to the Jewish identity his name represented. He might have perhaps even insisted that his first convert, Paul, change his name to "Saul." But the opposite in fact occurred. As Saul engaged a Gentile world that directly responded to the Gospel, he allowed his own identity to shift, according to the principle of "becoming all things to all people that I may by all means save some" (1 Cor 9:22). Whether the shift from "Saul" to "Paul" involved an actual name change (in which Saul took the name of his first Gentile convert) or more likely, involved a change to a name he already had as a Roman citizen, this apostle to the Gentiles would no longer be known by a Jewish name, but by the Greco-Roman name Paul. The Acts narrative would only briefly switch back to the name "Saul" when Paul was in the exclusively Jewish context of the Jerusalem Council. The people of his day would have understood that the transition from "Saul" to "Paul" involved an ethnically marked transition—a shift comparable today to a change from Guillermo to Bill, or from Charlie to Ziao. That is to say, the biblical narrative describing the name change from "Saul" to "Paul" illustrates the exact opposite of what later missionaries claimed that it demonstrated. No Gentile convert was asked to adopt a Jewish or "biblical name." Even when a convert's given name was explicitly religious, as with Apollos or Hermes, these names did not change upon conversion. This was not part of Paul's theology of conversion. Indeed, Saul, as Paul, a missionary to the Gentile world, embraced a non-Jewish identity that would position him favorably with his non-Jewish audience, and he himself called for no identity changes based purely on human convention or ethnic tradition. For Paul, Gentile conversion did not necessitate a change in ethnic identity to a Jewish one. To require this would be an act of hegemonic disrespect. In fact, Paul vigorously rebuked his fellow-Jew Peter, who personally did not regard Jewish customs as binding even on himself, but who nonetheless "compelled the Gentiles to live like Jews" (cf. Gal 2:14). Similarly, many nineteenth-century missionaries who came from Christian communities that did not themselves hold to a "Christian name" requirement nonetheless imposed such on converts by requiring them to adopt names from the missionaries' home culture. It was in response to this that President Mobutu outlawed the use of "Christian names" in Zaire in 1972. He did so not because the names were Christian, but because they were symbolic of cultural imperialism and a sign of disrespect for African heritage and identity.

Shakespeare wrote, "What's in a name? That which we call a rose, by any other name would smell as sweet." But Shakespeare was wrong. When a nineteenth-century Javanese man named Ajisaka was given the new "Christian name" Hendrik, to his family and friends he now seemed less sweet, less familiar, less trustworthy, more foreign, more threatening, and more of a moral traitor to his own family and people. As Hendrik, Ajisaka lost identifying links to his family, heritage, and ethnic group—and added identifying links and loyalties to a Dutch colonial order. We say in America, "Sticks and stones will break my bones, but names will never hurt me." But, like Shakespeare, we are also wrong. Names have the power either to wonderfully link us to family, parents, community, and friends—or to sever such links. Names do have the power to bring about negative consequences. Names that unnecessarily sever links with family are harmful. Names in a colonial order that require an African to adopt a non-African identity can be harmful. Names that honor a foreign culture can be harmful—and those that dishonor and stigmatize the culture of one's family and community are certainly so. To the extent that evangelization involves a requirement that people choose between being Christian and being Javanese or Chinese, harm results. And, contrary to the belief of many, such requirements are levied without biblical warrant and against the model of the first great missionary and theologian, the

Apostle Paul. Such requirements are, I argue, the result not of faithfulness to biblical theology, but of a failure to read our Bibles carefully, a failure to embrace good theology and missiology.

In looking at naming patterns of nineteenth-century missionaries, I intend merely to illustrate important the fact that the Gospel enters spaces where identities are already well established, and that the ideal relation of identities grounded in Scripture with identities already present is not a simple one to address, and cannot be addressed by a theology that is attentive only to Scripture and philosophy. Rather, there must be a triple hermeneutic: a careful and profound understanding of Scripture and what it reveals about both human and Christian identity, a careful and extensive understanding and knowledge of the identity discourses of any society in which the church is attempting to contextualize its message, and a solid understanding of the culturally-shaped and culturally-contingent identity assumptions of missionaries who first convey the Gospel elsewhere. Historically, it was disciplines such as anthropology, not philosophy, which forged methods and theories for understanding such cultural discursive identity patterns. A theology grounded in the triple hermeneutic described above must make disciplines such as anthropology core conversation partners.

Historically, missionaries did not sufficiently foster the theological reflections necessary for engaging contextual issues of identity. Missionaries did, however, sometimes stress the importance of mission-initiated churches becoming self-supporting, self-propagating, and self-governing. And these three aspects clearly had consequences for how Chinese Christians and their churches were perceived. But self-theologizing was not initially a desired goal. Missionaries thought of theology proper—the systematic, intellectual articulation of the Christian faith—as an acontextual project that was already complete. This is how their own theology professors had presented it to them. One studied the theological writings of Europeans and North Americans, paying minimal attention to the historically and culturally contingent contexts in which these writings were produced. Theological work was therefore not regarded as something to be actively carried out in diverse contexts in a way that was responsive to them.

In the late 1970s and 1980s, Charles Kraft and Paul Hiebert, two notable evangelical Christian anthropologists, began calling for theology to be carried out in dialogue with anthropology, as well as with philosophy.

Philosophy is abstract and acontextual, and theologians needed to begin dialogue with a field of study that fore-grounded human contextual issues. Their writings, addressed to fellow evangelicals, were largely either condemned outright by evangelical theologians, or simply ignored. Kraft's writings, especially, triggered swift and vigorous condemnation from theologians such as Carl F. H. Henry[6] and Kenneth Kantzer,[7] who framed Kraft's writings simply as an attack on biblical authority.

For example, at a 1982 conference held at Trinity Evangelical Divinity School in Deerfield, Illinois, Kantzer warned, in response to issues raised by Charles Kraft, that cultural anthropologists were creating "obfuscation of biblical authority" and that there were some "who wish to create an elite of professional cultural anthropologists who alone are effective to determine the meaning of Scripture for a particular community." He continued, "It's amazing how the church has communicated its message without that professional elite in the past . . . All that the average professional missionary needs of cultural anthropology is one good course." According to Kantzer, rather than study anthropology, the missionary would "do a lot better to study his Bible, learn good methods of exegesis, maybe read a few history books . . . and study theology. The current fad of overemphasizing the significance of cultural anthropology for missionary training is based on false premises as to the difficulty of the problem we face." In short, Kantzer was willing to grant that a professional career missionary could possibly justify a single course in cultural anthropology, but he did not believe the issues posed by human cultural variability posed challenges not easily answered. Furthermore, he sidestepped altogether the argument that theologians (and not just missionaries) need to have a sustained and constructive engagement with anthropology and with variable human cultural contexts.

It is interesting to contrast the views of Kantzer, the theologian, with those of the evangelist Billy Graham concerning this question. Graham was asked at the age of seventy seven whether he had any regrets in life, whether there was anything he might do differently. He replied, "I would

---

6. Carl F. H. Henry, "Review Article: The Cultural Relativizing of Revelation," *Trinity Journal* 1 (1980) 153–64.

7. Kenneth Kantzer, "Authority, Revelation and Contextualization" (presentation at Trinity Evangelical Divinity School's School of World Mission and Evangelism Conference, March 18, 1982).

have studied more. I would have gotten my PhD in anthropology."[8] Graham went on to tell of having majored in anthropology at Wheaton College, which he felt was enormously helpful to him as an evangelist. But while Kantzer suggested missionaries should not take more than a single course in cultural anthropology, Graham indicated that even the amount of anthropology he had taken was not nearly enough, given the challenges of wisely ministering in a diverse world.

While many career missionaries will easily resonate with Billy Graham's sentiments on the challenges and importance of understanding diverse human realities and contexts—and will thus be responsive to calls for constructively engaging the discipline of cultural anthropology—theologically conservative theologians, by contrast, have rather uniformly embrace the sentiments of Kantzer. Some, such as Radical Orthodoxy theologian John Milbank[9] and his followers, formally insist that it would be wrong to attempt to make the social sciences a dialogue partner. Evangelical theologian Alister McGrath,[10] while acknowledging that theologians have historically made philosophy their dialogue partner (their *ancilla theologiae*) and while setting forth a proposal to make the physical sciences a new dialogue partner for theologians (an *ancilla theologiae nova*), nonetheless insisted that the social sciences must not be allowed to play such a role.[11] Evangelical theologians rather consistently exemplify either an oppositional rhetoric vis-à-vis the human sciences, a rhetoric starkly at variance with their positive affirmation of the discipline of philosophy, or they are simply silent on the subject. When some theologians (one thinks of Kevin Vanhoozer or Miroslav Volf) do model helpful new ways of doing theology, their dialogue partners until now have at best included the humanities and cultural studies (a field emergent from the humanities, not from the social sciences). I have not been able to find a single evangelical theologian who writes out of a deep engagement with cultural anthropology as a dialogue partner.

---

8. Colin Greer, "'Change Will Come When Our Hearts Change': An Interview with the Reverend. Billy Graham," *Parade*, October 20, 1996, 6.

9. John Milbank, *Theology and Social Theory: Beyond Secular Reason*, Signposts in Theology (Oxford: Blackwell, 1993).

10. Alister E. McGrath, *A Scientific Theology*, vol. 1 (Grand Rapids: Eerdmans, 2001), 3–34.

11. Ibid., 15–18.

In short, while evangelical missiologists have been calling for contextualized theologizing for a quarter of a century, those who actually teach within evangelical departments of systematic theology articulate and model ways of doing theology that are inhospitable to the dialogue partners needed for knowledgeable contextual responsiveness. Only recently have we begun to see signs of a changing approach among evangelical theologians.[12]

The Christian Gospel provides theological information not only about God, but also about human selves. The call to conversion is a call to recognize and appropriately respond to theological truths about God, but also to recognize, confess, and appropriately respond to theological truths about the self. That is, to become a Christian requires a shift in how one answers the question, who am I?

Who am I? I am not an accident. I am a person, made in the very image of God, created for relationship with God and with others. Who am I? I am a sinner, fatally flawed, deserving of judgment. Who am I? I am mortal and am conscious that I will someday die. Who am I? I am forgiven, have a personal relationship with God, and am destined for eternal life with Him. Who am I? I am gifted by God and given to His body, the church, for service and witness. I have a calling before God. I am an ambassador of the King of Kings, but am also a clay vessel. Who am I? I am one who suffers, and I serve one who suffered on my behalf. Who am I? I am not my own; I have been bought with a price. Who am I? I am a follower of Jesus Christ—saved by grace, and indwelt and empowered by the Holy Spirit.

But while the Christian message affirms many such theological truths about human selves, these truths do not enter spaces that are vacuums with regard to identity, vacuums simply waiting to be filled with meaning. Rather, people around the world throughout time exist and have existed within cultural discursive spaces that have already constructed identities of all sorts—identities tied to gender and to culturally shaped ideas about gender; identities tied to age and to culturally shaped ideas about age; identities tied to wealth, status, and educational

---

12. Cf. David K. Clark, *To Know and Love God: Method for Theology*, Foundations of Evangelical Theology (Wheaton, IL: Crossway, 2003); Kevin J. Vanhoozer, "'One Rule to Rule Them All?' Theological Method in an Era of World Christianity," in *Globalizing Theology: Belief and Practice in an Era of World Christianity*, ed. Craig Ott and Harold Netland (Grand Rapids: Baker Academic, 2006), 85–126.

level; identities linked to skin color or to nationality; identities tied to the sports teams we support; identities tied to ancestry and genealogies and every possible kinship relationship; and identities tied to notions about race, language, accent, musical taste, caste, social class, geographical location, etc. Some identities are proudly embraced, and others are hatefully imposed by others—bringing assumed moral duties and obligations with them. For example, to be a son is not only to have a certain identity, it is to have an identity that prescribes specific ways of engaging people with corresponding identities, such as that of mother or father. These identities and corresponding notions of moral obligation vary significantly from one culture to another.

Theological truths about human selves must thus be instantiated in any given discursive community in ways that formally recognize and appropriately adjust to the discursive identity patterns already present. Christian truths must be appropriately articulated in each context. And since the Gospel is conveyed by fully human messengers, themselves deeply shaped in ways they are not fully conscious of by their societies' culturally contingent discourses on identity, it is not surprising that missionaries have sometimes contributed to profound identity problems faced by new or potential converts.

As mentioned previously, some Chinese ascribe to the equation, "one more Christian, one less Chinese." Many factors contribute to this slogan. Consider a single, small example of what may contribute to this perception for some.

In the lands surrounding Israel, one found mythic stories of sea monsters—Leviathan, Rahab, Tannin, or in Greek *drakōn*—fearsome serpentine creatures, chaos monsters. The image of a snake was central to these, although sometimes crocodilian features were described as present. In medieval Europe one found mythic stories of monsters called "dragons"—described as having the body of a reptile, the wings of a bat, and which breathed out fire. In China, for millennia there have also been mythic stories of *lóng*, a creature described as being comprised of body parts from various animals—the head of a camel, the horns of a stag, body of a snake, talons of an eagle, scales of a carp, etc.

If one examined images of these various creatures—the European dragon, the Chinese *lóng*, the semitic Leviathan, Rahab, or Tannin, and the Greek *drakōn* one would see some similarities between them, but also significant differences. Of course, the meanings of such mythic creatures are not to be discerned simply by staring at drawings of the mythic creatures and describing their physical attributes. Rather, the meanings of each creature are constructed through cultural discourses, and it is only through the study of such cultural discourses that the meanings may be reliably inferred.

European missionaries will have been raised on stories of dragons as vicious greedy creatures that spread plagues, abduct and eat young maidens, who burn homes, and steal cattle or crops. Heroes, like Saint George or Beowulf, are dragon slayers. Virtuous knights rescue virgin princesses from the dragons, killing them.[13] Dragons are things to be killed.

The writers of Scripture often referred to mythic monsters of surrounding cultures, chaos monsters of the sea, as symbols of evil power. And on one occasion, in the New Testament (Rev 12), a mythic monster-snake, a *drakōn* with seven heads and ten horns is identified as Satan, the enemy of God and of all good, the chief leader of all demonic forces. While the physical description of this creature, or of Leviathan, Tannin, or Rahab do not closely correspond to the European dragon image, any assumed equivalence between them is not found to be problematic. When European English speakers read in Isaiah 27:1 that God employs his mighty sword to slay "the dragon," this makes perfect moral sense even in terms of their own European imagery. Dragons are things that ought to be killed. That is what heroes do. But when the New Chinese Version (1992) translates this as *lóng*, with the Christian God a slayer of the dragon, this has other overtones.

While the Chinese *lóng* has both physical similarities and differences with the European dragon and with biblical serpentine monsters, it is at the level of discursive associations that the *lóng* diverges most markedly from the others. The *lóng*, in Chinese discourses and images, is a noble, blessed, auspicious, wise, friendly, powerful being—appropriate for joyful celebrations such as weddings. The *lóng* was historically associated positively with the Chinese emperor. Parents may express a wish for their son to have a glorious future, by saying they "hope the child becomes a dragon" (*wàng zi chéng lóng*). When opening a new home or business, one may invite dragon dancers to help celebrate an auspicious beginning. In New Year's celebrations, the mythic dragon helps drive

---

13. Recent fantasy novels and Hollywood movies are modifying the image of the dragon for Westerners, with dragons now often portrayed in more positive terms.

away evil spirits, ensuring a positive future. *Lóng* appear on everything from rugs or chopsticks to flower garden urns to tie pins and tapestries and pillowcases—and make their cultural appearance in everything from kite flying to weddings to boat races, to feeding the dragon dancers, to the Hong Kong brand, to songs such as "Children/Heirs of the Dragon" by Hou Dejian, "*Lóng de chuán rén*." The Chinese dragon so permeates Chinese culture that at least some Chinese proudly refer to their own culture and heritage simply as "dragon culture." Furthermore, discourses often construct the dragon as a core symbol of Chinese identity, a Durkheimian "collective representation," as in Hou Dejian's popular song of the late 1970s "Children of the Dragon":

> In the ancient Orient, there is a dragon
> The name of this dragon is called CHINA
> In the ancient Orient there is a race
> They are the children [heirs[14]] of the Dragon
> Under the feet of the dragon we grow up
> To be Children [Heirs] of the dragon
> With dark eyes, dark hair and yellow skin[15]
> Forever we will remain "Children [Heirs] of the Dragon"[16]

When translators of the Bible into Chinese reached Revelation 12, and encountered a reference to an apocalyptic vision of a snakelike monster with seven heads and ten horns, a *drakōn*, the translators faced a challenge—how to translate this. While this monster had seven heads, was not said to have four legs, had no feathered tail, no camel head, no catfish feelers and had cultural associations with chaos and evil which were there for the *Leviathan, Tannin, Rahab*, and *Drakōn*, but opposite to associations of the *Lóng*, the translators (beginning with Robert Morrison

14. Author's note: other translators use "heirs" or "descendents" instead of "children."

15. Author's note: Andrea Louie, "Re-territorializing Transnationalism: Chinese Americans and the Chinese Motherland," *American Ethnologist* 27 (2000) 646, 650, explores the ways in which modern Chinese identity is constructed around the racialized themes of sharing dark eyes, dark or black hair, and yellow skin. And again shared ancestry and solidarity are often invoked under the theme of being descendents of the dragon. Louie records a poem (p. 652) from a pamphlet at a 1995 Chinese youth festival, for example: "Descendents of the Dragon with Black Eyes/Gathered under the Blue Sky/Their hearts are linked to each other/They cherish the hope of unity, friendship, progress, and peace."

16. Quoted in Better Hong Kong Foundation, "Millions Singing with One Voice on July 1, 1997." Online: http://www.betterhongkong.org/eng/?section=pressRelease&page=pressReleasedetail&pressRelease_id=115/.

and including all subsequent translations) nonetheless chose to translate this monster as *Lóng*. This decision to translate *Drakōn* as *Lóng* rather than simply as *guai shou* (beast/monster), or "ancient serpent" or even to retain the word from the original text (as English translations do for certain creatures such as Leviathan)—introduced potentially profound ethnic and cultural identity tensions into conversion.

As early at the mid-nineteenth century one can find evidence that Chinese were disturbed by and struggling with this identification of Satan with the Chinese *Lóng*.[17] The fact that this *Lóng* was "red" in Revelation also was easily interpreted as applying to Communist China. Even today this identification of Satan with the Chinese *Lóng* raises challenges. The sociologist Jianbo Huang carried out research with Christian Chinese intellectuals in Beijing and Shanghai at the turn of the twenty-first century, and reports that when they become Christians they are "trapped" in an "identity crisis" which he describes as a "miserable and terrifying experience."[18] While he acknowledges that in theory one can be both a Christian and traditional Chinese, in fact one is seen as converting to a "foreign" religion, and becomes marginalized with reference to one's own culture. He identifies the core identity challenge as summarized in the proud claim to be "offspring of the dragon," a claim that is reconfigured in the Book of Revelation, which he says describes this Chinese dragon as "Satan himself, the ruler of dark forces." He says that "although some Christians hold that the evil dragon in the Bible is not the holy dragon in our culture, this explanation doesn't relieve the confusion and anxiety of the majority of believers." A PhD student of philosophy told Huang, "I love reading Revelation. But every time I get to chapter twelve and chapter twenty I feel upset. It's a feeling I can't describe . . . All these years I've identified the dragon as my ancestor. But I am also a Christian. I really don't know what I should do." Huang concludes, "We can say that his heart-felt situation truly reflects that of most Christians. Almost all the intellectuals that I have contact with have the same feeling. Also, there are some Christians who totally stand by the biblical definition,

---

17. Cf. Franz H. Michael, *The Taiping Rebellion: History and Documents*, vol. 2, University of Washington Publications on Asia (Seattle: University of Washington Press, 1971).

18. Huang Jianbo, "Who Am I?" Identity Tensions among Chinese Intellectual Christians," online: http://www.hartfordinstitute.org/sociology/huang.html/ (paper presented at the annual meeting of the Association for the Sociology of Religion, San Francisco, California, August 14, 2004).

maintaining that they are the same dragon, and that they shouldn't claim themselves "descendents of the dragon."[19]

The noted sociologist of religion Fenggang Yang, in his book *Chinese Christians in America: Conversion, Assimilation, and Adhesive Identities*,[20] discovered similar tensions over the dragon among Chinese Christians in America. Dr. Archie Lee, in his article,[21] "Religious Identity and Cultural Alienation: The Case of Chinese Christianity" describes his own childhood in China when his family converted to Christianity where church members descended on his home insisting that "art, literature, and household items including furniture, beddings, bowls and chopsticks that bore the dragon image, were to be surrendered and then destroyed, smashed and burnt completely in front of the house." He concludes that these Christians required his family to destroy the "symbols of our cultural heritage and especially the symbol of the dragon that once represented blessing and good in the culture of the new converts, but which was regarded as evil and wicked in the western Christian teaching of the time."

That is, when a symbol filled with positive associations and connected with Chinese ethnic identity, when this symbol is now linked through a biblical translation with Satan, the enemy of all good—this is not a minor linguistic act with minimal consequences. Rather, this equating of the dragon in Revelation with the dragon of Chinese heritage and culture, is consequential—seemingly entailing the implication that Han Chinese converts must reframe their valued heritage, culture,

---

19. One example of this view is seen in Chan Kei Thong, *Faith of Our Fathers: God in Ancient China* (Shanghai,: China Publishing Group Orient Publishing Center, 2006). For a more nuanced view, although still critical of the dragon, see Daniel Tong, "Appendix A: Long, The Chinese Dragon," in *A Biblical Approach to Chinese Traditions and Beliefs*, (Singapore: Genesis, 2003), 136–42. For an opposing view of the *lóng* as a holy seraph of God, see Ong Hean-tatt, *The Chinese Pakua: An Exposé* (Selangor Darul Ehsan, Malaysia: Pelandu, 2007). Another positive view of the Chinese dragon is found in the Chinese Christian artist He Qi, who paints a dragon face on the stomach of Moses, which he says represents "the power and unction of the Holy Spirit" [Susan Wunderink, "The Dragon in the Belly: Patriarchs, Judges, and Kings—The Old Testament Meets Beijing Opera in He Qi's Art," *Christianity Today* April 2008, online: http://www.christianitytoday.com/ct/2008/aprilweb-only/117-51.0.html].

20. Yang Fenggang, *Chinese Christians in America: Conversion, Assimilation, and Adhesive Identities* (University Park: Pennsylvania State University Press, 1999), 145ff.

21. Archie C. C. Lee, "Religious Identity and Cultural Alienation: The Case of Chinese Christianity," *Humanities Bulletin* 4 (December 1995) 97–99.

and identity, at its core, not as containing noble and positive elements to be enjoyed and celebrated, but as Satanic. And if the *Lóng*—a central figure in Chinese culture, art, marriage celebrations, heritage and ethnic identity—is really Satan, then prior positive valuations of Chinese ancestry and culture (celebrations, tapestries, art, music, dance, etc.) would seem to be quintessentially evil. To put this in somewhat overstated and extreme terms, if Chinese culture is dragon culture, and if Chinese ethnic identity is framed as being "heirs of the dragon," but if this dragon is really Satan, then the claim that "one more Christian" necessarily results in "one less Chinese" would appear to be subjectively plausible.

In this section of the paper, I have focused on the image of the dragon, not because this is the most important or pressing matter to be addressed, but primarily to illustrate the sort of identity challenges that must be addressed theologically in all different cultural settings. Just as there are some Chinese Christians who experience profound and deep identity challenges as a direct result of the way in which biblical texts and teachings about Satan come into engagement with identity discourses already present within the culture, so in all different settings there are complex and diverse issues raised when new Christian discourses enter social spaces already filled with identity discourses. Unfortunately, if Chinese or African or Korean theologians learn their methods and ideas from American and European evangelical systematic theologians, they will have learned methods that are attentive primarily to biblical texts and to philosophy, but that do not simultaneously interact with the fields of study (such as anthropology) that provide help in understanding the culturally variable human discursive contexts in which the biblical message must be articulated. That is, I believe that Chinese and Africans and Indians and Koreans need theologians who are addressing the distinctive identity challenges and opportunities provided within their own contexts out of a deep understanding of Scripture, but also out of profound skills in understanding the cultures both of their own societies and of the societies that first mediated the gospel to them and/or that continue to mediate theological training to them. A theology that attempts to do this, without an extensive and positive engagement with the disciplines that focus on social and cultural contextual patterns, will fail to provide the help that is needed. But when Chinese evangelical theologians, while retaining a deep knowledge of Scripture and submission to its authority, also direct their efforts towards contextual challenges of identity—honing their own skills in studying and exegeting culture, and doing so through a positive engagement with the human sciences—they will carry out theologizing that serves the Chinese Christian community and that also provides correctives for the global Christian community.

11

Chinese Contextual Theology

A Possible Reconstruction?

DAVID Y. T. LEE

INTRODUCTION

EVANGELICALS UPHOLD THE SUPREMACY and authority of the Holy Scripture. As noted by Anthony Lane, the *sola Scriptura* principle essentially holds that Scripture is the final authority or norm for Christian belief. As Lane acknowledges, the finality of Scripture should always be fiercely defended, but it is not the sole source or resource for theology. Lane further explains that there is no need to regard the *sola Scriptura* principle as antithetical to the validity of church tradition, Christian experience, human reason, or cultural understanding.[1] Without undermining the *sola Scriptura* principle, this paper asserts that it is possible to construct a Chinese theology that regards Chinese culture as an interpretative tool or communication vehicle that may be "allied" with the Bible. As a result, it is hoped that Chinese contextualized theology will be increasingly expressed as a way of religious lifestyle, that is, orthopraxy. The thesis of this paper is that doing Chinese theology beyond our past is to triangulate between the Bible, Chinese culture, and the world of sapiential wisdom.[2] Triangulation means treating both the Bible and

1. A. N. S. Lane, "Sola Scriptura? Making Sense of a Post-Reformation Slogan," in *A Pathway into the Holy Scripture*, ed. P. E. Satterthwaite and D. Wright (Grand Rapids: Eerdmans, 1994), 297–327.

2. *Sapientia* means the ability to go beyond the biblical text to act biblically with judg-

Chinese culture as subjects that interact communicatively with the world of wisdom. The anchor for such triangulation is Christology, specifically the recognition that Jesus Christ is both truly human and truly divine.

This paper will begin with a brief historical sketch of the three Abrahamic faiths, namely Jesuit Christianity, Chinese Hui Islam, and Chinese Judaism in late imperial China. Their methodological adaptations to Chinese culture will then be analyzed. Such evaluations will set the stage for the second part of this paper, which considers the possibility of Chinese theology in the twenty-first century.

LISTENING FROM THE PAST

The three Abrahamic faiths, namely Islam, Judaism, and Christianity, will be examined because they uphold a sacred, written, and authoritative text. A brief historical survey of pre-modern China (around sixteenth- to seventeenth-century Nanjing) will account for their methodologies in adapting to the Chinese tolerant and pluralistic culture.[3]

Jewish Diaspora in Pre-Modern China: Community in Kaifeng

The Jewish community in Kaifeng China had a continuous history for more than 800 years, undisrupted until the mid-nineteenth century.[4] Kaifeng was the capital of the Song Dynasty around the eleventh century. The golden age of the Kaifeng community was during the Ming Dynasty (1368–1644). Chinese Jews studied Neo-Confucianism and were able to enroll in the examinations and earn government positions.[5] They also began to adopt the seven commonly used Chinese surnames while still

---

ment. See Kevin J. Vanhoozer, *The Drama of Doctrine: A Canonical-Linguistic Approach to Christian Theology* (Louisville: Westminster John Knox, 2005), 252. Leonard Swidler defines *sapientia* as the knowledge that comes from experience, resulting in the ability to make judgments. See Leonard Swidler, "A Christian Historical Perspective on Wisdom as a Basis for Dialogue with Judaism and Chinese Religion," *JES* 33 (1996) 558.

3. This period of pre-modern China was chosen because it marked the golden era of Jewish, Jesuit, and Islamic activities. After the eighteenth century, Jesuit missions diminished abruptly, the Jewish community began to disappear, and Islamic rebellion resulted in imperial persecution and massacres.

4. The Kaifeng Jewish community is examined because this community has reliable extant records of its Jewish activities.

5. Xu Xin, "Jewish Diasporic Community in Kaifeng China," in *Jews in Asia: Comparative Perspectives*, ed. Pan Guang, Jewish and Israeli Studies Series 1 (Shanghai: Shanghai San Lian, 2007), 150–52.

loosely networking with other Jewish communities in Ningpo, Hangzhou, and Yangzhou. Reasons given for the decline of the Kaifeng community after the Ming Dynasty include syncretism, Confucianization, social and political upheavals. Both Xu Xin[6] and Stephen Sharot[7] argue that the Kaifeng community's disappearance was mainly the result of social and political factors. Xu asserts that multiple factors—natural horrific floods, suppression by the Qing emperors of both Huis and Jews, and the shifting of commercial prosperity toward the eastern region of China.[8] However, Sharot argues specifically that while the Kaifeng community was acculturated by the syncretistic Chinese religions and the tolerant pluralistic society, it was able to reformulate its Jewish distinctiveness by their communal and congregational religion. For Sharot, the community's extinction was due to the weakening of the imperial Qing government, which could no longer provide a stable base for the continued survival of the Kaifeng community's congregational form of organization.[9] In contrast to Sharot, Ho Wanli argues that it was syncretism that allowed the Kaifeng community to survive for eight hundred years. However, Ho believes its disappearance is solely due to isolation from other Jews and failure to emphasize the Jewish tradition.[10]

Confucianization of the Kaifeng community has been the subject of recent scholarly debate. Initially, Confucianization was supported by various stone inscriptions located in the synagogues. Stone inscriptions regarding Jewish history and teachings dated from the fifteenth to seventeenth centuries indicate a gradual indiscriminate use of overt

---

6. All Chinese names in this chapter follow the usual Chinese tradition of listing the surname first, followed by an additional name or names.

7. Stephen Sharot, "The Kaifeng Jews: A Reconsideration of Acculturation and Assimilation in a Comparative Perspective," *Jewish Social Studies: History, Culture, Society* 13 (new series [2007]) 179–203. While focusing on the Kaifeng Jews, Sharot also compares the adaptation of the Jesuits with that of the Hui Muslims in pre-modern China. However, he places too much emphasis on the social and political upheaval in explaining the disappearance of the Kaifeng Jewish community.

8. Xu Xin, *The Jews of Kaifeng, China: History, Culture and Religion* (Jersey City, NJ: Ktav, 2003), 47–61.

9. Sharot's argument is that "a minority group may retain its cohesiveness and social boundaries *because of* its extensive acculturation." Sharot, "Kaifeng Jews," 198–99. Sharot defines acculturation as "over a delimited period, the loss of distinctive beliefs and practices in the religious minority and the adoption of beliefs and practices of the host societies." See Sharot, "The Kaifeng Jews," 182.

10. Ho Wanli, "Jews in China: A Dialogue in Slow-Motion," *JES* 40 (2003) 199.

Neo-Confucianism. Donald Leslie points out that the "terminology of the Chinese inscriptions from the synagogue is highly Confucian... sometimes Jewish in Confucian garb... We hardly ever find any passages from the Jewish Law translated into Chinese."[11] Leslie's observation is further supported by Zhang Wianhong, who examined the inscriptions one by one. He asserts that inscriptions from 1676 and 1679 to 1688 indicated a mere record of Jewish history and an ever-increasing tendency toward identification of Jewish practices with Neo-Confucianism. For Zhang, there were no external pressures that forced the Jews to assimilate. Rather, the Kaifeng community gave up its Jewish identity due to, firstly, voluntary Confucianization with the Chinese losing their Jewish distinctiveness; secondly, lack of Jewish hall educational system and the failure to perpetuate their Jewish faith; and, lastly, no Chinese translations of the Torah and other significant Jewish literature and thus losing understanding of the authoritative texts.[12]

Andrew Plaks likewise analyzes the inscriptions' concepts of God and cosmology. He acknowledges the presence of various Neo-Confucian connotations, such as replacing the notion of God with the concept of heaven (*tien*) and the frequent references to "the way" (*dao*).[13] However, Plaks rejects the idea of simple assimilation. He regards the interaction between Kaifeng Jews and pre-modern China as a "creative cultural interaction." After a brief survey of recent scholarship by some leading Christian,[14] Chinese,[15] and Jewish[16] scholars on this subject,

---

11. Donald Leslie, *The Survival of the Chinese Jews: The Jewish Community of Kaifeng*, T'oung pao. Monographie 10 (Leiden: Brill, 1972), 102.

12. Zhang Qianhong, "From Judaism to Confucianism: Studies on the Internal Causes for the Assimilation of the Kaifeng Jewish Community," 世界宗教研究 [*Studies in World Religions*] (2007) 114–23.

13. Andrew H. Palks, "The Confucianization of the Kaifeng Jews: Interpretations of the Kaifeng Stelae Inscriptions," in *The Jews of China*, vol. 1, *Historical and Comparative Perspectives*, ed. Jonathan Goldstein (Armonk, NY: Sharpe, 1999), 41.

14. Daniel Chirot and Anthony Reid, ed., *Essential Outsiders: Chinese and Jews in the Modern Transformation of Southeast Asia and Central Europe*, Jackson School Publications in International Studies (Seattle: University of Washington Press, 1997); Hyman Kublin, ed., *Jews in Old China: Some Western Views* (New York: Paragon Book Reprint Corp., 1971).

15. Sidney Shapiro, ed., *Jews in Old China: Studies by Chinese Scholars* (New York: Hippocrene, 2001); Xun Zhou, *Chinese Perceptions of the "Jews" and Judaism: A History of the Youtai* (Richmond: Curzon, 2001).

16. Michael Pollak, *Mandarins, Jews and Missionaries: The Jewish Experience in the Chinese Empire* (Philadelphia: Jewish Publication Society of America, 1980).

Shalom S. Wald (following Xu, Sharot, Ho, and others) argues that the Kaifeng community disappeared as the result of a combination of various cultural and political factors including repeated disasters and the general turmoil and misery of the nineteenth century. Wald concludes: "There is no single, mono-causal reason for the disappearance of the Jewish community of Kaifeng. The so-called 'Confucianization' of the Jews, long believed to be the dominant reason for their disappearance, followed a pattern of cultural interaction that could also be found in other places and periods of Jewish history. Confucianization alone was not a death-sentence of Judaism."[17]

Jesuits in Pre-Modern China

The most well-known Catholic missionary to pre-modern China is Matteo Ricci (1552–1610).[18] Ricci took time to learn and research the Chinese geography, technology, and culture of his time. He appreciated some aspects, but found others were not up to European standards. Ricci embarked upon a program of Confucian-Christian synthesis, studying and translating Confucius's classics. He rejected Neo-Confucianism because of its pantheistic interpretation of God and, in response, synthesized the moral philosophy of classical Confucianism. This philosophy sought to foster moral self-cultivation and economic stability of the state and family. Thus, Ricci's synthesis was careful and strategic. Confucianism's five social relations, *Wu lun*, was consistent with Christian moral ethics. Ricci wrote that from "the very beginning of their history it is recorded in their writings that they recognized and worshipped one supreme being whom they called the King of Heaven . . ."[19] In Ricci's synthesis, classical Confucianism provided the social and moral ingredients for life whereas Christianity provided the spiritual ingredients. It is important to note that his synthesis was fairly accommodating to Chinese pagan and ancestral rites, and Ricci recognized that his strategy might there-

17. Shalom S. Wald, "The 'Confucianization' of the Jewish Community of Kaifeng: Jewish and Non-Jewish Historical Perspective," in *Jews in Asia: Comparative Perspectives*, ed. Pan Guang, Jewish and Israeli Studies Series 1 (Shanghai: Shanghai San Lian, 2007), 145.

18. Matteo Ricci is selected because of his strategic accommodation of Confucianism and the way in which his converted Chinese-Christian literati continued his Confucian-Christian synthesis.

19. David E. Mungello, *Curious Land: Jesuit Accommodation and the Origins of Sinology*, Studia Leibnitiana. Supplementa 25 (Stuttgart: Steiner, 1985), 63–64.

fore not be acceptable to all. The Jesuit program of accommodation in China was very successful, in part due to Ricci's articulate work in high standard literary Chinese and in part due to the Jesuits' importation of European science into China. The program declined with papal decrees in 1715 and 1742 that banned the Chinese Rites and prohibited further debate of the Rite Controversy.[20]

Erik Zürcher notes that the concept of God in the Confucian term *tien* (heaven) was used in western Jesuit writings in a way that was very similar to the Jewish inscriptions found in the Kaifeng community, which predated the Jesuits by more than 70 years.[21] Adaptation was unavoidable and did not necessarily result in Confucianization. Zürcher argues that Western Jesuits did not fully accommodate Confucianization because their writings insisted on the basic dogmas of the Christian creed. However, the same could not be argued for the converted Chinese Christian literati. Wang Xiaochao studied the writings of several influential first-generation Chinese Christian apologists, in particular Xu Guangqi (1562–1633). According to Wang, Xu asserted that in addition to the God of heaven, there were many other Christian 'gods.' The Virgin Mary was a Christian goddess. Most troublesome was Xu's concept of the Trinity, which held that Jesus was simply synonymous with God.[22] Undoubtedly, the parallels between Christian ethics and Confucianism facilitated the Jesuits' mission.[23] Due to doctrinal incompetence, Xu and other Chinese Christian literati began an era of Sinicization of Christianity.[24] Progressively, the Chinese Christian literati saw themselves

---

20. For an account of the Rites Controversy, see D. E. Mungello, "An Introduction to the Chinese Rites Controversy," in *The Chinese Rites Controversy: Its History and Meaning*, ed. D. E. Mungello, Monumenta Serica Monograph Series 33 (Nettetal: Steyler, 1994), 3–14.

21. Erick Zürcher, "Jesuit Accommodation and the Chinese Cultural Imperative," in *The Chinese Rites Controversy: Its History and Meaning*, ed. D. E. Mungello, Monumenta Serica Monograph Series 33 (Nettetal: Steyler, 1994), 34.

22. Wang Xiaochao, *Christianity and Imperial Culture: Chinese Christian Apologetics in the Seventeenth Century and Their Latin Patristic Equivalent*, Studies in Christian Mission 20 (Leiden: Brill, 1998), 187–88.

23. Wan Junren, "Why Was It Easier for Christianity to Enter into Chinese Culture? The Close Cultural Relationship between Religion and Ethics according to Matteo Ricci's Entry," in *Christianity and Chinese Culture: A Sino-Nordic Conference on Chinese Contextual Theology*, ed. Miika Ruokanen and Paulos Huang (Beijing: China Social Sciences Press, 2004), 103–23.

24. The same cannot be said of another influential Chinese Christian literati, Yang Tingyun (1562–1627). See N. Standaert, *Yang Tingyun: Confucian and Christian in*

and their Christian teachings as entirely consistent with Confucianism and Neo-Confucianism.²⁵ D. Mungello argues that these Chinese apologists saw Christianity as part of, if not the fulfillment of, Neo-Confucian orthodox thought.²⁶

Islam in Pre-Modern China

Soon after the death of the prophet Muhammad, Islam was spread into China by traders via the ancient and well-known Silk Road to Northwestern China, as well as by sea traders traveling to seaports in Southeastern China. In the seventeenth century, Nanjing remained prosperous. Muslims numbered around one hundred thousand. Educated Hui Muslims were well trained in both Chinese and Islamic philosophy. The key feature of sixteenth- and seventeenth-century Chinese Islam was vigorous scholarly activity by the Chinese Muslim literati such as Wang Daiyu (1573–1619), Ma Zhu (1640–1711), Liu Zhi (1662–1730), and Ma Dexin (1794–1874). This activity produced scholarly Muslim literature in Chinese and was paralleled by the impressive development of the

---

Late Ming China, Sinica Leidensia 19 (Leiden: Brill, 1988); Xiaolin Zhang, 張曉林著, 天主實義與中國學統, 上海: 學林出版社 *[The True Meaning of the Lord of Heaven and Chinese Philosophical Study: Interaction of Culture and Interpretation]* (Shanghai: Shanghai Century Press, 2005), 211–51. Yang Tingyun is argued to have developed Confucian monotheism.

25. Wang Dingan argues that Xu Guangqi accepted Christianity because he lost confidence in his own Confucian heritage—that is, the school of mind (Xin Xue), and he (Xu) preferred science and theology offered by the Jesuit missionaries. Xu's theology, then, became very pluralistic due to his former school-of-mind training. Wang Dingan, "To Achieve Unification because of Difference: The Role Played by Xin Xue in the Cultural Communication between China and the West in Ming and Qing Dynasty," *Logos and Pneuma* 27 (2007) 149–51.

26. D. E. Mungello, *The Forgotten Christians of Hangzhou* (Honolulu: University of Hawaii Press, 1994), 144. Liu Yunhua wrote a substantial work on the Jesuit interpretation of Confucianism and subsequent reinterpretations of Ricci's writings by converted Chinese literati. Liu's argument is that Ricci avoided the differences between Christianity and Confucianism and strategically emphasized the similarities. Subsequent converted Chinese Christian literati did likewise. For Liu, there was no genuine synthesis, and Chinese Christian literati did not undergo any Confucianization. Liu Yunhua, *The Circularity of Interpretation* (Beijing: Beijing University Press, 2005), 6–9. His argument is not tenable because evidences from primary sources by these literati have indicated otherwise. See Wang Xiaochao, *Christianity and Imperial Culture: Chinese Christian Apologetics in the Seventeenth Century and Their Latin Patristic Equivalent*, Studies in Christian Mission 20 (Leiden: Brill, 1998); N. Standaert *Yang Tingyun: Confucian and Christian in Late Ming China*, Sinica Leidensia 19 (Leiden: Brill, 1988).

scripture hall educational system in all major Chinese cities.[27] The Hui Muslim literati's goal was Islamic reform by translating the sacred text and popularizing the educational hall system based in the mosque.[28]

Wang Daiyu's goal was to use Neo-Confucianism to explicate and propagate Islamic faith. He defended his approach by arguing that words and languages were merely earth and wood. These were included among the materials to build the mosque. For Wang Daiyu, the motive and purpose of such usage were just the tools.[29] Born in Yunnan, Ma Zhu traveled widely in China because of political uprising in his birthplace. He tried three times to submit his works to the Qing court and hoped to win imperial approval. His motive was to gain legitimate status for Islam once imperial approval was granted. Liu Yihong asserts that Ma Zhu's main goal was to illustrate that both Neo-Confucianism and Islam are mutually illuminating traditions.[30] In Liu's study of these important Hui

---

27. For a short history of the Scripture hall educational system, see Li Xinghua, et al., *History of Islam in China*, Zhe xue zong jiao yan jiu xi lie (Beijing: Chinese Academy of Social Science Press, 1998), 415–54.

28. A recent study by Zvi Ben-Dor Benite based on primary sources confirms the Islamic educational movement involved thousands of Muslims between the mid-sixteenth and eighteenth century. Zvi Ben-Dor Benite, *The Dao of Muhammad: A Cultural History of Muslims in Late Imperial China*, Harvard East Asian Monographs 248 (Cambridge: Harvard University Asia Center, distributed by Harvard University Press, 2005). Benite believes that the emerging and flourishing Hui Muslim literary work was not due to accommodation of Islam into Chinese culture. Rather, these literati presented their scholarship out of the context of their educational networks. The primary source is known as the *Register of Lineage and Transmission of Classical Learning*, or named by Benite as genealogy, authored by Zhao Can prior to 1697. This work consists of twenty-six chapters and three appendixes, covering 150 years between 1550 and 1700. It is a study of various networks with biographical details of some teachers and scholars. Benite, *Dao*, 30–31. Another source is Yuan Guozuo's (b. 1717) bibliography, namely, *An Introduction of Collected Islamic Books*, from 1780. See Benite, *The Dao of Muhammad*, 155. Yuan also published Liu Zhi's books. Yuan assumed the task of compiling a bibliography of Muslim Chinese books written up to his time. In addition, he also provided biographical information on these authors and their networks (teacher-student or intellectual relationships). See ibid., 27, 154–59.

29. The modern scholar Liu Yihong regards Wang Daiyu's methodology as "using Neo-Confucianism to explain Islam." See Liu Yihong, 劉一虹著, 回儒對話, 北京: 宗教文化出版社 *The Dialogue between Confucianism and Islam* (Beijing: Religion and Culture Press, 2006), 115.

30. Ibid., 117–21. Sinicization of Chinese Muslims may be defined simply as the acculturation and penetration of Han culture into the Hui daily life.

Muslim literati, she fails to note the importance of Muslim cultural and scholarly networking based on mosques in major cities.[31]

Again, the majority of scholarly debate focuses on the Confucianization of Islam in late imperial China.[32] Was Islam in China tempered by Neo-Confucianism in the seventeenth century? Liu Yihong's comparative work between Chinese Islam and Neo-Confucianism provides a methodological analysis of the works by Wang Daiyu, Liu Zhi, and Ma Dexin. She argues that three models of dialogue can be identified. Firstly, Wang Daiyu used Neo-Confucianism to explicate Islam—that is, he explained the doctrine of Islam through Neo-Confucianism. Wang Daiyu nevertheless maintained that Islam was unique. Secondly, Liu Zhi perceived Neo-Confucianism and Islam as mutually complementing each other. Thirdly, Ma Dexin believed that Islam could enhance Neo-Confucianism. For example, Islam enriched certain aspects of Neo-Confucianism, especially Islamic teaching on the afterlife.[33] Thus, the three models are ones of explication, mutual complement, and enhancement, respectively. Although Liu Yihong's model is perceptive in nature, the conclusion of her study at the end of her book seems one-sided and contrary to her data.

> While it is necessary [for the Chinese Muslim literati] to integrate Islamic and traditional Chinese philosophy, certain unsolvable problems of Islamic philosophy can be better explained by borrowing the wisdom of Chinese thought. Mystery is then solved and propagation of Islam is then enabled. This lays the foundation for Chinese Islam to spread and develop. The creative element of Chinese Islamic thought is due to the result of dialogue between cultures and civilizations.[34]

---

31. Benite has made distinctive contributions in this area. He argues that Chinese Muslim scholarship in the seventeenth century must be understood "against the backdrop of broad Chinese intellectual trends and within the context of their intellectual networks, educational system, lineage, and pedagogy." See Benite, *The Dao of Muhammad*, 123. He also insists that the Muslim school "has its starting point a filiation in Islam but insists that Islam be viewed through the lenses of dominant Chinese cultural categories" (ibid., 125).

32. Jean A. Berlie, *Islam in China*, translated by Min Chang, Zhongguo zong jiao ji ben qing kuang cong shu (Bangkok: White Lotus, 2004), 8.

33. Liu Yihong, *The Dialogue between Confucianism and Islam*, 11–12.

34. Ibid., 178.

On one level, Liu Yihong argues that Hui Islam is enhanced and enriched by Chinese religious thought. On another level, the articulate, masterful, and architectonic system of Neo-Confucianism provides not only the linguistic and conceptual tools to reveal the meaning of difficult Islamic terms, but also enables traditional Arabic and Persian Islamic metaphysical terms to be imbued with fresh meanings, with the ability to solve mystery. Such localized Islam with Chinese characteristics[35] is understood as Confucianized Islam. Liu Yihong's view represents a consensus among many scholars that Chinese Islam is localized and qualitatively different from its Middle Eastern origin.

An opponent to the majority view is explicated by Zheng Wenquan. Zheng chose the Islamic reformer Liu Zhi (1662–1730) as the focus of his study. Zheng emphatically disagrees with the common consensus that Hui Islam in pre-modern China underwent Confucianization. His main argument is that the concept of God (i.e., the "Real One") does not originate from Neo-Confucianism, as the majority view asserts. Zheng maintains, rather, that this concept already existed in Sufi Islam in thirteenth-century Eastern Asia. Secondly, it is not so much that Islamic philosophy was Confucianized, but that Liu Zhi's work actually reinterpreted the well-known medieval Islamic theologian Ibn Arabi's cosmology and humanity that were resonant with Neo-Confucianism at that time. Thirdly, while Liu Zhi used plenty of Neo-Confucian terms, the dynamic meaning of the translated terms remains Islamic and not Chinese. It was just natural for Liu Zhi to use Neo-Confucian linguistic tools because they were the only ones available. Furthermore, Zheng argues that the Hui Muslim literati in the sixteenth and seventeenth centuries achieved the beginning of a new age of Chinese Islamic philosophy for the Hui. This existential Islamic philosophy in the Chinese language context included primarily a re-presentation of Ibn Arabi-like philosophy and secondarily a dialogue with non-Arabi philosophy current at that time.[36]

The most persistent opponent to a superficial reading of seventeenth-century Islamic reformers work is another Chinese scholar, Yang Zhongdong. He has conducted several studies comparing Zhu Xi and

---

35. The following phrase is commonly found in popular Chinese religious literature: "Islam with Chinese characteristics."

36. Zheng Wenquan, "Islamic Philosophy in China," Online: http://arts.cuhk.edu.hk/~hkshp/zhesi/zs7/gart3.htm/.

Liu Zhi and also investigated Liu Zhi's own Sufism. Yang emphatically asserts that while Liu Zhi quite often used Neo-Confucian terms, he infused such terms with Islamic meanings. While Liu Zhi's teachings on the return of humanity and reunion with the divine being via the Sufi path might have parallels with Zhu Xi's principle *li*, Liu clearly had a specific and different concept in mind than did Zhu. Thus, Yang asserts that familiar Neo-Confucian terms did not carry the same meaning after Liu's redefinition.[37] Consistent with Zheng Wenquan, Yang argues that Liu Zhi's Islam was firmly rooted in Sufi mysticism. He also traces the Sufi source of Liu's concept of divine effusion. The source was *Mirsad* and was unrelated to Neo-Confucianism's humanistic concepts of *li* and *qi*, or *yin* and *yan*.[38] These Neo-Confucian terms were used to interpret Ibn Arabi's principle of divine effusion in Liu's Sufi sources. Yang's conclusion is that Liu's Islam is existential Sufi Islam. Liu edited, adapted, and translated his source into Chinese.[39] For Yang, then, it is permissible to say that the Chinese language context affected Liu's choice and edition of Sufi source materials. However, it cannot be said that Liu Confucianized his Islamic source materials.

A Preliminary Comment

The above brief comparative study is significant because little research has been done comparing the three Abrahamic faiths in seventeenth-century pre-modern China. While the historical contexts were localized in famous ancient cities such as Nanjing and Beijing, these faiths shared very similar social, political, linguistic, cultural, religious, and philosophical contexts. Their different responses to acculturation, assimilation, and Confucianization are informative in formulating a Chinese theology beyond the past into the future. The Chinese followers of each faith were under tremendous syncretistic pressure to Confucianize in their local pluralistic settings.

37. Yang Zhongdong, "Pilot Study of Liu Zhi's Idealism in Life and Difference between Liu Zhi and Zhu Xi," *Journal of Xinjiang University (Social Science Ed.)* 29:1 (2001) 55–56. Yang Zhongdong, "Similarity in Forms and Dissimilarity in Content: A Comparative Study of Liu Zhi and Zhu Xi," *Journal of Xinjiang University* 31.1 (2003) 48–51.

38. Yang Zhongdong, "Mirsad and Liu Zhi on the Creation of the Universe," *Journal of Ningxia University (Social Science Ed.)* 24.4 (2002) 26.

39. Yang Zhongdong, "Arabian Principles of Nature and Sufist Mysticism," *Journal of Xinjiang University (Social Science Ed.)* 30.1 (2002) 86–90.

The Kaifeng community survived for more than 800 years in China. Such a history is unique for Diaspora Jews outside Palestine. The community's survival is most likely due to its constant reformulation of Jewish distinctiveness based on a synagogue-type community. Its disappearance is not solely due to Confucianization, but may be explained by various other factors. Illiteracy in the Hebrew language may likely have played a more significant role than previously thought.

The Jesuits' program of synthesis declined around 1710, after more than 100 years of mission success. Ricci's success was due to his careful interpretation of the Chinese culture and strategic adaptation of Biblical truth by selective use of Confucian philosophy. Another reason for his success was his explication of Biblical truths using exquisite Chinese. Ricci did not compromise any essential Christian doctrines while making great efforts to become a learned scholar of Chinese culture. He was a committed missionary, articulate Bible interpreter, and effective cultural agent. The Jesuits' program ended primarily due to political forces, rather than Confucianization.

While Hui Islam suffered regular setbacks, including political massacre by the imperial army and religious intolerance by the Hans in late imperial China, the religion gradually grew after Hui reform in the seventeenth century. Several historical factors deserve careful deliberation. Firstly, great emphasis is placed on transmission of sacred text into indigenous language. The authority of sacred text was not diminished by translation or transmission. Rather, this effect of reform made the Islamic faith more distinctive in the Chinese culture.[40] Secondly, while the fear of acculturation was real and the tremendous power of

---

40. Benite briefly compares the contextualization of Christianity and Islam between Chinese Christian and Muslim literati in the seventeenth century. Chinese Christian apologists such as Yang Tingyun in the seventeenth century had to make sense of Christianity through Chinese categories. "The process by its very nature was a binary or, at the very least, dialogic one, because two separate entities, one 'Chinese' and one 'foreign.'" However, the Chinese Muslim reformers never configured the relationship between China and Islam as oppositional. In addition, the major advantage of the Chinese Muslim literati was the accompanying educational network that further "underscored their sense of themselves as true members of Chinese literati culture." It is important to note that such a widespread and complex education system in major Chinese cities allowed the Muslim Chinese reformers "a powerful sense of themselves as members of a community of knowledge, tied together by familial, geographic, and pedagogical ties, which behaved according to the norms of Confucian literati society." See Benite, *The Dao of Muhammad*, 169–70.

Sinicization should not be underestimated, the Islamic reformers demonstrated that faith and culture are not necessarily in antithesis.[41] Rather, the Neo-Confucian values, lexicons, anthropology, and philosophy were, and continue to be, exploited in an effort to present Islam as a credible religious and distinctive faith in a pluralistic society.

This first part of this chapter has set the stage for its remainder. Valuable lessons are to be learnt from the three Abrahamic faiths in pre-modern China. Interactive relationships exist among the urgent need for careful transmission of sacred text into indigenous meaningful and contemporary language, the ubiquitous and transformative influence of indigenous culture, the ongoing reformation of the local religious community, the necessary networking of different communities with key religious bases in major strategic cities acting as communication hubs, the vital importance of community education systems linking with nationwide networks, and the constant reformulation of religious distinctiveness in various cultural settings. We shall probe into such interactive relationships with a helpful hermeneutical analysis as put forward by Kevin Vanhoozer.

THE BIBLE AND CULTURAL IDENTITY

Hermeneutical Methodology

In his earlier research, Kevin Vanhoozer studied the hermeneutics of Paul Ricoeur. Vanhoozer believes that Ricoeur's hermeneutical philosophy has opened up the world of the text and its role in the transformation of the reader's world. Vanhoozer cautiously supports some aspects of Ricoeur's hermeneutic philosophy. For Vanhoozer, the sacred text is more than a mere collection of propositional revelations. Firstly, Vanhoozer explains that orthodoxy is not merely a systematization of information contained in the biblical statements. In addition, doctrines are not written in the language of heaven, but in time-bound and culture-bound languages, governed by the dialogue we find in Scripture. Interpretation of Scripture is important, and so is the culture. Readers should be active when they

---

41. Liu Zhi and other reformers portrayed the prophet Muhammad as a sage or righteous ruler. Thus, Islam is not so much a foreign culture, but is part of Chinese knowledge itself. The "quintessential category of the Muslim world—the prophet—is in the Chinese Muslim instance converted into the quintessential category of China's intellectual elite—the sage" (ibid., 171).

read the Bible. Vanhoozer states, "What the reader receives according to Ricoeur is not the author's intention but the 'world of the text'—that is, a proposed way of being-in-the-world. Reading is a process by which the world of the text intersects with the world of the reader. Interpretation is fulfilled only when the 'world' is appropriated through the words. The act of reading is thus a war of the worlds: 'Reading is, first and foremost, a struggle with the text.'"[42]

Readers should seek to ascertain the nature of the text's communicative intent before making attempts at appropriation. Readers should be active in the sense that they should accept, appropriate, and respond responsibly to the sacred text. Clearly, Vanhoozer asserts a close relationship between the communicative action of the text and the responding appropriation of its readers. Thus, when a text is transmitted and interpreted, interpretation "is doubly part of theological work: not only the Word but the world itself must be interpreted."[43]

Secondly, Vanhoozer believes firmly that transmission of text to different cultures must be done cautiously with full recognition of the local culture. Contextualization, for Vanhoozer, is not primarily a matter of communication: decoding the essential components of truth from the host culture and encoding it to a new culture. Vanhoozer asserts, rather, that cultural adaptation involves actually *doing* theology in a new context.[44] A major component of doing theology is to interpret the meaning of the local culture. For Vanhoozer, culture is itself a text that calls for interpretation.[45] It is made up of works and worlds of meaning.[46] He even coined the term cultural text, which refers to any human work that, precisely because it is something done purposefully and not by reflex,

---

42. Kevin J. Vanhoozer, *First Theology: God, Scripture & Hermeneutics* (Downers Grove: InterVarsity, 2002), 243. See also Vanhoozer, "Paul Ricoeur," in *Dictionary for Theological Interpretation of the Bible*, ed. Kevin J. Vanhoozer (London: SPCK, 2005), 693.

43. J. Vanhoozer, *First Theology*, 309.

44. Kevin J. Vanhoozer, "'One Rule to Rule Them All'? Theological Method in an Era of World Christianity," in *Globalizing Theology: Belief and Practice in an Era of World Christianity*, ed. Craig Ott and Harold A. Netland (Grand Rapids: Baker Academic, 2006), 100–101.

45. Vanhoozer, *First Theology*, 316.

46. Kevin J. Vanhoozer, "What Is Everyday Theology? How and Why Christians Should Read Culture," in *Everyday Theology. How to Read Cultural Texts and Interpret Trends*, ed. Kevin J. Vanhoozer et al., Cultural Exegesis (Grand Rapids: Baker Academic, 2007), 26.

bears meaning and calls for interpretation. Text is equated with meaningful action, and a library is like a culture where "texts are classified by value and shelved in corporate memory."[47] For Vanhoozer, then, culture is not a static and neutral human network of events, traditions, arts, science, history, and philosophy. Culture is instead quite dynamic, possessing the ability to communicate, express, objectify human concerns and even to transform humanity. It embodies the worldviews of all who are in that culture.

How does culture influence us? It is "not by explicit arguments but rather by displaying them in concrete forms. The world-of-the-text is often not demonstrated by logic but displayed in the products and practices that comprise our everyday life."[48] Any translator of sacred text or even any cross-cultural worker is a cultural agent. Not only should such an agent know his own theology well, he must also be able to read and interpret the culture. In addition, Vanhoozer asserts that a cultural agent should never work alone. He should work with his own community of interpreters. As a corporate body, they work to create forms of life that correspond to the scriptural teaching in contemporary cultural contexts.[49]

Thirdly, Vanhoozer argues emphatically that the proper end of theology or theological hermeneutics is sapiential systematics. Because the Bible is more than a book of written information, the reader who interprets it will have wisdom. Wisdom is "lived knowledge, performance knowledge. The ultimate justification for the study of theology is that doctrine is good for our selves and good for our souls . . . the most important preliminary question is how to become right with God."[50] Vanhoozer asserts that anyone doing theology, whether cross-culturally or systematically, must help people of faith obtain wisdom. That is, he or she should not merely produce a literal translation or theoretical system of knowledge, but must cultivate followers who learn and embody sapiential systematics.[51] Taking into full consideration the authority of the

---

47. Vanhoozer, *First Theology*, 314.

48. Vanhoozer, "What Is Everyday Theology?" 51. An example given by Vanhoozer is the world of advertisements. It is a world in which one can seemingly succeed because of the clothes one wears or the drugs one takes to be happy.

49. Vanhoozer, "What is Everyday Theology?" 55.

50. Vanhoozer, *First Theology*, 40.

51. Vanhoozer, "On the Very Idea of a Theological System: An Essay in Aid of

sacred text and the transformative role of the cultural setting, wisdom is the ability to say and do what is religiously fitting.

The Bible as Divine Discourse and Propositional Truth

Vanhoozer's methodological approach is theodramatic systematics by triangulating Scripture, church, and world.[52] Firstly, he argues that Scripture is the church's theodramatic script that governs Christian doctrine. As Scripture is played out as drama, people are drawn into action. Thus, knowledge of God always results in evangelical action, creating a church that embodies the truth of Jesus Christ.[53] Secondly, Vanhoozer also emphasizes the important role of the Holy Spirit. It is the Spirit speaking in and through Scripture that holds Scripture, the church, and the world together. Alternatively put, theodrama triangulates the Spirit's speaking in Scripture, the belief practices of the church, and the world made new in Jesus Christ. It is not the community's discourse that is primary. Rather, God's discourse or canonical triangulation is the norm for ecclesial triangulation. Vanhoozer emphasizes that it is the divinely authored biblical discourse that has epistemic primacy. The vocation of the church, therefore, is to embody the Bible in new contexts and tradition is conceived in terms of Trinitarian deed.[54] Undoubtedly, the strength of Vanhoozer's argument is that whereas he upholds the *sola Scriptura* principle, he also emphasizes that the Bible has a built-in "sapiential norm that provides direction for one's fitting participation in the great evangelical drama of redemption."[55] That is, if the Bible is identified as a divine discourse, it would invariably lead to Christians' participation in the life of the church and testimony of God's kingdom in various cultural settings of the world.

Quite often, Vanhoozer asserts that the Bible in its canonical context is not merely propositional information.[56] Does he diminish the

---

Triangulating Scripture, Church, and World," in *Always Reforming: Explorations in Systematic Theology*, ed. A. T. B. McGowan, 182.

52. Ibid., 125–82.

53. Ibid, 173.

54. Kevin J. Vanhoozer, "Scripture and Tradition," in *The Cambridge Companion to Postmodern Theology*, ed. Kevin J. Vanhoozer, Cambridge Companions to Religion (Cambridge: Cambridge University Press, 2003), 164.

55. Ibid., 167.

56. Ibid., 166.

propositional character of the Bible as traditionally understood by the church after the Reformation? Vanhoozer does not deny that truth is the agreement of language or ideas with reality. Does he run the risk of passing by the correspondence theory of truth? Does he really locate the truth in the community rather than the Bible? The answer to these queries is negative. Firstly, as clearly indicated by the above point, the Bible is primary and community serves to interpret the divine discourse. Secondly, by saying that the Bible's revelation is not merely propositional, the premise that the Bible reveals God's truth both propositionally and personally is highlighted and emphasized. Not only does the Bible convey intentional truth claims, the proclamation of the Bible also confronts the hearers in a personal way.[57] A. B. Caneday forcefully defends Vanhoozer's hermeneutical methodology. He says, "Vanhoozer's approach preserves Scripture as the church's foundation of faith, retains the correspondence theory of truth, and reclaims the priesthood of individual believers as capable of doing theology rightly."[58]

Chinese Christian theology should be based on a fundamentally dynamic and yet careful transmission and interpretation of the Bible.[59] Lai Pan-chiu (also known as Lai Pin-chao) recently rekindled the hermeneutical debate regarding the relationship between Sino-theology and the Bible. He also argues that the rich Chinese cultural resources, including the Buddhist method of doctrinal criticism, may point the way forward for Biblical studies.[60] Whereas Liang Jia-lin (also known as Leung Ka-lun) opts for a linear and irreversible hermeneutical approach from

---

57. D. Groothuis asserts that the Bible conveys intentional truth-claims. "They are *directed* at a state of affairs, and, if they are true, they capture the state of affairs conceptually. 'God exists' is a statement about God's being there as opposed to being absent. God, then, is the intentional object of the intentional statement 'God exists.'" See Douglas Groothuis, "Truth Defined and Defended," in *Reclaiming the Center: Confronting Evangelical Accommodation in Postmodern Times*, ed. Millard J. Erickson et al. (Wheaton, IL: Crossway, 2004) 66.

58. A. B. Caneday, "Is Theological Truth Functional or Propositional? Postconservatism's Use of Language Games and Speech-Act Theory," in *Reclaiming the Center*, ed. M. Erickson, P. K. Helseth, and J. Taylor (Wheaton, IL: Crossway, 2004) 157.

59. Whereas Vanhoozer triangulates the Bible, culture, and the world, this chapter modifies his triangulation. Both the Bible and culture triangulate with the world of wisdom. The triangulation is based on a pivotal Christological standpoint. The Holy Spirit is active in every aspect of such triangulation.

60. Lai Pan-chiu, "Sino-Theology, the Bible and the Christian Tradition," *Studies in World Christianity* 12 (2006) 266–81.

exegesis through systematic theology to practical theology[61], Lai suggests an alternative approach of a non-linear, reversible hermeneutical circle of exegesis, theology, and practice.[62] This chapter takes a *via media* approach between Liang and Lai in light of Vanhoozer's hermeneutical methodology and insights from historical analysis of various contextualized adaptations in seventeenth-century China. Neither Liang's linear, irreversible approach nor Lai's reversible hermeneutical spiral is satisfactory. Triangulation of the Bible, culture, and the world of wisdom, emphasizing the Bible as the ecclesial community's foundation of faith and the vital role of the faith community, will prove to be efficacious.

Attempts to translate the Jewish Torah into Chinese in the Kaifeng community were never made due to the belief that it was too heavenly and had little earthly use. The Jesuits' program failed to continue partly due to incompetent appropriation of technical Christian doctrines by the Chinese Christian literati. They were scholars in Neo-Confucianism, but were not able to articulate God's unity in three persons. The Hui Islamic reformers were competent Arabic/Persian readers and Neo-Confucian scholars. The impact of their reform has continued until the present day.

This chapter views the Bible as both divine discourse and propositional truth that requires cautious and conscientious translation by articulate cultural agents who speak the language of both cultures. Simultaneously, they also belong to the pool of community interpreters, namely, the Christian church with its local, nationwide, and global perspectives. Admittedly, the local and global churches always affect and are affected by both local and worldwide postmodern culture.

Culture as Works and Worlds of Meaning

Culture may be defined in various ways. It can be defined broadly as the body of knowledge shared by the members in that society. A more sophisticated discussion of culture presented by Charles H. Kraft illustrates the mutual, interactive relationship between culture and human beings. Kraft says that humans "thus may be regarded as culture-shaped

---

61. Liang Jia-lin, "Another Debt We Owe?" in *Cultural Christian: Phenomenon and Argument*, ed. Institute of Sino-Christian Studies, Han yu Jidu jiao wen hua yan jiu suo cong kan, 1 (Hong Kong: Institute of Sino-Christian Studies), 108.

62. Lai Pan-chiu, "Sino-Theology, the Bible and the Christian Tradition," *Studies in World Christianity* 12 (2006) 268, 279.

and culture-transmitting beings. But we not only are shaped by and participate in the transmission of our culture; we also influence it and contribute to its reshaping."[63] The Chinese culture is a syncretistic, pluralistic, and tolerant culture with a mighty power to confucianize foreign cultures. Foreign invading cultures then reappear as different forms of sinicized culture or ethnic minorities.

Contemporary Chinese society is encountering many postmodern challenges and powerful changes. Economic successes have tremendously improved the standard of living for the Chinese people, especially in major cities. However, the traditional and indigenous ways of thinking and feeling do not always succumb to the challenges, and the changes can be sinicized. As noted by Julia Ching, the Confucian tradition has lost ground in modern times but it is not dead.[64] Moreover, Cheng Chung-ying even argues that modern Confucianism has global significance in "its revival of the ethical value and cultural form of humanity and in its placement of these concerns within modern scientific and technological culture."[65] While modernization and globalization are inevitable, traditional Chinese culture is retaining its basic tenets and revitalizing its focus on self-cultivation and self-transformation. "Chinese philosophers are paying attention to nature and ultimate reality and, hence, are nature-centered in ecology and *dao*-centered or universe-centered in cosmology. Their sense of human centrality does not imply an anthropocentrism, but rather a tendency toward a holism and organicism of the human person, nature and heaven. It is a reflection and articulation of their perception of the cocreativity of nature or heaven and the human."[66]

The powerful syncretism of Chinese culture stems from its propositions about what it means to be human. Culture is recognized by some Chinese scholars to be a *living* tradition.[67] As Vanhoozer puts it, culture does not only communicate, express, or objectify human concerns, but

63. Charles H. Kraft, *Christianity in Culture: A Study in Dynamic Biblical Theologizing in Cross-Cultural Perspective* (Maryknoll, NY: Orbis, 1979), 47.

64. Julia Ching and Hans Küng, *Christianity and Chinese Religions* (New York: Doubleday, 1989), 89.

65. Cheng Chung-ying, "An Onto-hermeneutic Interpretation of Twentieth-Century Chinese Philosophy: Identity and Vision," in *Contemporary Chinese Philosophy*, ed. Chung-ying Cheng and Nicholas Bunnin (Malden, MA: Blackwell, 2002), 385.

66. Ibid., 398.

67. Chinese Confucian scholars like Shuxian Liu and Weiming Tu.

also leads to a process of spiritual formation.[68] Clearly, culture is not merely a static and neutral object. Both the Bible as sacred text and culture as cultural text[69] are both subjects triangulating with the world of religious and cultural practice.

It is possible and necessary to contextualize the Middle Eastern Bible into the Chinese culture. Yet, caution and care are required to carry out authentic and effective contextualization. After acknowledging Charles Kraft's creative dynamic-equivalent model of contextualization as well as other models, David J. Hesselgrave and Edward Rommen conclude, "Christian contextualizations that are both authentic and effective are based on careful attention to both the biblical text and the respondent culture . . . Both the decontexualization and the contextualization tasks are best accomplished by persons who are expert in the cultures and languages involved, who understand cultural dynamics, and who are themselves bicultural."[70] Ideally, the mission of contextualization should not be furthered merely by individual effort. Rather, the work of the Holy Spirit should empower the ecclesial community.[71] As argued by Vanhoozer, the Holy Spirit not only empowers the translators or the ecclesial community, but also illuminates readers of the canonical text. "[T]he Spirit ministers God's *general* discourse embedded in creation and the human conscience as well as the special divine Christ-directed canonical discourse . . . It follows that there may be vestiges of truth, goodness, and beauty outside the church—in culture."[72]

By contextualizing Christian theology in the Chinese culture, the *sola Scriptura* principle is not necessarily lost. Lai Pan-chiu has argued from a global perspective that it is possible to integrate both Christian

---

68. Kevin J. Vanhoozer, "What Is Everyday Theology?" 28–31.

69. According to Vanhoozer, culture is made up of work and worlds of meanings. Culture is what we get when we work. Vanhoozer refers to the products of such work as "cultural texts." He uses this term because texts are intentional human action that communicates meaning and calls for interpretation (ibid., 26).

70. David J. Hesselgrave and Edward Rommen, *Contextualization: Meanings, Methods and Models* (Leicester, UK: Apollos, 1989), 211.

71. The community aspect was well illustrated by the seventeenth-century Islamic reformers. The seventeenth-century Muslim Hui reformers did not work alone. They were in continuation of the Islamic traditions, part of the literati networks, and supported by the elaborate and extensive educational systems in major cities.

72. Kevin J. Vanhoozer, "What is Everyday Theology?" 43.

and Chinese traditions without violating either.[73] In addition, such integration fosters the development of both traditions.[74] This paper, however, has argued from an evangelical perspective. The Bible and culture should not be viewed as a dichotomy. They are sacred and cultural texts, respectively, that require careful interpretation by community-based interpreters. By the empowering of the Spirit, both the translators and the Christian community can inculturate the way of Christ in specific contexts.[75]

Sapientia as the World of Wisdom[76]

Hermeneutically, the Bible and Chinese culture as subjects are in dialogical triangulation with the world of wisdom, which is expressed by both exoteric and esoteric religion. Wisdom and religion are closely related terms, but they do not mean the same thing. Religion is a loaded word often associated with powerful, greedy totalitarian regimes; sterile observance of rigid rules; and obsolete creeds filled with archaic terms that lack contemporary relevance. While wisdom may sound mystical to some, it is a word associated with the practice of human self-cultivation and transformation according to Confucian thoughts. As Kirill Thompson puts it, Confucius understood wisdom to be knowledge of the

---

73. Lai Pan-chiu, "Inheriting Chinese and Christian Traditions in Global Context: A Confucian-Protestant Perspective," *Religion and Theology* 10 (2003) 1–23.

74. A similar argument was presented by Lai Pan-chiu in 2001. Lai Pan-chiu, "Chinese Culture and the Development of Chinese Christian Theology," *Studies in World Christianity* 7 (2001) 219–40. He argues that Chinese Christian theology can enrich Western concepts of Christology and ecology.

75. A similar strategy was deployed by the seventeenth-century Hui Muslim reformers with the aims to expand and continue specifically the Muslim Chinese body of knowledge (i.e., the "Dao" of Islam). Benite investigates the relationship between the Hui Muslim reformers and the extensive, complicated, and elaborate mosque education systems in major Chinese cities. He reveals the interactive relationship between transmitters of sacred texts (as interpreters of culture also) and the local religious communities. Benite argues that the Hui reformation was successful because, firstly, Hui Muslim literati did not work alone. They involved their own Muslim communities, communities in other regions, and also non-Muslim intellectual surroundings. Secondly, their transmitted texts entered into direct dialogue with other texts (e.g., classical Confucian texts). Thirdly, published texts were supported or legitimized by preface, postface, greetings, or editorship from the broader Chinese literati community. See Benite, *The Dao of Muhammad*, 161.

76. Huston Smith, "Chinese Religion in World Perspective," *Dialogue & Alliance* 4.2 (1990) 4–14. Smith emphasizes the social emphasis of Chinese religion.

actual state of affairs. Thus, the wise person is able to penetrate obscurity and change to comprehend the hidden, true state of affairs. Thompson asserts that while Zhu Xi's notions of knowledge and wisdom were to inform life practice, Zhu's purpose in seeking and exercising wisdom was "to cultivate a nuanced, holistic, responsive sensitivity to the immanent patterns of change and transformation."[77] Yao Xinzhong, another Confucian scholar, also asserts that Confucian wisdom is a "progress from 'what is below' to 'what is above' and the interrelationship between knowing human nature, human destiny, and heaven . . . 'higher realms' that are initially beyond the reach of ordinary people but can be fully realized in their effort to know, understand, and appreciate."[78] Furthermore, after exploring the concept of Yi (righteousness) in Confucius's *Analects*, Yu Jiyuan concludes that "while appropriateness [righteousness] is about practical affairs, wisdom seems to be both theoretical and practical. It is theoretical because it is knowledge of the *ming* [destiny] of heaven, the ontological premise of the good life; it is practical because at A. 12:22 . . . wisdom is to 'know one's fellow human beings' . . . Wisdom is about what is appropriate [righteous] in human affairs . . . to have wisdom is to know the social rites and their ontological grounds, while appropriateness [righteousness] is more closely associated with the agent's choosing and determining."[79]

If this understanding reflects the consensus of Confucianism and contemporary Chinese tradition, then such concepts can be helpfully developed. Admittedly, wisdom in Confucian and Neo-Confucian contexts has minimal religious connotation but extensive ethical-moral character. Wisdom can be acquired by practice and becomes a habitual attitude. Interestingly, Confucian wisdom resonates with Christian sanctification, righteous attitudes, and works. The Christian rites of baptism as initiation and the Lord's Supper as continuation can possibly be interpreted as methods of acquiring righteousness. Wisdom language, as well as philosophical and anthropological concepts, may form helpful

---

77. Kirill O. Thompson, "The Archery of 'Wisdom' in the Stream of Life: 'Wisdom' in the Four Books with Zhu Xi's Reflections," *Philosophy East and West* 57 (2007) 336.

78. Yao Xinzhong, "From 'What Is Below' to 'What Is Above': A Confucian Discourse on Wisdom," *Journal of Chinese Philosophy* 33 (2006) 359–60.

79. Yu Jiyuan, "Yi: Practical Wisdom in Confucius's Analects," *Journal of Chinese Philosophy* 33 (2006) 342.

bridges and offer useful lexicon tools to develop a Chinese Christian theology.[80]

The apostle Paul is very explicit and boldly identifies Christ as "our wisdom" (1 Cor 1:30) in contrast to the Corinthians' human wisdom (1 Cor 1:20). Christ is the definitive self-expression of God (Col 1:19; 2:9). Paul argues that wisdom is no longer embodied in the Torah as understood in Palestinian Judaism. Rather, it is embodied in Christ. In particular, Paul refers to Christ's crucifixion as the definition of divine wisdom (1 Cor 1:24). James Dunn equates the Johannine Logos/Wisdom with God in that it is *"precosmic existence with God* (e.g., Prov 8:27–30; Sir 24:9; Wis 9:9) and precisely by virtue of its close identity with God (e.g., Ps 33:6; Wis 7:25; Philo, *Opif.* 24; *Sacr.* 64). The point of distinctiveness being that Wisdom/Logos is *not* a heavenly being over against God, but is *God himself.*"[81]

While Paul identifies Christ with divine wisdom, he deliberately does not identify the Holy Spirit with such wisdom, although the Spirit is virtually synonymous with wisdom in pre-Christian Judaism. It is the apostle John in his gospel who sheds greater light on the relationship between Christ as the divine wisdom and the Holy Spirit who acts as Christ's advocate, that is, as the continuing presence of God in the mode of Christ after Christ's ascension. According to Cornelis Bennema, the role of the Holy Spirit in relation to Christ the divine wisdom is multifaceted, centering upon the theme of Johannine soteriology: "The Spirit is active in/through Jesus' revelatory teaching and somehow mediates life to people. In fact, the Spirit seems to function as the facilitator of cognitive perception and understanding, which enables a person to make an adequate (i.e., authentic and sufficiently salvific) belief-response that results in entering into a life-giving relationship with the Father and Son. The Spirit is also expected to sustain the believer's saving relationship."[82]

---

80. A worthy attempt to develop such a theology has been made by Leonard Swidler. See Leonard Swidler, "A Christian Historical Perspective on Wisdom as a Basis for Dialogue with Judaism and Chinese Religion," *JES* 33 (1996) 557–72.

81. James D. G. Dunn, *The Christ and the Spirit: Collected Essays of James D. G. Dunn*, vol. 1, *Christology* (Edinburgh: T. & T. Clark, 1998), 367. A similar argument has been offered by Michael E. Willett, *Wisdom Christology in the Fourth Gospel* (San Francisco: Mellen, 1992), 149–50.

82. Cornelis Bennema, "The Power of Saving Wisdom," *TynBul* 52 (2001) 296. See also Cornelis Bennema, *The Power of Saving Wisdom: An Investigation of Spirit and Wisdom in Relation to the Soteriology of the Fourth Gospel*, WUNT 2/148 (Tübingen: Mohr/Siebeck, 2002), 38.

Wisdom, self-cultivation and mind-heart[83] are common categories in Chinese culture. Careful contextualized interpretation of the Bible can imbue these categories with fresh Christian meanings.[84] Christ is unquestionably unique and can be presented in Chinese context as divine wisdom. The work of the Spirit is also equally significant and yet different from Christ. The Spirit informs, empowers the Christian community in its missionary effort of transmitting the Biblical text prophetically and illuminates those outside the community into saving wisdom cognitively and experientially.

Christology as the Basis of Triangulation

While the Chalcedonian definition upholds both the divinity and humanity of Christ, the development beyond Chalcedon has not favored a deeper theological exploration of Christ's humanity. In the nineteenth-century West, Christ's humanity was emphasized at the expense of his divinity by liberal scholars. Rather than indiscriminately importing nineteenth- and twentieth-century Western religious thought, Chinese Christian interpreters and cultural agents may explore the God-man—the human and divine Christ—as the pivotal stand on which they can triangulate Scripture, culture, and the world of wisdom. It is not necessary to pursue solely a Christology from below, emphasizing the exaltation of merely a holy sage. This may risk the Logos Christology. Rather, Jesus Christ must be regarded as both the divine wisdom and holy human sage. He is not firstly a sage who then achieves divine wisdom at the end of his human life. Rather, he is both the exemplary holy sage who teaches divine revelation. Simultaneously, Christ also embodies saving wisdom in his personhood. From the beginning of his life's journey to his eventual spiritual presence (he is now exalted in heaven), the role of the Holy Spirit is vital. Through the Holy Spirit, Christ the divine wisdom and

---

83. According to Tu Wei-ming, mind-heart may be interpreted as a creative reason through which self-transformation may be achieved. Tu Wei-ming, *Centrality and Commonality: An Essay on Confucian Religiousness*, SUNY Series in Chinese Philosophy and Culture (Albany: State University of New York Press, 1989).

84. Benedict Kwok believes that a dialogue on humanity between Neo-orthodox Karl Barth and Neo-Confucian Yangming Wang (1472–1529) can be mutually enriching. Interreligious dialogue must not necessarily dilute the foundation of the Christian faith. Benedict Hung-biu Kwok, "The Christological Doctrine of Reconciliation of Karl Barth and the Dialogue with the Neo-Confucian Understanding of Self-Cultivation: A Response to Heup Young Kim," *Ching Feng* 41 (1998) 105–6.

holy sage continues to be present with us. It is the Spirit-enabled church that testifies to Christ's presence in concrete social settings.

Late in his life, the seventeenth-century Hui Muslim reformer Liu Zhi wrote a fairly free translation of the life and teaching of Muhammad. Liu exalted Islam based on the story of Muhammad. In his careful re-interpretation of Persian sources, namely, *Tarjama-yi Mustafa*,[85] Liu almost divinized the Islamic sage. "The Prophet was first established in the pre-existent heaven and earth, his designation then being Ahmad, and he was the progenitor of all creation. When he was born into the later heaven and earth as the Completer of the work of all the prophets, he was named Mohammed."[86] "Pre-existent" and "later" heaven and earth refer to two forms of existence. They correspond to primordial/spiritual and consequent/physical existence. Liu's portrayal of Muhammad was strategic, as Muhammad came close to being portrayed as a divine being in addition to a sage. His exaltation of Muhammad reinforced both the pre-existent and divine origin of Islam, which served his goal to raise the credibility and status of Islam in late imperial China.

While Liu Zhi tried to make the prophet Muhammad divine though he was not, Chinese Christian interpreters should affirm the holy sage Jesus Christ as divine and truly the Son of God. Contextualized theology can simultaneously assert that Christ is divine (from above) and that He is human (from below). Sagehood in Neo-Confucianism is a common conceptuality, as Liu Zhi employed such a notion to identify Muhammad with the Neo-Confucian sagehood tradition. Contextualization of Christ, the holy sage, by transference may be carried out with lesser difficulty. A Christology from below can be contextualized as holy sagehood, emphasizing the humanity of Christ. That is to say, Christ, as the second Adam and a particular representative of the entire human race, lived exemplarily. In addition, his teaching reveals divine wisdom. More than that, he himself embodies the divine wisdom.

Christ as the Divine Wisdom, rather than any abstract Greek concept of *hypostasis, ousia* makes greater sense to Chinese people in the postmodern world. In addition, the wisdom concept in the Pauline

---

85. Sachiko Murata, *Chinese Gleams of Sufi Light* (Albany: State University of New York, 2000), 34.

86. Isaac Mason, trans., *The Arabian Prophet: A Life of Mohammed from Chinese and Arabic Sources. A Chinese-Moslem Work by Liu Chai-Lien* (Shanghai: Commercial, 1921), 11.

and Johannine texts can be cautiously contextualized for the Chinese culture. The Confucian notion of wisdom is fluid enough to be reinterpreted with new meaning. If Christ is set within the contemporary Chinese context, it must be stressed that He is both wholly other (God and incarnate wisdom) and holy human (exemplary prophet-sage).[87] Undoubtedly, it is the concept of Christ as truly divine that demands greater care and articulation by contemporary Chinese theologians. Notions of penal substitution and the total depravity of humanity are foreign to mainstream Chinese traditions.[88] While the Divine Wisdom may be expressed as the Logos or God incarnate, Confucianism in all its forms provides few resources on such theistic concepts. However, indigenous Daoism does have clear concepts of a creator and transcendence.[89] It should be noted that Daoism is a topic still in need of careful research by Chinese evangelical Christians, who should always strive to be effective cultural agents.[90] Research on Daoism by Chinese Christian scholars

---

87. Benedict Kwok helpfully emphasizes both the immanence and transcendence of the Christian God in his correction of the view of Liu Shu-hsien, who misunderstands the Christian understanding of God as pure transcendence. See Benedict Hung-biu Kwok, "The Christian Understanding of God as Transcendence and Immanence: A Response to Liu Shu-hsien's Understanding of the 'Pure Transcendence of God,'" *Ching Feng* 42 (1999) 36.

88. After comparing Karl Barth and Wang Yangming, Benedict Kwok reasons that the dialogue between Confucianism and Christian theology should avoid Christology as a starting point. Fallen humanness would be a better entry point. See Benedict Kwok, "The Christological Doctrine of Reconciliation of Karl Barth and the Dialogue with the Neo-Confucian Understanding of Self-Cultivation: A Response to Heup Young Kim," *Ching Feng*, 41.1 (1998).

89. Russell Kirkland is a distinguished Western scholar on Daoism. His introductory book is *Taoism: An Enduring Tradition* (New York: Routledge, 2004). He emphatically insists on using reliable texts and translations because few contemporary scholars have a nuanced and appreciative view of Daoism. Significant advances in careful and detailed scholarship have been made only during the last ten years. James Miller and Elijah Siegler assert that scholarly advances regarding the construction of the religious authenticity of Daoism have recently been made and should be further encouraged. James Miller and Elijah Siegler, "Of Alchemy and Authenticity: Teaching about Daoism Today," *Teaching Theology and Religion* 10 (2007) 102–3.

90. Very few well-informed, comparative, book-length studies on Christianity and Daoism have been published by evangelical Christians. However, admirable contributions have been made by Julia Ching (see Hans Küng and Julia Ching, *Christianity and Chinese Religions* [London: SCM, 1993], 129–58; Julia Ching, *Mysticism and Kingship in China: The Heart of Chinese Wisdom*, Cambridge Studies in Religious Traditions 11 [Cambridge: Cambridge University Press, 1997].) Short articles by evangelical Christians are increasingly common. (See Arnold M. K. Yeung, "Union with Tao in Tao

might quite possibly yield rich linguistic, philosophical, and anthropological resources in constructing a Chinese Christian theology.

CONCLUSION

Evangelical scholars engaging in contextualization must avoid direct transference of philosophical concepts to the Chinese context, simple parallels of linguistic terms, and superficial resonance of ideas from the western Christian tradition.[91] Is the task of doing Christian theology in a Chinese context possible? The thesis of this paper is affirmative. As Lai argues, "To be a Chinese Christian, it is not necessary to take an antagonistic attitude against the western theological heritage—assuming that everything from western theology must be either irrelevant or harmful. Nor is it necessary for Chinese Christians to identify western theology as the norm or totality of the Christian tradition."[92]

Indeed, there is an urgent need to construct or reinherit an evangelical Chinese theology, taking into full consideration the contemporary Chinese postmodern culture with the aim of developing an ethnic theology while affirming the final and pervasive authority of the Bible. The adaptation of Biblical truth and interpretation of culture do not necessarily diminish the *sola Scriptura* principle. Evangelical transmitters of Biblical texts and cultural interpreters of cultural texts are not lone workers in their attempts at theological construction. The role of the church is vital in the process of contextualizing the Christian message. In the end, the mission of the Christian church in China is to demonstrate that the world of wisdom is found only in the person and work of Jesus Christ, who is both the Divine Wisdom and holy sage.

Te Ching: A Dialogue between a Taoist and a Christian," *Dialogue & Alliance* 5:1 (1991) 68–80; Jason H. Yeung, "The Flesh Becoming Dao: A Comparison of the Soteriologies of Confucianism, Daojiao and Christianity," *CGST Journal* 34 (2003) 95–120; Paul S. Chung, "The Mystery of God and Tao in Jewish-Christian-Taoist Context," in *Asian Contextual Theology for the Third Millennium*, PTMS 70 (Eugene, OR: Pickwick Publications, 2007) 243–66. From an evangelical Lutheran perspective, Paul Chung has contributed many articles on Christian-Asian religious dialogues.

91. Ying Fuk-tsang warns of focusing merely on similarities between the Christian faith and Chinese ethos. He insists on the uniqueness and heterogeneity of Christian faith and that Christian faith can transform the Chinese culture. See Fuk-tsang Ying, "Grace and Merit: Christian Doctrine of Salvation against Chinese Culture," *Jian Dao* 19 (2003) 39–58.

92. Lai Pan-chiu, "Chinese Culture and the Development of Chinese Christian Theology," *Studies in World Christianity* 7 (2001) 234.

12

Forging Evangelical Identity

Integration of Models of Theological Education in the Global Context

CARVER T. YU

PORTRAYING THE GLOBAL CONTEXT

IN THE LAST FIFTY years, the world has witnessed some rather drastic changes. From the Christian perspective, the most significant changes may crudely be epitomized by two juxtaposed pictures. One picture is the unrelenting acceleration of secularization disseminating from the West, or, more accurately, from the North. The other is that of Christian expansion in Africa, Latin America, and Asia. Combined, these two pictures pose a serious challenge for theological educators.

Secularization has been with us for the last three hundred years, but the speed with which it is now transforming fundamental values, as well as the basic structure of our society, is unprecedented. Three main components contribute to this trend: market capitalism, liberal humanism, and information overload. What really matters in the process we call globalization is the global dissemination of these three components of secularization.

Globalization of market capitalism is foundation shaking. The logic of operation, or sets of rules and assumptions for the proper functioning of the market, are being implanted everywhere in the world. Once the principles and assumptions of market capitalism are globalized, wherever the market is, functional rationality becomes the norm of the day, efficiency becomes the highest virtue, and moral values are on the way of becoming marginalized. People are driven by market dynamics to consume, resulting in a consumer culture in which economics becomes a religion and its article of faith is that the entire world is driven by an economic rationality based on self-interest. In other words, people's basic motivation for doing things is the belief that their actions will offer them greater positive benefits than the costs incurred. Market fundamentalists like those who adhere to the Chicago School of Economics would unashamedly exclude non-market values as driving forces even in non-economic arenas of life. From the economic perspective, marriage and sex are nothing more than transactional arrangements that provide mutual benefits for the involved parties, with the logical conclusion that marriage is no different from prostitution.[1] As George Soros points out, "Market fundamentalists have transformed an axiomatic, value-neutral theory into an ideology, which has influenced political and business behavior in a powerful and dangerous way . . . the idea that some values may not be negotiable is not recognized or, more exactly, such values are excluded from the realm of economics."[2] The implication, as Soros sees it, is that "our contemporary society seems to be suffering from an acute deficiency of social values . . . Market values have penetrated into areas of society that were previously governed by non-market considerations."[3]

Inseparable from the globalization of market capitalism is the globalization of the liberal humanist concept of freedom. Isaiah Berlin's *Two Concepts of Liberty* and John Rawls's *A Theory of Justice* may be regarded as the two most powerful essays in shaping the idea of freedom in our culture. Berlin defines freedom as negative liberty, i.e., freedom from constraints or interference imposed on the individual, whether by society or private persons, even for the sake of realizing the common good that is preconceived by society as a whole. To avoid any possible encroachment of the state or collective ideology, the idea of the common

---

1. Gary Becker and Richard Posner, both committed adherents to the Chicago school, try to reduce marriage and sex to economic terms so as to incorporate them into a system of economic rationality; cf. Robert Nelson, *Economics as Religion: From Samuelson to Chicago and Beyond* (University Park: Pennsylvania State University Press, 2001), 179–81.

2. Cf. George Soros, *The Crisis of Global Capitalism: Open Society Endangered* (London: Little, Brown, 1998), 43.

3. Ibid., 73.

good must be shunned. Liberty conceived in such a way is liberty with no definite moral discrimination; it is a liberty of indifference.

Rawls follows Berlin's line of thought, but brings back the Romantic ideal of selfhood with radical autonomy as the absolute value. Freedom is defined as freedom for any free agent to exercise her rights to define the good for herself within the boundary of justice. Freedom here is freedom to realize the ends chosen by one's autonomous will. The autonomous self is therefore the Alpha and the Omega of all values.

An almost imperceptible change, which proves to be highly significant, took place in the twentieth century. It is the change in the nature of industry. The industry of manufacturing tangible material goods is gradually being taken over by the manufacturing of ideas. In the sixties, discussions about the "production and distribution" of knowledge and the "uses" of the university in this manufacturing process were already underway.[4] Changes in the concept of knowledge and the role of the university coincided with the coming of the "post-industrial society" and the "economics of information."[5] Knowledge is now being increasingly perceived as a commodity fabricated to serve the needs of a consumer society. It is no longer primarily regarded as a mirror of reality or truth, but merely as conglomerates of information freely assembled to serve certain socio-economic functions.

British sociologist Anthony Giddens describes modern self-identity as post-traditional, as it is no longer built around a set of clearly defined traditional values. The self is, rather, a reflexive project, an ongoing story that proceeds by continually sorting out and integrating events in the external world. There is no magnetic center, no core in the self. Instead, the self is now "liquid": it changes as it flows along. "A person's identity is not to be found in behavior, nor—important though this is—in the reactions of others, but in the capacity to keep a particular narrative going."[6] But what exactly is in the narrative? Flooded by advertisements, the so-called "private" life is thoroughly

---

4. Fritz Machlup, *The Production and Distribution of Knowledge in the United States* (Princeton: Princeton University Press, 1962); Clark Kerr, *The Uses of the University*, The Godkin Lectures at Harvard University 1963 (Cambridge: Harvard University Press, 1963).

5. Daniel Bell, *The Coming of Post-industrial Society: A Venture in Social Forecasting*, Colophon Books (New York: Basic Books, 1976).

6. Anthony Giddens, *Modernity and Self-Identity: Self and Society in the Late Modern Age* (Stanford: Stanford University Press, 1991), 54.

invaded by consumer images, which have become the main substance of the self. German sociologist Wolf Dieter-Narr sums up the problem for us most vividly, "The change in behavior long observed by Riesman, Mitscherlich, Weber and many others consists in a destruction of 'inwardness,' in a loss of the individual's mechanism for reflection and for the process of experience... Our modern society has become a society of conditioned reflexes, a society where the individual is important only as a bearer of attributes—with reference to this or that attribute but not to what these attributes constitute: the person."[7]

The globalization that is prevalent today is fundamentally the globalization of functional rationality, fragmented identity in the deluge of information, and liberty of indifference in the guise of democracy. In such scenarios, traditional spiritual values are being supplanted. Caught in this process, the Church seems to be fighting a losing battle, particularly in that the Church herself is being infected by secularization as well as market logic. The drastic eclipse of the Christian religion seems inevitable, as suggested by the religious condition of the West, particularly in Europe.

There is, however, another picture of the global context deemed highly relevant to Christian educators. It is the picture of the astounding expansion of Christianity in the last fifty years. Take Africa as an example: it is estimated that the Christian population in 1900 was about eight to nine million, or about 8 percent of the continental total. By 1950, this figure had risen to thirty four million, or 15 percent of the population. By 1965, there were seventy five million Christians in Africa, a quarter of the entire population, and by 2000 there were 360 million Christians, comprising nearly half of the continent's population.[8] As we look at Latin America, the growth is equally astounding. About 480 million Christians are currently living in Latin America. Protestants, who in 1950 made up merely a fraction of the general population, now account for 12 to 15 percent of the population. Of the Protestants, 75 percent

---

7. Wolf Dieter-Narr, "Toward a Society of Conditioned Reflexes," in *Observations on the "Spiritual Situation of the Age": Contemporary German Perspectives*, ed. Jürgen Habermas, trans. Andrew Buchwalter, Studies in Contemporary German Social Thought (Cambridge: MIT Press, 1984), 33, 36.

8. David B. Barrett et al., *World Christian Encyclopedia: A Comparative Survey of Churches and Religions in the Modern World*, 2nd ed. (Oxford: Oxford University Press, 2001). Cf. Philip Jenkins, *The Next Christendom: The Coming of Global Christianity* (Oxford: Oxford University Press, 2002), 56.

are Pentecostals. Phenomenal growth has also occurred in China. In 1949, fewer than two million Christians (both Roman Catholics and Protestants combined) were living in China. Now, Christians in China are estimated to number from fifty million to one hundred million. The Amity Press recently celebrated the printing of fifty million copies of the Bible (of which just eight million are for use outside China). The new printing plant that opened in May of 2008 is planning to print twelve million Bibles each year. This number reflects the impressive number of active Christians. Nepal boasts another totally unexpected explosion of the Christian faith. Fifty years ago, only a handful of Christians were living in this land, which had long been tightly closed to Christian missionaries. Now Christians constitute about 1.5 to 2 percent of the total population of twenty six million. The Christian church in other parts of Asia, such as Korea, has also experienced phenomenal growth. Christians in Asia are now estimated to number 313 million.[9] Africa, Latin America, and Asia combined are home to 1.2 billion Christians, whereas there are only about 560 million Christians living in Europe as a whole. The significance of such a comparison does not lie in sheer numbers, but in the underlying trends. As Jenkins observes, "Over the past century . . . the center of gravity in the Christian world has shifted inexorably southward, to Africa, Asia and Latin America . . ." While the church in Europe has been in unrelenting decline for more than a century due to the onslaught of secularization, the young church in Africa, Latin America, and Asia is thriving most vibrantly. According to Jenkins' prediction, by 2050, only one-fifth of the world's three billion Christians will be non-Hispanic Whites living in Europe and North America. What do these trends tell us? Are there significant implications for theological education?

CAUGHT IN THE MIDDLE

Without being overly triumphant, it is safe to say that Christian expansion in the South is largely due to the zeal of missionaries to proclaim the Gospel. Such zeal is fueled by the deep conviction that true liberation of the human person and transformation of society comes only through God's revelation in Jesus Christ as proclaimed in Scripture and by the church. The missional orientation of the church seems to be key.

---

9. Ibid., 3.

However, the picture may not be as simple as that. Missional orientation without sound biblical-theological reflection can be detrimental to those both inside and outside the church. At the same time, the South is, for the time being, relatively unravished by market capitalism and untested by liberal humanism in the guise of democracy. However, when globalization pervades nations like China and Brazil, will such Christian expansion continue? Will the existing Christians in these nations be able to withstand the uprooting of values central to their faith? Core values that define evangelical identity and spirituality, such as faith in biblical authority, personal piety, evangelistic zeal, and moral character, may disintegrate under the overwhelming impact of market logic. The crisis of evangelical identity may come from the inside once secularization has made its subtle inroads.

Indeed, we do not need to go very far back in history to understand this concern; in fact, we need only to look more closely at our own contemporary scene. Evangelical churches in North America have been growing impressively over the last five decades. Yet their spiritual impact on contemporary culture and thought seems rather feeble. Not only has the church failed to stem the tide of secularization and individualism, she has actually been held captive by such an ethos.[10] David Wells has rightly pointed to the fact that increasing numbers of evangelical churches "are adapting themselves to the felt needs in the congregation much as a business might adapt its product to a market." Such adaptation "has enabled evangelicalism to orient itself to our consumer culture and the habits of mind that go with it."[11] However, in a narcissistic culture like ours, many people are not looking for personal salvation but psychological well-being. They come to the church as religious consumers who are free to define their needs and express their demands. Those who best understand the trends in contemporary society are able to draw the greatest crowd. "When the religious audience is thus sovereign, its leadership is appropriately refined. The best pollster now makes the best leader, for all ideas must find their sanction, even their legitimacy, in the audience, and who knows the audience better than a pollster?"[12] With the intrusion of the market ethos, "the importance of theology is eclipsed by the clamor

---

10. Cf. David F. Wells, *No Place for Truth, or, Whatever Happened to Evangelical Theology?* (Grand Rapids: Eerdmans, 1993).

11. Ibid., 173.

12. Ibid., 214.

for management skills, biblical preaching by entertaining story-telling, godly character by engaging personality, and the work of the ministry by the art of sustaining a career." Professionalism of the ministry gradually sets in, and training for ministry becomes more and more professionalized. "It is being anchored firmly in the middle class, and the attitudes of those who are themselves professionals . . . who are increasingly defining who the minister is. Once again, it is the old market mechanism at work—ministers defining themselves as a product for which there is a market." They are tempted to adopt "the role of passive agent of process." Their competence is measured by managerial skills rather than theological insights or spiritual depth.[13]

The erosion of the role of theology in the life of the evangelical church and the evasion of theological reflection in response to socio-cultural trends is costly. The confessional character of theology is becoming more and more questionable, as common consensus of and communal commitment to faith have become so fragmented that theological expressions are now often treated as personal opinions or ideologies.

The Lausanne Conference on World Evangelization in 1974 was originally a watershed event for evangelical theology. Lausanne put culture and society back where they belonged—in the evangelical theological agenda. Evangelical leaders were convinced that personal salvation and cultural redemption were inseparable, and that there could be no true proclamation of the Gospel without prophetic judgment on our human condition as manifested in social, political, economic, and cultural realities.[14] However, after three and a half decades, evangelical reflections on culture seem to remain merely on the surface, leaving the ideological core, or the "soul," of our culture untouched. The result is that our culture continues along in its secular way as our theologians continue to offer monologue in their inner circles. If evangelical theology today is perceived to lack vitality and a sense of direction, it is largely due to the fact that our evangelical movement has somehow lost its vision for reshaping our culture and redirecting our history. Because of this, the evangelical church is paying a heavy price. Abandoning culture to itself, letting it become deleterious, we are in effect putting the church under a collapsing wall. In fact, the evangelical movement, and evangelical theology along

---

13. Ibid., 233–34.

14. C. Rene Padilla, ed., *The New Face of Evangelicalism: An International Symposium on the Lausanne Covenant* (Downers Grove, IL: InterVarsity, 1976).

with it, are being attacked from all directions. Biblical authority is being undermined in an unprecedented way due to the trend of nihilism in hermeneutics. When objective meaning is in doubt, Biblical authority cannot hold. Without a common reference and under the influence of diverse ideologies, the evangelical movement is in danger of becoming increasingly fragmented. When objective truth is eroded, the subjective begins to dominate our faith. Consumerism, which is well poised to cater to individual orientation and preference, begins to subtly shape pastoral and church leadership practices. Even evangelicals with the greatest missional-evangelistic zeal will be threatened by socio-cultural conditions that have been "nurtured" by their neglect. Such socio-cultural disintegrations will continue to boomerang, so, while we celebrate the Christian expansion in the South, we should not congratulate ourselves too soon. We should also not jump to the conclusion that conservative biblical faith alone is the key to Christian expansion. We need, rather, to probe more deeply into our evangelical identity.

BACK TO THE BASICS FOR EVANGELICAL IDENTITY

Before we discuss what theological education for the evangelical church should consist of, we need to revisit some basic questions. What is the church? What is theology? What is theological education? These questions are fundamental to assessing our evangelical identity.

What is theology? Karl Barth, in my view, provides by far the most insightful and relevant understanding of evangelical theology. Theology, according to Barth, is a science. What sort of a science? It is a science of critique (examination, test). Critique of what? It is a science of critique of the proclamation of the church, to examine and test whether it is faithful to the Word of God. "The primary task of the Church is to proclaim the Christian gospel, and theology functions first of all as a test and a corrective to measure the integrity of this proclamation."[15] Theology is deemed to be vital only if the church regards proclamation of the Word of God as essential to her identity. For a church that ceases to proclaim the Word of God, theology is deemed to be irrelevant and therefore obsolete.

As the Word of God is nothing but the Word Incarnate, being faithful to the Word of God necessarily means being relevant and prophetic

---

15. Karl Barth, *Church Dogmatics*, I/1, trans. Geoffrey W. Bromiley (Edinburgh: T. & T. Clark, 1975), 82–83.

to human constructs, which oppress and distort humanity. Theology, therefore, in its critique of the church's proclamation, is inevitably a critique of culture—not only culture that is "outside" the church, but also culture that has been integrated with the life of the church. Culture that captivates humanity can hijack the church unless she is faithful to the Word of God.

Theology should serve as the reflection of the church in action, reaching the world and showing it a new life that is completely different from its old way. When the church collides with the world, placing herself in danger of losing her distinctive identity, theology should offer a prophetic critique of the church.

Positively, theological education should serve to cultivate the ability of the whole church to expound the Word of God as *Gospel* for the world. It is only when the Word is so expounded that it truly is the Word Incarnate. When the Word of God is expounded merely for the self-definition and self-justification of the church (as in the case of hair-splitting doctrinal debates), it will no longer be the Word of Life, but becomes *words of human tradition*. Theological education should thus prepare the church to listen to the Word of God while simultaneously listening to cries of spiritual desperation. In such a way, the Word may be expounded as Gospel for the world. Therefore, the world—its cultural constructs and spiritual condition—must be the medium in and through which the Word of God is heard. *Consequently, the world must be structured as a significant part of our theological curriculum.*

What is the church? If we are true to biblical teachings, we cannot define the church as anything other than an *Eschatological Charismatic Covenantal Eucharistic Community*.

The church is, first and foremost, an *eschatological* community. It has the Kingdom of God as the foundation of her existence and the *telos* of its realization. The church not only exists in the light of the *eschaton*; it is also both witness to and the manifestation of the reality of the *eschaton*. The coming transformation of the world is being revealed in and through the church, as the firstfruit of transformed humanity. The church exists for the Kingdom of God, and her ministry is always Kingdom ministry—seeking to expand the reign of God over the world. As an eschatological community, the church is history-oriented. She has a deep sense of history, being conscious of the fact that she is part of a larger historical movement seeking the complete manifestation of the Kingdom of God.

The church is a *charismatic* community. All power and spiritual gifts have been given to her freely by Christ through the Holy Spirit for the service of the Kingdom. The reality of spiritual gifts has to be taken seriously both for the life of the church and for the Kingdom. Such gifts must be identified and coordinated in such a way that the church functions in unity as a body. The church as a body is a structure of spiritual gifts, and should not be mistaken as a structure of authority.

The church is a *covenantal* community. It is a community where the reality of God's covenantal love is being manifested through human relationships. The church is a community where self-centeredness is being overcome, where a person's being as being-with-others-and-for-others is to be experienced, nurtured, exercised, and realized. Covenantal humanity is humanity restored to its original mode.

The church is a *Eucharistic* community. The Eucharist is a celebration of the ultimate gift of God to humankind, God giving Himself. It is a celebration of self-giving to the point of death. As a Eucharistic community, the church celebrates self-giving to the point of giving up her life.

THEOLOGICAL EDUCATION FOR THE CHURCH

The church is an eschatological community. Theology thus ought to test whether the church is proclaiming the gospel of the Kingdom and whether she is part of the historical movement toward the *eschaton*, when the reign of God will be complete. The eschatological perspective runs through both the Old and New Testament. In his essay "Malkuk YHWH," Old Testament scholar Viktor Maag points to the fact that Israel's "*Weltgefühl und Daseinsverstandnis*" has a historical-eschatological consciousness deeply ingrained in it.[16] Israel's religion thus has a "vectoral-kinetic" character over against the static character of Canaanite religion. The sense of "becoming" and the forward-looking motif, in short a strong sense of movement toward a specific destination, is clearly apparent in Israel's perception of history. Israel's God "leads to a future which is not just a repetition and confirmation of the present,

---

16. Viktor Maag, "*Malkût Jwhw*," in *Congress Volume: Oxford 1959*, VTSup 7 (Leiden: Brill, 1960), 134–35.

but the goal of on-going events."[17] "Sedentarization" (becoming static) in Israel's life was considered to be the foundational cause of corruption in the Kingdom of Israel. The same can be true for the church today. To avoid "sedentarization," the church must maintain a clear eschatological sense. It is therefore essential to inculcate in the whole church an awareness of the historical movement toward the *eschaton*. However, there has been too little eschatological awareness in our theological education, and theological reflection on history as the arena where God and his people act to bring forth his Kingdom can hardly be found in theological curriculum. In fact, attempts to uncover such would result in an embarrassment to scholarship. Yet, for several centuries now, history has been moving toward radical secularization on a global scale in accordance with the Enlightenment cultural project. The church has been held hostage to this trend because it lacks vision about what direction history should be moving. The church needs to understand the driving forces behind such a movement in order to discern how its proclamation of the Word of God may become part of God's means to turn the tide. The eschatological vision of reality brings hope and judgment together. The preaching of the Gospel, the Gospel of redemption and transformation, inevitably brings prophetic judgment on our cultural trends. Theological education fails if it does not help the church to maintain her prophetic edge. The lack of cultural reflection in biblical studies, in theological discussions, and in pastoral explorations explains why the church is becoming less and less capable of responding to cultural trends that are detrimental to humanity.

The problem with theological schools does not lie in their emphasis on scholarship; rather, it lies in their lack of a sense of history, and, therefore, a sense of purpose for their existence, or the mission of scholarship. While liberal humanism is running wild in our culture, greatly compromising the moral substance of our society's laws, how is biblical scholarship on the biblical concepts of law responding? Endless studies on historical or exegetical problems have been conducted that are totally irrelevant to what is happening in our culture. Why? Our theological scholarship lacks the eschatological, historical, and prophetic senses that are so critically needed to effectively engage our culture.

The church is a charismatic community. As such, it has been blessed with enormous gifts endowed by the Holy Spirit. Are these gifts being

---

17. Ibid., 140.

taken seriously and put to use for the Kingdom? Or would the sheer mention of "charisma" raise concerns about the charismatic movement? Are we merely paying lip service to the work and power of the Holy Spirit, or do we truly believe that the Holy Spirit is always ready and eager to empower us to serve the Kingdom? In what way have our theological schools helped the church to understand the nature, allocation, identification, confirmation, and coordination of spiritual gifts in the Christian community? How have our theological curricula helped the church to amplify and maximize these gifts for the Kingdom? How may the exercise of these gifts from the Holy Spirit be subjected under the authority of the church as a whole? How can obedience and freedom work together in the exercise of these gifts? There seems to be little in our theological curricula that speaks to these questions or to the charismatic dimension of the church in general.

The church is a covenantal community. How can our theological seminaries help educate our pastoral leadership to nurture covenantal awareness and commitment within the church? Ironically, theology, whether it be biblical studies or dogmatics, has been a lonely enterprise. More often than not, theological reflection or biblical scholarship bears the mark of individualism that is so symptomatic of our age. That is why our theological endeavors suffer from fragmentation. Theological seminaries are rarely a team of unified purpose and mission. Theological curricula are rarely integrated, and there seems to be little interdisciplinary effort. When seminaries fail to reflect the covenantal life of the church, their students can hardly develop a covenantal orientation for their future pastorate. This, however, is vital, as the exercise of covenantal love among the people of God is the antidote to the narcissism prevalent in our culture. If the church fails to convey such love, she will also lose her distinctive character. The training of covenantal communal life must therefore be part of our theological curriculum. Theological educators like us must give careful thought as to how to incorporate such training.

The church is a Eucharistic community. In our culture, Christians often appear to be a strange bunch of people. They celebrate death, self-giving death. This, in fact, is a radically distinctive characteristic of the church. She is herself a self-giving community. The church thus fails when she is inward-looking and overly concerned about her own well-being, her rights as a community, and her enterprise as a successful institution. How does the church cultivate a Eucharistic outlook on life among the people of God? How do our theological schools cultivate a Eucharistic character in our future pastors? The issue here is much deeper than that of liturgy or theological understanding of the Eucharistic bread and wine. It is about life that reflects the self-giving death of our Lord Jesus Christ. Have not our theological schools put too much effort into cultivating professional competence at the expense of inculcating a Eucharistic approach? How can seminaries begin to cultivate a spirit of celebration, specifically the celebration of giving up one's self?

AN INTEGRATED MODEL FOR THE GLOBAL CONTEXT

What have we gained from the above discussions? Fluid identity and the loss of inwardness is the hallmark of our age. The autonomy of the will, held so dear by many, is a myth. What we are faced with is a form of individualism that is completely void of individual identity. Theological students coming into seminaries today can be expected to have been deeply affected by such fragmented identity. How can we nurture such a generation of students and prepare them to respond effectively to a generation of fragmented identity? If integrity of personhood and character has always been important to effective ministry, then they are much more so in the present age. How can we inculcate inwardness in our students so that they too may become inculcators of inwardness? Can our present theological education that is modeled after university education effect such inculcation? Or, does it stand as an obstacle to the whole concept of knowledge, giving insufficient consideration to the person and his or her character formation? Or, worse, has the enterprise of knowledge been hijacked by secular humanism and functional rationality? The concept of theological education as *paideia* for the cultivation of a person's mind, spirit, and character has largely been eroded in Western theological seminaries. Edward Farley points to the fragmentation of theological education and the eclipse of *theologia* (theological wisdom) in the training of ministers.[18] In recovering *theologia*, we need to redirect our understanding of what constitutes knowledge and scholarship.

---

18. Cf. Edward Farley, *Theologia: The Fragmentation and Unity of Theological Education* (Philadelphia: Fortress, 1983).

Restoring Piety in the Loss of Inwardness

What can we learn from, for example, the Asian context? What is the orientation of theological education in Asia, and what can we draw from it? In the Chinese context, even when highly Westernized, the concept of knowledge is still quite different from that in the West. From both the Confucian perspective and the perspective of the Chinese Christian tradition, which has a strong pietistic inclination, knowledge is not the sheer objective understanding of things. Rather, knowledge is always personal knowledge; it has deep personal meaning and implications. The highest form of knowledge is that which makes life authentic and whole. Acquiring truth is one and the same as identifying with truth and living it out. Acquiring knowledge and character, or spiritual formation, are not separate entities. As such, spiritual formation cannot be considered a mere supplement to biblical-theological knowledge. To the contrary, it must be integrated in biblical research and theological reflection.

Chinese evangelical theology and Chinese tradition have a common language, the language for life-transforming truth and authentic humanity. In the Chinese tradition, the human person is at once a partner with, as well as the concrete manifestation of, Dao. "Participating in the transforming and nurturing process of Heaven and Earth" (贊天地之化育) and "being in unity with Heaven and Earth" (與天地參) are one and the same thing.[19] Therefore, learning in the highest order is learning for the fulfillment of humanity. As Yang Xiong (揚雄) puts it, learning for the refinement of humanity far surpasses learning how to transform metals into gold (君子問鑄人, 不問鑄金).[20] Any genuine pursuit of knowledge should lead ultimately to the fulfillment of an unadulterated manifestation of truth in the life of the knower. Similarly, for Chinese evangelicals, all theological understandings lead to a life that is the concrete manifestation of the Divine Logos.

---

19. *The Doctrine of the Mean*, #22. "Only those who possess absolute sincerity can give full development to his nature. He who is able to give full development to his own nature can give development to the nature of other men . . . he who can give full development to the nature of all beings can assist the transforming and nourishing powers of Heaven and Earth . . . he may with Heaven and Earth form a triad." Cf. William Theodore de Bary et al, ed., *Sources of Chinese Tradition* (New York: Columbia University Press, 1960), 134–35.

20. 法言義疏, Fa-yan Yi Shu *[Words concerning the Principle of Life—A Commentary* 香港: 中華書局, 1987, 頁(Yang Xiong, Fa-yan Yi Shu, Hong Kong: Chung Hwa Book Company, 1987), 15.

For the Chinese tradition, the self is a great gift from Heaven and Earth. One has to recognize its given-ness and receive it with a sense of gratitude and reverence (*Jing*, 敬). Out of gratitude, one strives to preserve one's integrity and authenticity. Such an orientation in life is called *Cheng* (誠).[21] Yet, to maintain one's true authenticity, one has to empty oneself of self-centeredness and desires that result from external sensual attractions.[22] Only then can the self be filled with the "mind" of Heaven and Earth.[23] Thus, "emptying" is a fundamental exercise in life. To attain the state of "emptiness" (虛), one needs to exercise quietude. It is in the absence of the anxiousness to talk, to express oneself, that one begins to hear the Way. Ch'eng Hao once said to his pupils, "You come together here and only learn the way to talk. Therefore in your learning, your minds and words do not correspond . . . You should therefore practice quiet sitting."[24] In fact, long before the Neo-Confucianists, the emphasis on quietude as the beginning of wisdom was already highly significant. In the I-Ching, a sage aims to establish his humanity or stand on the ground of his humanity (君子立心); to do so, he ought to be still before he makes a move (to bring himself in line with Dao), he ought to change his heart before he speaks (君子安其身而後動, 易其心而後語).[25] Hsuen Tzu (荀子) understands well that our hearts house hidden ideas and diverse orientations; our hearts are always driven to motion. The contents of our heart can be stumbling blocks on our way to true knowledge. To remove these, the sage strives to cultivate "emptiness, unity of knowing and being, quietude" (虛, 壹, 靜). For Hsuen Tzu, these qualities are the wellspring of true knowledge.

Theology needs to recover the long-forgotten practice of "emptiness, unity of knowing and being, quietude" in the Christian tradition.

---

21. According to Ch'eng I (程頤), the student of truth "should hold fast to the mind with reverence. He should not be anxious. Instead he should nourish and cultivate it deeply and earnestly, and immerse himself [in the Way]. Only then can he have a sense of fulfillment and be at ease with himself. If one seeks anxiously, that is merely selfishness" (de Bary et al., *Sources of Chinese Tradition*, 168).

22. Ibid., 167.

23. *Ming-Ju Hsueh An* (明儒學案), II, 7/10, (ibid., 186). Also refer to *Chin-ssu Lu*, 4/2a, in *The Unfolding of Neo-Confucianism*, by William Theodore de Bary and the Conference on Seventeenth-Century Chinese Thought, Studies in Oriental Culture 10 (New York: Columbia University Press, 1975), 186.

24. Ibid., 170.

25. 【周易繫辭下】, 第四章 (Zhou-yi Xi-Xia, book 2, chapter 4 *I-Chuan* (易傳).

Spiritual exercises for inculcating piety have for centuries been at the core of evangelical theological training. We need to recover such a tradition to build "inwardness" of the self among our future ministers. The terms *piety* and *pietism* have become derogatory terms associated with fundamentalism. However, Chinese evangelicals by and large remain pietist in orientation. We need not apologize for that. We see the cultivation of personal piety as highly significant, especially in a time when the loss of inwardness has become detrimental to society. Reclaiming the pietist root of the evangelical tradition is an essential step in the reorientation of our theological education.

Theological Education with a Missional Orientation

After years of what seemed to be rather fruitless efforts, and amidst accusations of complicity with imperialism and colonialism, the missionary movement was on drastic retreat following World War II, with a deep sense of guilt and remorse. In 1949, Protestants in China numbered just 700,000 and were stigmatized, in disarray, poised to be eliminated under Communist suppression. Yet in barely fifty years, Christians in China numbered more than fifty million. The missionaries were gone, but the missional orientation of faith they left behind proved to be highly explosive. The numerical or physical foundations built by missionaries were almost negligible, but the evangelical understanding of the Gospel and the evangelistic zeal that accompanied it, as actualized in the life of missionaries, was, and continues to be, very powerful. Several years ago, I met a professor in Beijing. He told me that he had just received Christ and immediately said, "I intend to lead all my colleagues in my department to Christ." In Sichuan, about four years ago, I met two former professors who had accepted Christ. They told me that they left their jobs soon after their conversion to become evangelists. Through them, many have come to Christ. Where does such evangelistic zeal come from? Here I cannot but think of the massacre of missionaries in Shandong or the Oberlin Band of missionaries brutally murdered in Shanxi during the Boxer Uprising. The blood of these missionaries is the seed of the church in China. The phenomenal growth of Christianity in China has its root in the missional orientation of Christian faith inculcated by missionaries. The church in China has the evangelistic zeal of missionaries stamped on her life. We see a glimpse of such missional orientation in the motto of the Hong Kong Alliance Bible Seminary. The motto, "Be tough, dare to pioneer in mission, and burn with evangelistic zeal," says it all.

Restoring the missional orientation to our theological curriculum is the real answer to the fragmentation in our theological education. How can we instill such an orientation in the way we teach the Bible, systematic theology, and practical theology? Simply patching up our existing curriculum with one or two more courses in evangelism and missions will not do. Rather, our entire curriculum must be infused with missional concern and reflection.

A Prophetic Critique of Culture

Evangelicalism before Lausanne had been largely perceived as pietistic in an individualistic sense. The Lausanne Congress of 1974 has been regarded as a watershed event for evangelical theology. Redemption in the social and cultural dimensions has become vital in the agenda of world evangelization. How has such concern been translated into theological curriculum? In many evangelical seminaries, the impact of Lausanne has hardly been felt. Most Bible scholars and theologians continue to go about their business of scholarship as usual. Little discussion about curriculum change has occurred in response to the 1974 congress. Theologians and biblical scholars are largely oblivious to the sociocultural changes that have been emerging and surrounding them. The greatest challenge to evangelical identity thus comes from the inertia of evangelicals themselves.

Perhaps we need to rethink the way we are bringing up a new generation of systematic theologians. Instead of routinely sending bright young persons to research doctrinal issues in systematic theology or historical theology, should we not send some of them to study the theology of economics, aiming prophetically at the Chicago School of Economics? Can we not ask our theologians to write on the idea of covenant with an objective of developing a covenantal economics? Why are so few theologians interested in engaging John Rawls or Isaiah Berlin? Can we not have Old Testament professors who do research on Old Testament Law with the objective of critiquing the "amoral" foundation of modern law? Can theological seminaries consider developing partnerships with leaders in the marketplace to probe into issues of life in the marketplace philosophies? Would not such partnerships help us mentor our students to become ministers who can look beyond the four walls of their churches?

These are the questions we need to reflect on when we think about the new direction of evangelical theological education in the twenty-first century. We should not do so for the sake of self-preservation, but for the sake of the prophetic edge of the Gospel. The Gospel is to be preached for the transformation of the world. In what sense is the Gospel relevant to dehumanizing socio-cultural structures, behind which lie dehumanizing ideologies? Theological education must empower future ministers to be able to think through these issues.